# ROUTLEDGE LIBRARY EDITIONS: SOUTH AFRICA

Volume 9

# AN ECONOMIC HISTORY OF SOUTH AFRICA

# AN ECONOMIC HISTORY OF SOUTH AFRICA

D. M. GOODFELLOW

LONDON AND NEW YORK

First published by George Routledge & Sons in 1931.

This edition first published in 2023
by Routledge
4 Park Square, Milton Park, Abingdon, Oxon OX14 4RN

and by Routledge
605 Third Avenue, New York, NY 10158

*Routledge is an imprint of the Taylor & Francis Group, an informa business*

© 1931 D. M. Goodfellow

All rights reserved. No part of this book may be reprinted or reproduced or utilised in any form or by any electronic, mechanical, or other means, now known or hereafter invented, including photocopying and recording, or in any information storage or retrieval system, without permission in writing from the publishers.

Trademark notice: Product or corporate names may be trademarks or registered trademarks, and are used only for identification and explanation without intent to infringe.

*British Library Cataloguing in Publication Data*
A catalogue record for this book is available from the British Library

ISBN: 978-1-032-30347-5 (Set)
ISBN: 978-1-032-32692-4 (Volume 9) (hbk)
ISBN: 978-1-032-32791-4 (Volume 9) (pbk)
ISBN: 978-1-003-31672-5 (Volume 9) (ebk)

DOI: 10.4324/9781003316725

**Publisher's Note**
The publisher has gone to great lengths to ensure the quality of this reprint but points out that some imperfections in the original copies may be apparent.

**Disclaimer**
The publisher has made every effort to trace copyright holders and would welcome correspondence from those they have been unable to trace.

This is a reissue of a previously published book. The language is reflective of the time in which this book was published. In reissuing this book, no offence is intended by the Publishers to any reader.

# A MODERN ECONOMIC HISTORY OF SOUTH AFRICA

BY

D. M. GOODFELLOW

B.Sc. (Econ.) London

Formerly Senior Lecturer in Economics
in the University of Cape Town

LONDON
GEORGE ROUTLEDGE & SONS, LTD.,
BROADWAY HOUSE : 68-74, CARTER LANE, E.C.
1931

PRINTED IN GREAT BRITAIN BY THE DEVONSHIRE PRESS, TORQUAY

To
**MY PARENTS**

# CONTENTS

| | PAGE |
|---|---|
| PREFACE | ix |
| INTRODUCTION | 1 |

## SECTION I

A Survey of Development Before 1892
- (a) Preliminary Observations . . . 13
- (b) Population . . . . . . 14
- (c) Trade Statistics . . . . . 20
- (d) Customs Policies of the South African States . . . . . . 24
- (e) Early Transport in Cape Colony . . 33
- (f) Agricultural Development . . . 40
- (g) Early Land Settlement Policy . . 51
- (h) Early Native Economic Policy . . 62

## SECTION II

CHAPTER I.—EARLY RAILWAY AGREEMENTS . 81

CHAPTER II.—CUSTOMS AND TRADE IN THE GOLD DISCOVERY PERIOD . . . . . 94
- (a) Inter-colonial Tariff Relations . . 94
- (b) Foreign Trade . . . . . 96

CHAPTER III.—AGRICULTURE IN THE MINING DEVELOPMENT PERIOD, 1887 TO 1899. . 103
- (a) Types of Land and Farming Methods in Cape Colony . . . . . 103
- (b) Irrigation . . . . . . 114
- (c) Marketing Methods of South African Farmers . . . . . . 117
- (d) Agriculture in Native Areas . . 119
- (e) Natal . . . . . . 124

## CONTENTS

| | PAGE |
|---|---|
| (f) The Orange Free State | 127 |
| (g) Farming Methods in the Transvaal and Changes Consequent on the Gold Discoveries | 130 |
| (h) Summary of Agricultural Development in South Africa as a Whole | 134 |

CHAPTER IV.—THE DEVELOPMENT OF ECONOMIC CONTACT BETWEEN EUROPEAN AND BANTU 1890 TO 1899 . . . . . . 138
  (a) The Inter-action of Recruitment with Native Modes of Life . . . . 138
  (b) The Glen Grey Act . . . . 148
  (c) Natives Outside Reserves . . . 158

CHAPTER V.—THE INDUSTRIAL DEVELOPMENT OF THE SOUTH AFRICAN STATES FROM 1887 TO 1899 . . . . . . . . 168

CHAPTER VI.—THE RECONSTRUCTION OF SOUTH AFRICA AFTER THE ANGLO-BOER WAR . . 185
  (a) Introductory . . . . . 185
  (b) The 1904 Census . . . . . 187

CHAPTER VII.—THE RAILWAYS AND FINANCES OF THE FOUR COLONIES . . . . . 193

CHAPTER VIII.—LAND SETTLEMENT AND AGRICULTURE IN THE RECONSTRUCTION . . . 203

CHAPTER IX.—MINING AND LABOUR QUESTIONS IN THE POST-WAR PERIOD . . . 214

CHAPTER X.—CUSTOMS PROBLEMS WITHIN THE CUSTOMS UNION . . . . . 219

### SECTION III

CHAPTER I.—NATIVE LAND AND RECRUITMENT 223
  Recent Developments . . . . 223
CHAPTER II.—LAND SETTLEMENT, AGRICULTURE AND IRRIGATION . . . . . 242
CHAPTER III.—CONCLUSION . . . . 254
INDEX . . . . . . . . 259

# PREFACE

My greatest indebtedness, for any value which this book may have, is to Professor Leslie, of the University of Cape Town. Himself slow to publish, the depth and perspicacity of his observations upon the economic development of South Africa, give to those who are fortunate enough to be associated with him great opportunities of having new light thrown upon old facts and of finding the significance of new facts well appraised. Any failure on my part to derive full benefit from my association with Professor Leslie must recoil entirely upon my own head.

I am deeply indebted to several librarians, more especially to Mr Freer, now of the Library of the University of the Witwatersrand. For three years I had the great advantage of his unfailing patience and expertness. Three librarians in Cape Town went out of their way to make matters easy for me—Mr Graham Botha, keeper of the Archives in Cape Town; Mr A. C. Lloyd, Librarian of the South African Public Library; and Mr Riebeck, Librarian to the Union Parliament. On returning to England I made use of the Library of the Colonial Office and wish to record the great assistance which was given me there.

To the University of Cape Town I am deeply indebted for very liberal financial assistance in the collection of information.

Mr R. H. Tawney first suggested that I should undertake the work, and his encouragement, though given from a distance of six thousand miles, was a factor of the greatest value, while on my return to England Professor Malinowski at once offered me every assistance.

## PREFACE

No one engaged upon a piece of research could ever have been more fortunate in his colleagues than I was at the University of Cape Town. Professor Plant and Mr Hutt of the Department of Commerce, Professor Walker of the Department of History, and Professor Fred Clark of the Department of Education are some of those, constant contact with whose special knowledge and enthusiasm for their subjects leave me dull indeed if I have not woven into this book some little at least of their influence.

D. M. GOODFELLOW.

1931.

# A MODERN ECONOMIC HISTORY OF SOUTH AFRICA

## INTRODUCTION

OUR object is to trace the development of that part of the Southern end of Africa which in 1910 became the Union of South Africa. We begin our study, not with early attempts at colonization, nor with the first evidences of industry, but with the development of those great industries which after 1886 began to give unity to what had previously been a barren sub-continent. Our study will commence with the establishment of the gold industry of the Transvaal and of the railway development to which it gave rise.

The economic history of the sub-continent before 1886 had been a simple one and has frequently been described. For our purpose however, we must recapitulate its main features. In the first place was the great pastoral industry which was spread over almost the whole area; in the second place was an agricultural industry of which the chief example was at the Cape, and which was to be found only where good arable land happened to be in communication with a sea port or other consuming centre; in the third place was the exotic diamond industry centred in only one colony, but affecting others slightly, and rendered less exotic than it might have been by the fact that prospectors from the diamond field had spread over all of South Africa, and indeed had discovered the Witwatersrand. We might add a fourth, namely the transport industry, for this, whether ox wagon or railway, had for some ten years before 1886 been affecting the process of development and unification.

The pastoral industry was one which had betrayed very little progress within the memory of man. The most widespread of occupations, it was the least intensively practised. Pioneer colonists, wherever they had penetrated and settled, had adopted a mode of life depending mainly upon the size of the flocks which they could keep. This, curiously enough, applied almost equally to semi-desert land such as that of Namaqualand and to fertile grass land such as that of the Eastern Province; the reason was that with every type of land, lack of communication was the dominating factor. Each colonist who reached fertile land was able to claim his share of it according to pioneer custom, and then, having become possessed of some 6,000 acres, he felt no pressure of any kind—neither from other colonists nor from any difficulty in making ends meet. He was able to subsist by cultivating patches of arable land on his farm, and, according to the usage of primitive peoples the world over, he would accumulate cattle and sheep and goats and horses, more for the satisfaction of being able to count a large number of head of stock than because he attached any market value to them. Nevertheless it was the pastoral products and not the arable which formed the main commercial staples of the agricultural community.

Under the transport conditions in the pre-railway age in South Africa none but pastoral products could be sent for any considerable distance by the farmers. And the distances were very considerable. A Karroo sheep farmer might be anything up to 100 miles from the nearest market centre. The farmers of the Eastern Province were more fortunate; but those who lived in the Orange Free

State and the Transvaal might be anything from 200 to 400 miles from any central market. Food growing for commerce was quite impossible, excepting, as has been said before, in the actual neighbourhood of a seaport or of a manufacturing centre like Kimberley. A trade in wool and hides grew up simultaneously with the settling of the land from 1830 until the period with which our study commences. This trade was most diverse in character. It varied from the comparatively high quality products of the farmers who were lucky enough to possess sheep land at the eastern end of the Karroo, where grass was plentiful, and so transport easy over the few hundred miles which separated them from Algoa Bay, to the crude products of Transvaal farmers, who scarcely succeeded in exporting wool at all, but only hides and tallow. The chief wool producing districts in South Africa were the Orange Free State and the Eastern Province of the Cape. Wool, it is true, came from many other parts, but only from those two areas was it of any uniformity, and of exportable quality. Had the Transkeian districts been available for white possession they would doubtless have produced fine wools; but they were fully occupied by the natives and scarcely enter into our culculations in this respect. The Transvaal High Veld is not grass-land of a piece with the Orange Free State. It is land with arable possibilities, given water and scientific cultivation. But these had not been realized by the time our study begins. Sheep grazing was possible only in the summer months; and in the winter the sheep had to be trekked, sometimes over great distances, toward coastal land. This trekking effectively prevented development, and even if farmers in those regions had attempted to provide winter fodder and so to improve the strain of the sheep, the transport to the coast, involving as it did the traversing of great distance of land, frequently grassless, must have made their efforts uneconomic.

Even in the favoured grass districts of the Orange Free State and the Cape Eastern Province, wool production could scarcely be described as a progressive industry.

### WOOL EXPORTS OF CAPE COLONY.
(000 omitted throughout)

|      | lbs.   | £     |
|------|--------|-------|
| 1871 | 46,279 | 2,191 |
| 1872 | 48,822 | 3,275 |
| 1873 | 40,393 | 2,710 |
| 1874 | 42,620 | 2,948 |
| 1875 | 40,339 | 2,855 |
| 1876 | 34,861 | 2,278 |
| 1877 | 36,020 | 2,232 |
| 1878 | 32,127 | 1,888 |
| 1879 | 40,087 | 2,156 |
| 1880 | 42,468 | 2,420 |
| 1881 | 42,770 | 2,181 |
| 1882 | 41,689 | 2,062 |
| 1883 | 38,029 | 1,992 |
| 1884 | 37,270 | 1,745 |
| 1885 | 34,432 | 1,426 |
| 1886 | 47,454 | 1,590 |
| 1887 | 44,758 | 1,674 |

As may be seen from this table, exports between 1871 and 1887 through the Cape ports fluctuated according to season, without showing any sustained increase. This shows that once the land had been settled even in the most primary fashion, as it was by 1850, there was very little tendency to improve breed, or to increase the carrying capacity of the land. We shall attempt to account for this in another part of this study.

The arable land of South Africa, as may be seen from a glance at any good economic map, is found only in small areas scattered over the whole sub-continent. Such a map will show cultivation at the extreme south-west corner where vines and wheat will be marked. The next areas of cultivation are scattered eastward along the south coast for about 300 miles between the coast and the ranges of mountains beyond which is found the Karroo. In this strip of land the soil is of excellent quality, but depends upon spasmodic river waters which make its cultivation dependant upon storage works, and these are very expensive and difficult. So that areas,

# INTRODUCTION 5

although marked as arable on the map, are in reality of a somewhat speculative value, and up to 1880 they were very largely undeveloped or were used as pasture.

Next, stretching right up the East Coast and lying between the coast and the Drakensburg mountains, is an immense area of land marked "fertile" on the map but very largely given up to grass and tropical woodland, mostly occupied by natives, and only in one part, namely Natal, actually brought under cultivation for economic purposes. Natal is a kind of cross piece cut out of this tropical belt between the Native areas on the South and Portuguese territory to the north. The Natal area changes in nature as it runs from the coast inland; at the coast only purely tropical products are possible; but as the land approaches the Drakensburgs maize becomes the staple crop and on some of the high land wheat is possible. But maize-growing on any but the smallest scale developed only in the first decade of the twentieth century, and at the opening of our period Natal had only just managed to establish the cultivation of tropical products on her coastal belt.

Basutoland has valuable high lands, but is occupied almost entirely by natives, and it is only on her borders that white colonists have succeeded in establishing a foothold. It is here that the only real wheat growing district of the Orange Free State, the Conquered Territory, is found. The centres of cultivation in the interior are seen to be on the High Veld of the Transvaal and to be small in area and few in number. These were the districts such as Potchefstroom, Rustenberg, and Zeerust in which the early Transvaal settlers found a good water supply, making the land exceedingly fertile and so enabling them to establish their homes. But these districts, fertile though they were, passed through many vicissitudes until they finally became prosperous regions in the course of the twentieth century. We may say that at the opening of our period there were thus two kinds of agricultural lands; those which were near the coast and so had a chance of real development through being in touch with passing ships, and those which were inland and were required to do little more than to meet the needs of any population which might find itself there. The primitive commerce of the interior of South Africa was not uninteresting and had some few characteristics which indicated the future lines of development of the country. In the first place we find inland centres of trade growing up. These centres were generally found on the agricultural patches and maintained connections with farmers over vast areas. Very often the trade with these farmers would consist in mere barter of such articles as coffee and firearms in exchange for hides and would be effected on the occasion of an annual visit paid by the farmer to the store-keeper. Apart from this comparatively fixed trade however, there was a commerce maintained by pioneering travelling traders who would keep in touch with settlers in the most outlying parts, and, not less important, with the native tribes who were found all over the north and the north-east of the Transvaal. It was the existence of these two kinds of traders which facilitated the work of prospectors, and when any hopes of successful mines were raised the traders would at once settle in the neighbourhood and primitive but effective communications would be established. The travelling type of trader also met the needs of those colonists who never settled permanently, but merely hunted and drove small flocks in the bush-veld, and of the more settled colonists who, although they had permanent holdings, yet found it necessary to spend part of every year in trekking between the High and the Low Veld. It would appear that in the transactions between traders and colonists coin was scarcely ever used. This is easily understandable in the outlying semi-barbarous regions where ivory and skins were the staple product until as late as the eighties. Even in the more settled regions major transactions were often carried through without coin, since the farmers generally called twice a year at the store and then, in exchange for products which they brought, would carry away house-

# INTRODUCTION 7

hold products sufficient to last the whole family until the next visit.

Even in very good years, when the value of skins and wool brought in might greatly exceed the normal value of articles actually required in exchange, the balance would probably be taken in the form of some permanent equipment such as a new piece of harness for the ox wagon or even a new wagon itself. But very often such a surplus would be required to meet a debt which had been contracted with the trader in an earlier year of drought. Even in the settled agricultural regions it became the custom for farmers to keep permanent accounts with their store-keepers and so recently as the first or second decades of the present century this custom retained its grip with considerable effect upon the agricultural economy of the country. It was found not only in the Transvaal, but, with apparently equal force, in the Orange Free State and the Eastern Province of the Cape.

From this introductory description it may easily be seen that the southern part of the African Continent up to 1890 was in no sense a unified economic area. It consisted of some 475,000 square miles with a total White population of 577,000 and a Black population of 1,458,000. Thousands of square miles were practically unoccupied. Hundreds of square miles were occupied only by natives in their original semi-barbarous state. The whole of the Karroid Plateau and the High Veld of the Transvaal were settled so thinly that each family would know of the existence of scarcely a dozen other families, was totally without literature, excepting religious literature, and had no touch with civilization excepting through occasional contact with traders and missionaries. Political units were correspondingly loose. The territory of Cape Colony stretched indefinitely into the north. When diamonds were discovered in a district known as Griqualand West it was possible for the Cape to dispute its possession with the Orange Free State. It was north of a line beyond which the Cape had agreed not to go, but neither power had previously surveyed the land or indeed taken any notice of its existence. Equal difficulties of political possession would have been encountered had the diamonds been discovered in many other parts of the sub-continent. Cape Colony was the oldest and the most definite of the political units. But even apart from its Northern boundaries it was by no means definitely rounded off at the date (1886) of which we speak. Indeed it was only in 1894 that its area was definitely demarcated by the annexation of Bechuanaland and Pondoland. Up to the date of the latter annexation the possession of almost the whole of the lands occupied by natives between Algoa Bay and Natal had been not so much in dispute as merely unsettled. Their possession was a matter of minor importance. It was only when the native territories, with their supply of native labour, became essential for the development of the Witwatersrand that actual disputes occurred between the two British Colonies as to political ownership. These disputes were settled in summary fashion when Rhodes, the mining magnate, achieved the annexation of Pondoland. The most concrete political units were Natal and the Orange Free State. The former was definitely bounded on the one side by the sea, on the other by the Drakensbergs, to the south by the Cape, (after 1895); only its northern boundary was indefinite. Here Natal territory ran into land occupied by Zulus near the coast and by territory included in the South African republic to the north. After the Anglo Boer War Zululand was included in Natal and also a slice of territory cut from the Transvaal. The South African Republic was the most sprawling and indefinite of the States. This was inevitable from its very nature. It had one stretch of fairly uniform land known as the High Veld, then shaded indefinitely into bush veld and into desert on its North-West and West and into the semi-tropical grass lands of the coast on its East. To the North across the Limpopo River was more fertile land into which Dutch pioneers were gradually penetrating. Apart from its indefinite boundaries, even the interior of the South African Republic had very little economic or social life to give it cohesion. Its area was great and its means of communication small. Widely scattered farming communities owed but little allegiance to any central government. Only such major issues as a threat of annexation by the British or serious trouble with natives could cause the Boer farmers to act under the leadership of the government of their State. Here we need only describe briefly the boundary questions in which the South African Republic was involved. We have already seen that part of its territory bordered on Natal and was consequently always in some dispute. More serious was the fact that the South African Republic was entirely land-locked. Its more far-sighted leaders had seen the disadvantages of this from the very early pioneering days of the thirties and forties. They had at first hoped to maintain Natal as a Boer Republic, so giving the Dutch access to the sea, no matter how far inland they might penetrate from their starting point. This idea had been frustrated by the British. The next hope and the one which held sway at the opening of our period was that a means of communication might be found through Swaziland to St. Lucia Bay, but this again was frustrated by British influence. The best natural harbour was Delagoa Bay and this was in the possession of the Portuguese. As early as about 1875 an enlightened Transvaal statesman had bargained with the Portuguese for the right to build a railway line through their territory. Had this project succeeded it would have provided the first example in South Africa of a railway line traversing the territory of two separate powers and worked by an agreement between them. But finance was not forthcoming. Much as the South African Republic needed a railway, it did not have the economic produce to guarantee its success. Indeed there was no clear sign that the railway would so develop the country as to provide a payable traffic. On the discovery of gold in the Witwatersrand, the first condition made by the

President of the Republic to those who wished to build railways connecting the Witwatersrand with the British colonies, was that a corridor through Swaziland should first be granted. This may be taken to show the main significance of Swaziland for the Transvaal.

On the other side of her territory, was the vast district known as Bechuanaland, not fertile except toward the south, but still a good continuation of the Transvaal Bush-Veld and being gradually settled by Dutch pioneers. The southern more fertile portion came rather within the sphere of influence of Cape Colony. But the fate of Bechuanaland was decided by quite different factors. It was the route along which a railway could be built on purely British ground, if it were annexed by Britain, leading to the land north of the Transvaal. It was this land to the north that was the vital factor. Its economic importance merely as grass land, settleable by whites and highly mineralized, was considerable, but its strategic importance as a stepping stone to penetration into the interior of Africa was even greater. This was appreciated by the more far-sighted among the Dutch, but it is highly improbable that the Dutch State of the South African Republic would have ever used it for any other purpose than to settle colonists and to safeguard the value of their Witwatersrand by having a prior claim into the territory on which any potential competitor might be found. To the British, however, it was a much more vital concern both to discover minerals on British land and to obtain access to the North. Bechuanaland was annexed, the railway built, and the territory to the north settled by means of a chartered company.

These boundary disputes became important only when it was known that a really first rate gold reef had been discovered in the Transvaal in 1887. It was only after that date that the first inter-state railway lines were proceeded with.

Our study opens with the building of these lines. Before they were built no such thing as a South African economy could be said to exist. After they were built

# INTRODUCTION

all parts of the sub-continent were brought into such vital contact that it could well be said that a vast new economic unit had been created. Prior to 1887 there had been one highly developed industry and one good railway system serving it. But this had only been in one colony, namely the Cape Colony. It had not been without its importance for the sub-continent as a whole, but only in secondary ways. We shall attempt, by way of introduction to our main theme, a description of these Cape Colony activities. But we shall see that their chief importance lay in their being a stepping stone, and only a stepping stone, to the sub-continental developments which it is our chief object to describe.

### REFERENCES

Lucas, *Historical Geography of the British Empire*.
Walker, *History of South Africa* and *Historical Atlas of South Africa*.
Wallace, *Farming Industries of Cape Colony*.
*Report of the Transvaal Indigency Commission*, 1906, Historical Section.
*Report of the Imperial Commission on Land Settlement in South Africa*, 1901, and evidence laid before it by several witnesses.

## SECTION I

## A SURVEY OF SOUTH AFRICAN DEVELOPMENT PRIOR TO 1892

### (a) *Preliminary Observations*

FROM its very lack of unity it is very difficult to make a survey of the economic and social conditions in South Africa before 1892. None of the states, not even Cape Colony, kept records of births and deaths or of immigration or emigration. Census machinery had been developed in Cape Colony and Natal to the point of some usefulness, but in the other two chief states only the crudest numbering of the people (white people only) had been attempted. Trade statistics were equally defective and misleading. In many cases goods classed as exports from Cape Colony were really only sent through Cape Colony in transit; they were really the exports of the Orange Free State or the Transvaal, but these two states kept no record of them. Even between 1900 and 1910, when trade statistics were of the most vital importance to the discussions preceding Union, we find on referring back to the Blue Books that all kinds of gaps and discrepencies exist. This is easily understandable if we keep in mind the undeveloped and un-unified state of the country as we have tried to describe it in chapter I. If states do not have regular boundaries then they cannot have accurate import and export statistics. The inland states in South Africa both erected customs boundaries in the course of the nineteenth century, and by the opening of our period we find the Transvaal with a customs policy of its own, and the Orange Free State also attempting to collect customs on imports, both for its own consumption and for transit to the South African Republic. But we may appreciate the true nature of these customs boundaries when we realize that the Orange Free State did not even have a customs department, while the Transvaal collected monies on imports only at a few selected outposts.

Any survey must be prefaced by such remarks as these. The present writer has read many accounts of early South African conditions which seem to treat the statistics available as if they completely represented all the facts. All the facts cannot be known. We attempt here to set out and to estimate the importance of those that are known.

### (b) *Population*

The Cape Colony and Natal had developed census systems by the opening of our period. It would be a mistake, however, to accept these figures at their face value. The Cape Colony had taken censuses in 1865, 1875, and in 1891. These were taken with considerable care and comparative figures may be used as furnishing at least some information. But the boundaries of Cape Colony had changed considerably between 1865 and 1891. A number of wars, those most upsetting features in census results, had taken place. They had even been in progress while the censuses were being taken. Apart from movements of troops, the colonial districts near the native borders inevitably contained shifting populations of pioneers. These could not be numbered at any one census date so as to give a true conception of the settlement of the lands. But if the white population was shifting and fluctuating the black population was even more difficult to handle. As each census period passed, the officials learned more and more about the means of numbering the native people. This meant that at each census more natives would be counted, whether or not there were actually more to be counted. But to complicate this still further the native population, especially in such border districts as those between the

## DEVELOPMENT PRIOR TO 1892

Cape Eastern Province and the Transkei, was a very drifting one.

Male natives especially, but also females and children, would move very considerable distances in the hope of finding new land, or to work for white farmers, or merely to satisfy their whims. Estimates of native population made under these conditions, while they may be better than nothing, are to be used only with the greatest of care. In the case of Natal the conditions applying to these considerations were slightly different. The main difference was, that the Natal natives, as we may see when we come to deal with them in another part of the book, were much more firmly settled, for the most part, in mountainous land. But though their people moved about less they were much more difficult to find. The Natal white population was so small that we may hope that it was accurately counted, while its Asiatic population would be accurately counted, at least at the ports.

The Orange Free State had attempted two censuses before 1892. These aimed at no fuller particulars than the mere counting of the people, their classification according to sex, and their age grouping. They also attempted to enumerate the native population, but when we realize that at harvest and sowing times there is a great influx of natives from Basutoland, and that in between those seasons the natives go in large numbers back to their own country, we see that in order to make anything of the census result we must know not merely at what period of the year they were taken but whether the year was a good one or not agriculturally, and whether this applied over the whole of the Orange Free State or only in parts.

The Transvaal had been much the most modest in its census attempts. It had merely collected figures, without using any specially constructed census machinery, as to the number of white people in the various parts of the republic. No further details were collected. The data is given almost entirely in round numbers, and the native population is completely ignored. Various unofficial estimates of the native population had been made, but when we examine their bases we may learn to appreciate the wisdom of the Transvaal Government in attempting little.

In the Cape Colony an effort was made to render comparable the census figures of 1875 and 1891 by dividing the Colony into three parts, first the Colony as it was in 1875, second Griqualand West, and third the Transkeian districts which were in the main added between the two dates. It was not till the census of 1904 that the final annexations, those of Pondoland and Bechuanaland, were counted.

The early Cape censuses show the following results:

(1) CAPE COLONY PROPER.
as constituted and bounded in 1875 (excluding Griqualand West and the Native Territories.
(000 is omitted throughout)

| Year. | All Races. | | | European or White. | | | Other than European or White. | | |
|---|---|---|---|---|---|---|---|---|---|
| | Persons | Males | Females | Persons | Males | Females | Persons | Males | Females |
| 1891 | 956 | 485 | 470 | 336 | 174 | 162 | 619 | 311 | 308 |
| 1875 | 720 | 369 | 351 | 236 | 123 | 112 | 484 | 245 | 238 |

(2) GRIQUALAND WEST.
(annexed 1880)
(000 omitted throughout)

| Year | All Races | | | European or White | | | Other than European or White. | | |
|---|---|---|---|---|---|---|---|---|---|
| | Persons | Males | Females | Persons | Males | Females | Persons | Males | Females |
| 1891 | 83 | 49 | 34 | 29 | 16 | 13 | 53 | 32 | 20 |
| 1887 | 45 | 27 | 17 | 12 | 7 | 4 | 32 | 20 | 12 |

(3) NATIVE TERRITORIES
(East Griqualand, Tembuland, Transkei and Walfish Bay)
(annexed after 1875)
(000 omitted throughout)

| Year | All Races | | | European or White | | | Other than European or White | | |
|---|---|---|---|---|---|---|---|---|---|
| | Persons | Males | Females | Persons | Males | Females | Persons | Males | Females |
| 1891 | 487 | 232 | 254 | 10 | 5 | 4 | 476 | 226 | 250 |
| 1879 | 269 | 125 | 137 | 2 | 1 | 1 | 260 | 124 | 136 |

# DEVELOPMENT PRIOR TO 1892

As the early censuses in the three sections were taken in different years, they cannot be totalled. We give the total for 1891.

### CAPE COLONY
(as constituted in 1891)
(000 omitted throughout)

| Year | All Races | European or White | Other than European or White |
|---|---|---|---|
|  | Persons | Persons | Persons |
| 1891 | 1,527 | 376 | 1,150 |

An attempt was made, progressively successful, we may believe, with each census, to enumerate the occupational activities both of the white and of the non-white populations. These returns as affecting the natives must be radically discounted, for it was not until well into the twentieth century that any considerable number of natives had definitely adopted occupations classifiable along with those of the whites. In all early census attempts they were merely returned in bulk as "Agricultural," "Pastoral," "Domestic," and so on.

As regards the white population, its occupations, as will be seen from the following table, were classified under eight headings, and we give the results for the census of 1891

### CAPE COLONY
Occupations of the European White Population, 1891
(000 omitted throughout)

| Class | Persons | Males | Females |
|---|---|---|---|
| (1) Professional | 14 | 10 | 4 |
| (2) Domestic | 77 | 7 | 74 |
| (3) Commercial | 17 | 16 | 1 |
| (4) Agricultural | 74 | 59 | 14 |
| (5) Industrial | 31 | 26 | 4 |
| (6) Indefinite | 4 | 1 | 3 |
| (7) Dependents | 155 | 77 | 77 |
| (8) Unspecified | 2 | 1 | 1 |
| Total White Population | 376 | 195 | 181 |

It will be seen from this table that, as one would expect in a country in which native and coloured labour was plentiful, a very considerable proportion of the white people are classed as commercial and professional. Yet the great bulk of the white population lived on the land and so is classed as agricultural. Between 1870 and 1891, however, the commercial element grew at a much greater rate than the agricultural. This is easily accounted for. Between 1865 and 1875 the diamond mining industry of Kimberley was opened up; between 1875 and 1891 the gold mining industry of the Witwatersand was established. These two events had precisely similar effects upon the figures with which we are dealing. They both increase the commercial activity of the Cape ports and, despite all speculations to the contrary, appear to have withdrawn population from agriculture. This tendency would have been even more marked, we may safely say, had it happened that the Witwatersrand gold mines were in Cape Colony. In that case the net transfer of population from the one occupation to the others would have been shown. As it is, the agricultural population is not added to the others but is transferred out of the Colony. We know nothing of the movements of population between one South African State and another. We only know that these movements were at times of very great importance. Doubtless the gold-mining industry attracted people of all occupations from Cape Colony to the Transvaal, but the commercial and professional people in Cape Colony actually increased in number, while the agricultural people underwent a slight decrease. We must remember again that by 1891 the movement to the Transvaal was by no means complete. The deep level mines had not yet been proved and the migration was very much in process, thus vitiating the census result as definite data and leaving them with value only in so far as they indicate tendencies.

All these considerations must apply with redoubled

# DEVELOPMENT PRIOR TO 1892

force when we use the census result in comparing the increases or decreases in the White and non-White populations. Both were actively engaged in migration between the Cape Colony and the Transvaal at the time of the 1891 census. How they are respectively affected the present writer has never been able to determine. He can only suggest an abstention from over hasty attempts and generalizations on the subject of the increase of any one race relatively to any other. We know that there was a very considerable immigration of Whites into South Africa via the Cape and Natal ports. We do not know what happened to that immigrant population once it was in South African territory. The only thing that could have told us anything about it would have been immigration statistics kept by the Transvaal government. These were not kept.

We shall now give tables of the Natal population corresponding to those we have just given for the Cape:

### NATAL CENSUS RESULTS, 1891
(000 omitted throughout)

|      | White Population | | Coloured Population | | Indians and Asiatics | |
|------|-------|---------|-------|---------|-------|---------|
|      | Males | Females | Males | Females | Males | Females |
| 1891 | 25    | 21      | 216   | 239     | 18    | 12      |

### OCCUPATIONS OF THE WHITE AND ASIATIC POPULATION, 1891
(000 omitted throughout)

| Classes of Occupation | White | Asiatic* |
|---|---|---|
| Professional | 3 | 0.1 |
| Domestic | 0.7 | 1 |
| Commercial | 1 | 0.3 |
| Agricultural | 3 | 4 |
| Industrial | 6 | 6 |
| Indefinite and Dependents | 29 | 17 |
| Totals | 46 | 30 |

* Excluding Indians under indenture, and including mixed races.

We need scarcely say that all of the considerations

pointed out in connection with the Cape Colony figures apply with equal force to those for Natal.

### (c) *Trade Statistics*

In 1905 a customs statistical bureau was established to facilitate the keeping of accurate statistics as to the over-sea trade of South Africa as a whole. Even that bureau, however, did not attempt the recording of the overland trade of the different states in South Africa. This was indeed an almost impossible task, even after the achievement of customs unification (1903). In the earlier period with which we are now dealing it was quite impossible. Each state made certain returns as to its dealings in the transit of goods with its neighbours. It is probable that some of the most important of these returns have some reliability ; for example, the imports of mining goods into the Transvaal were probably accurately returned owing to a somewhat stringent collection of customs duties upon them. But in the main we know nothing of inter-colonial trade in detail. We know that all parts of South Africa sent food-stuffs first to Kimberley and later to Johannesburg. There is evidence that cultivation in the Orange Free State, both of cereals and of beef and mutton, received a great stimulus from the growth of the Johannesburg market ; but no statistics were kept to show the extent of this trade. The Cape Colony, as might be expected, had much the best trade statistics service. Yet by looking at just a few of the clearer facts we may see how very limited it was. Under the heading of Exports, all exports through the Cape ports were included, and also all exports over land. These were not differentiated ; they were returned in one lump sum. We may guess that exports such as wool went entirely overseas ; indeed we know that as a fact from the port returns. And we may also guess that the great bulk of her exports of food-stuffs went over land. But we do not know definitely. In the case of some commodities, notably wine, the figures of exports overseas were

## DEVELOPMENT PRIOR TO 1892

carefully kept, while we have no figures whatever as to the considerable quantities which must have gone into the Transvaal. Again, the exports from Cape Colony were merely the goods which were sent out of the Colony; no record was ever taken showing what proportion of those were the produce of the Colony and what proportion were re-exports. Thus the wool found in the export tables came partly from the pastures of Cape Colony, but very largely also from the Orange Free State, and to some extent from Basutoland; while the whole of the interior was also drawn upon. This practice of classing re-exports simply as exports caused considerable amusement after the opening out of the Witwatersrand Gold Field when the tables showed that the Cape Colony had a great export both of diamonds and of gold, the diamonds in fact coming actually from Cape Colony but the gold proceeding entirely from the Transvaal. This failure was not due, however, to any accident, and still less to mere carelessness or desire to achieve high paper exports for the Colony. It was due to the fact, which we have already noticed, that over-land trade statistics were almost a physical impossibility.

We give here the main tables of South African trade as they are available up to 1890. In the first place is a table of the imports and exports of Cape Colony since 1850.

TABLE OF IMPORTS FOR THE CAPE COLONY, 1850–90
(excluding gold)
(000 omitted throughout)

| Year | Imports £ | Exports £ | Year | Imports £ | Exports £ |
|---|---|---|---|---|---|
| 1850 | 1,277 | 637 | 1862 | 2,785 | 1,957 |
| 1851 | 1,675 | 651 | 1863 | 2,275 | 2,224 |
| 1852 | 1,861 | 772 | 1864 | 2,471 | 2,594 |
| 1853 | 1,651 | 1,264 | 1865 | 2,111 | 2,222 |
| 1854 | 1,548 | 764 | 1866 | 1,940 | 2,590 |
| 1855 | 1,175 | 1,061 | 1867 | 2,405 | 2,514 |
| 1856 | 1,588 | 1,327 | 1868 | 1,956 | 2,306 |
| 1857 | 2,637 | 1,988 | 1869 | 1,953 | 2,225 |
| 1858 | 2,495 | 1,798 | 1870 | 2,352 | 2,569 |
| 1859 | 2,579 | 2,021 | 1871 | 2,585 | 2,531 |
| 1860 | 2,665 | 2,083 | 1872 | 4,388 | 6,069 |
| 1861 | 2,605 | 1,972 | 1873 | 5,130 | 5,531 |

## TABLE OF IMPORTS—continued.

| Year | Imports £ | Exports £ | Year | Imports £ | Exports £ |
|---|---|---|---|---|---|
| 1874 | 5,558 | 5,538 | 1883 | 6,470 | 7,151 |
| 1875 | 5,731 | 5,755 | 1884 | 5,249 | 6,945 |
| 1876 | 5,556 | 5,012 | 1885 | 4,772 | 5,811 |
| 1877 | 5,158 | 5,356 | 1886 | 3,799 | 7,125 |
| 1878 | 6,151 | 5,615 | 1887 | 5,036 | 7,858 |
| 1879 | 7,083 | 6,385 | 1888 | 5,678 | 8,876 |
| 1880 | 7,662 | 7,710 | 1889 | 8,446 | 9,269 |
| 1881 | 9,227 | 8,396 | 1890 | 9,366 | 9,837 |
| 1882 | 9,372 | 8,506 | | | |

It will be seen from this table that imports and exports were affected radically by the opening up of the diamond mines in the early seventies and the gold mines in the late eighties. In these two periods, however, we see that the imports are increased more greatly than are the exports. In both tables Cape Colony appears as a country with an excess of exports. This was inevitable in an undeveloped state, all of whose shipping services and capital requirements were supplied from overseas.

We now show the same table for Natal, to which very similar remarks will be seen to apply.

## IMPORTS AND EXPORTS OF NATAL, 1850-90
(000 omitted throughout)

| Year | Imports £ | Exports £ | Year | Imports £ | Exports £ |
|---|---|---|---|---|---|
| 1850 | 111 | 17 | 1871 | 472 | 562 |
| 1851 | 125 | 21 | 1872 | 825 | 622 |
| 1852 | 103 | 27 | 1873 | 1,011 | 651 |
| 1853 | 98 | 36 | 1874 | 1,121 | 779 |
| 1854 | 112 | 43 | 1875 | 1,268 | 835 |
| 1855 | 86 | 52 | 1876 | 1,022 | 657 |
| 1856 | 102 | 56 | 1877 | 1,167 | 689 |
| 1857 | 184 | 82 | 1878 | 1,719 | 694 |
| 1858 | 172 | 100 | 1879 | 2,176 | 583 |
| 1859 | 218 | 103 | 1880 | 2,336 | 890 |
| 1860 | 354 | 139 | 1881 | 1,912 | 768 |
| 1861 | 420 | 199 | 1882 | 2,213 | 731 |
| 1862 | 449 | 127 | 1883 | 1,751 | 831 |
| 1863 | 473 | 158 | 1884 | 1,675 | 957 |
| 1864 | 591 | 220 | 1885 | 1,518 | 877 |
| 1865 | 455 | 210 | 1886 | 1,367 | 960 |
| 1866 | 263 | 203 | 1887 | 2,263 | 1,056 |
| 1867 | 269 | 225 | 1888 | 2,890 | 1,417 |
| 1868 | 317 | 271 | 1889 | 4,527 | 1,656 |
| 1869 | 380 | 363 | 1890 | 4,417 | 1,379 |
| 1870 | 429 | 382 | | | |

# DEVELOPMENT PRIOR TO 1892

Similar tables for the Orange Free State, for the Transvaal, for Swaziland, for Basutoland, are not available.

The exports, apart from minerals, were entirely of goods from the land, and after 1868 almost entirely pastoral. Prior to 1868 there was a slight export, depending entirely upon seasonal fluctuations, of food stuffs. With the establishment of the first mineral industry this export is changed immediately into a heavy and regular import. One of the permanent tendencies in the development of South African trade up to the present day is the recovering of the export of food stuffs. We cannot conclude from these tables that either Cape Colony or Natal were failing to feed themselves, although it is quite possible that that was so; the decrease in the numbers "agriculturally employed" in the census returns would seem to support this assumption. It receives further support from our knowledge that some of those who remained on the land devoted their attention to transport riding, especially just at this period until the railway system was developed, instead of to cultivation. On the other hand much land in both coastal colonies was capable of more intensive cultivation, and some of it received this. What we do know is that the Transvaal was falling very far short of supplying its new population with food stuffs and that South Africa as a whole was not meeting these needs either. This, as we shall see later, was easily to be accounted for, partly by the nature of South African agriculture, both as regards its soil and its methods, and partly by the nature of the transport available; for the railway lines that were built aimed almost entirely at connecting the mineral fields directly with the ports, and the agricultural regions were fortunate if they did not have to depend for years to come on the lumbering ox-wagon.

### REFERENCE
Cape Colony and Natal Government Gazettes.

### (d) *The Customs Policies of the South African States.*

Up to 1889 there was no customs agreement between any two South African States. The Orange Free State had no clear customs boundary. The Cape Colony and Natal were both in the extremely fortunate position of having sea-ports by means of which customs duties could be levied. The South African Republic had had a customs department for some time but had succeeded only in deriving a small revenue from goods entering the State by fords and other recognised out-posts. She had never attempted to enforce any real customs policy. The two inland States had been in the unfortunate position of having to buy over-sea goods at prices enhanced by the Cape customs duties, but from which they themselves derived no revenue. As early as 1855 the Orange Free State had begged Cape Colony to regard itself merely as a collector of customs for the inland State. The Cape had recognised this claim in principle and had agreed to accept an estimate of the amount which should be repaid to its neighbour in respect of customs duties collected on goods which ultimately went to it. Collection costs were to be charged by the Cape and deducted from this sum. But in the absence of knowledge of the overland trade this sum could only take the form of an agreed estimate. An amount was agreed upon but in fact never paid. The Cape Colony was in an overwhelmingly powerful position and could afford to ignore the Orange Free State. The opening up of the Witwatersrand changed all this. It now become necessary for the Cape to build railways through the Orange Free State, and customs and railway agreements went hand in hand. The same applied soon afterwards to the Transvaal.

It might be said without a great deal of exaggeration that South Africa had no customs history before 1886. The two coastal colonies had their customs tariffs but they did not affect each other and each of them was much more an empirical revenue-raising affair than the result of any coherent policy. The exception to this is to be found in Cape Colony, and it is an exception which proves the rule. Cape Colony's customs collections before the opening of her diamond industry had been of the most primitive kind. The rates had been low and had been levied upon imported articles such as carriages and shoes and candles—articles of general consumption by the farming population over the whole colony, who bought only small quantities of these articles and were not taxed in any other way. Local industries were still on the smallest parochial scale, making up local materials for village consumption and being unaware of any impact from imported goods. This policy, if such it can be called, had one decided feature: it aimed at protecting the producer of raw materials. The duties on imported timber worked out at a higher rate than those on carriages; and the duties on imported leather were similarly higher than those on imported boots and shoes. There was also a duty on the import of grain which undoubtedly tended to simulate wheat growing in the coastal regions. This state of things continued unaltered through the changes brought about by the diamond industry. But these changes had far reaching effects. One of these, little noticed at the time but not unimportant, was the stimulation of local manufacturing industry. Throughout the seventies people such as carriage manufacturers found an unprecedented demand for their goods at very high prices. The same applied to practically all manufactures carried on in South Africa. The mining region of Kimberley created a demand which had to be almost entirely met by imports, but which incidentally greatly stimulated local manufacturers. Throughout the prosperous seventies these local manufactures enjoyed their prosperity and little or no attention was paid to the existing customs tariff, although it was unfavourable to them and by now of little use even to the farming community, who had found a new market which was of much greater importance to them than the protection they had enjoyed.

But in the early eighties depression set in. The manufacturing interest built up during the seventies found itself among the interests most affected by the slump. The diamond miners were no longer buying on a great scale; prices of all commodities were falling as a result of concentration of interests at Kimberley which meant that fewer people there were actively engaged in buying development materials; worst of all, the railway had largely replaced the ox-wagon, which consequently greatly diminished the demand for carriage materials and harness. The depressed manufacturing industries at once sought redress through tariff changes. They drew attention to the fact that the tariff, while openly protective, was protective only of the farming interest; that that interest scarcely now needed protection, but that a new industry had been created by circumstances despite the unfavourable tariff and that the tariff policy of the colony would have to be reformed so as to protect, or at least to cease penalising, the new industries.

The claim, as such claims go, was a strong one. The local manufacturing industry was spread over nearly the whole of the colony; it had undoubtedly been a factor in cheapening costs of production in the diamond mines by preventing a monopoly of imported produce. It does not appear that it had grown to any considerable size. No reliable data was given as to the capital invested in the various industries or as to the number of people employed in them. Most of the factories concerned were in the coastal towns of Cape Town, Port Elizabeth and East London. They appear to have been conducted on a small scale. Other factories existed inland, some of them near to the mining centres, and others near the more prosperous agricultural centres. While their claim to protection was strong, it was evident to observers that the grant of protection to them might be the first step in a protective policy that would have to become more and more stringent as time went on, for the manufacturing industries depended upon the diamond mining and if they fluctuated along with the ups and downs of the diamond market then protective policy would have a hard job to keep pace with their needs in the future. Again, the protection which was demanded might take one or both of two forms. It might reduce duties on imported raw materials or it might impose duties on other imported articles. The former proceeding would be to the disadvantage of the farmer who produced the hides, the tanning material, the tallow, and the timber used by the manufacturers. The second measure would enhance the prices of the carriages and harness and boots and shoes, not to mention agricultural implements which the farmers had to buy. Whatever was done it appeared that the farming community would suffer. The mining interests, as far as one could see, stood to lose rather than to gain, but not very definitely, for while they wished for free imports they were not adverse to the existence of local manufacturers to compete with the imported article. The mercantile interests in the sea-port towns were, needless to say, entirely free trade. The farmers were the main consideration. If any protection, even protection by reduction of duties, were given to the manufacturers, it would be to the detriment of the agricultural community.

The farmers themselves, however, had grown somewhat dissatisfied with the old tariff which, now that conditions had changed, met their needs much less fully than it had previously done. In the main, as we have already indicated, they were much less dependent upon tariff protection than they were before the diamond discoveries. They now had an unlimited market for the whole of their agricultural products, which consisted chiefly in wine and wheat from the South Western Cape, and of maize and miscellaneous grain products from the many inland farmers who found a market in Kimberley.  It cannot be over-emphasized that, excepting in the south-west corner, agriculture was very spasmodic and nearly always on a very small scale.  This will be explained when we come to deal with the agriculture of Cape Colony.  There were no extensive wheat lands either on the south coast or in the Karroo.  Nor was maize grown extensively.  Indeed it is very doubtful whether any farmers except those in the south west ever subscribed to a protectionist policy.  All that was wanted was good access to the inland market.  On the other hand most of the Karroo farmers and all of the Eastern Province farmers, as well as those of the Orange Free State, did definitely want low costs of production in order to be able to dispose of their wool with a good margin of profit.  Had it not been for the fact that the industrial depression of the eighties, depriving the farmers as it did of their easy access to good markets, was accompanied by drought and so brought on an agricultural depression, it is doubtful whether the agricultural community would have voiced their demands in the tariff agitation of that decade. As it is it appears that they were mainly intent upon a *quid pro quo* to offset any higher tariff which might be granted to the new manufacturers.

A select-committee, which reported in 1883, fully recognised the existing tariff as being unfavourable to the development of colonial manufactures.  It is noticeable, however, that any increase in the general tariff rate was carefully not recommended.  A reduction of rates upon raw materials would be a decided first step toward encouraging manufactures, for supplies of raw materials had to be imported.  As to agriculture, it was clearly stated that its revival was contingent upon the commercial activity of the colony and that cheapness of agricultural production would actually benefit the farmer as well as contribute materially toward the necessary trade revival.

No action was taken.  The manufacturing industry were not as yet a powerful influence in the State.  The

## DEVELOPMENT PRIOR TO 1892

government, though in some financial distress, and tempted to raise duties merely for revenue purposes, was afraid that any increase might still further diminish its railway traffic and so cause a possibly greater shrinkage in income. Its railway position at the moment was not a happy one. Any decided demands from the farmers might have brought about a change, but these, as we have seen, were not forthcoming.

No fresh developments in the tariff question are found until after the Transvaal gold mines had once more given a new direction to the economy, not only of Cape Colony, but of the whole of South Africa. The establishment of the Witwatersrand industry once more provided new activities and new markets for the farmers of South Africa. Again the small manufacturing industries of the Cape were revived. But once more, after a few years of intense activity, the mining industry slowed down its buying while transport riders were again displaced by the railway, and depression set in. The tariff enquiry of 1883 was repeated in 1891 and the ground covered and the demands made were remarkably similar. But by this time the government of Cape Colony was in a very different position. The Ministers had made a railway arrangement with the Orange Free State which necessitated customs-union with that State; and intense competition with Natal for the inland carrying trade had begun. Both the value of this union and the necessity of victory in the carrying war with Natal were only increased by the trade depression.

The competition with Natal indeed became the dominating factor, for the Cape Colony government had invested all its substance in an elaborate railway system designed in the first place to give its three chief ports equal shares in the trade to the diamond fields. This trade had proved insufficient to support the mileage built. A serious financial collapse had almost certainly been averted only by the timely discovery of the Transvaal gold. The existing lines, by being extended through Orange Free State territory, were by great good fortune the best that the Cape could ever have built for the Rand trade, but the geographical position of Natal, as a glance at the map will show, was much more favourable than that of Cape Colony. The Cape had the advantage of being first on the spot with a railway system already fully developed. But the capital sunk had strained the resources of the Colony and it was only by keeping the whole mileage working at high pressure that a dividend could be obtained. Actually while trade was good rich profits had been reaped, but their continuance was no less necessary, and the impending competition with Natal may be said to have dominated the customs question in Cape Colony.

As matters stood, Natal had the advantage of a much lower tariff than the Cape. She was a much less developed colony with only one small group of tropical plantation industries to demand anything in the nature of a protective tariff. Her government expenditure also was much smaller than that of the Cape ; before building her line to the Transvaal she was not saddled with any substantial public debt, and that line always paid for itself. So that Natal's low tariff promised to confirm her geographical advantages and make her a really powerful competitor.

The inherent weakness of Cape Colony, a weakness which existed up to the moment of her absorption in United South Africa, was now apparent. Her financial position depended to an overwhelming extent upon her railway and her customs revenues, but her railways were threatened with competition and her customs policy was almost equally taken out of her own hands. At the same time she of all South African States had the most strongly developed agricultural and manufacturing industries demanding favours through railway or customs.

The occasion of her custom's union with the Orange Free State had, however, been used for a revision of her tariff (1889). The new tariff conceded the demands of the industrialists by radically reducing the duties on

## DEVELOPMENT PRIOR TO 1892

imported timber, leather, and similar goods. The internal market for these was now quite good enough to use up all the local products in addition to free imports. This, however, was one of the least important of the features of the new tariff. The main questions involved were the granting of favours to the farming community and the cheapening of the transit of imported produce for the Transvaal. So far as machinery and mining implements were concerned the problem was a fairly simple one and the rates on these were considerably reduced. Agriculture was satisfied by means of a retention of existing duties on wheat and wine but was really to be given protection by railway preferences on the carriage of agricultural produce. On the whole, the revision meant a reduction in tariff, but this still stood at about seven per cent. average rate. A minor feature of the tariff was that the Cape now consented to refund to the Orange Free State the money in respect of goods to be consumed in that State.

Natal customs policy has already been indicated. Its sugar planters on the coast had demanded and obtained fairly substantial protection. Its upland wheat and maize farmers were chiefly concerned with securing free access for their products through the Orange Free State to the Witwatersrand, for this was the route favoured by the ox-wagons before the building of the railway. Thus with protection demanded on only one product, and with its main agricultural population free-trade, its main policy could easily be the commercial one of a very low tariff. When, in 1895, competition with Delagoa Bay set in seriously, and Natal was angling for the favours of the Transvaal railway administration, the tariff was further reduced to the point of only transit duties being imposed on goods going to the Transvaal.

A factor of great importance yet to be dealt with is the customs policy of the Transvaal itself. As we have already seen, the existence of any such policy was virtually impossible so long as the Transvaal was a mere inland area without many of the attributes of a state and unable to collect taxes from its own white population. Its trade with the outside world was so slight, and conducted through so many points of entrance, that its customs collections were almost non-existent. This was immediately altered on the establishment of the Witwatersrand industry. The routes by which goods were imported became few and well marked. The Cape railway brought the whole of its produce across the border at one point. Customs could easily be collected here. Doubtless some smuggling was conducted by means of ox-wagons, but it was only a question of time until railways from three great centres would supersede these. An entirely new customs tariff was put into force in 1889. In the early twentieth century the customs policy of the Transvaal was not without its complications, but in 1889 the situation was simple. The farmers were enjoying prodigious prosperity from transport riding, from the sale of whatever small quantities of produce they might have for disposal, and by the sale of options on their farm to prospectors. They had no strong tariff demands. The commercial community and the gold mining industry were completely free-trade, since low costs of production and the resulting development meant everything to them. Manufacturing industries were non-existent, excepting for a few quasi-industries completely protected by concessions. The government had the single aim of deriving the highest possible income from customs revenue and their position to do this was very strong. They did not need to bargain with either of the coastal colonies. For now the disadvantages of its land-locked position were changed into the advantages of a central state whose business was competed for by several coastal states. The tariff adopted was entirely empirical, being slightly below that of Cape Colony as regards its general average, but differing from it in that the highest duties were imposed on goods used by the mining industry and by the commercial community in general. Food-stuffs did not escape, and it was one of the chief

# DEVELOPMENT PRIOR TO 1892

misfortunes of the new Transvaal population that almost the whole of these had to be imported. A slight preference was given to the Dutch population in that the duty on coffee was lower than that on tea while such luxuries as wines were heavily taxed.

It was now strongly in the interests of the Cape Colony to promote customs unification. It was equally in the interest of Natal to keep a lower tariff. The Transvaal was able to pursue her own line. While the Orange Free State, the only intermediary among the States, was in the position of having united with Cape Colony on account of railway necessity, but still attached considerable importance to a free entry of her agricultural produce into the Transvaal, which had been granted in the Transvaal tariff.

### REFERENCES

Annexure to The Report of the Collector of Customs of Cape Colony, 1899. This gives a full Resumé of Important Customs Matters since 1806.

Report and Evidence of the Select Committee on the Trade and Industry of Cape Colony, 1883.

The same for the Committee on the same Subject of 1891.

Annual Reports of the Customs Department of Cape Colony and Natal.

Some valuable evidence is to be found in the files of the *British and South African Export Gazette* for its first few years of issue, say 1892 to 1895, in which earlier conditions are sometimes described.

### (e) *Early Transport in Cape Colony*

As Cape Colony was the oldest part of South Africa so, in the main, she was the most highly developed part. Her development required three systems of transport; one to connect Cape Town with the agricultural land of the south west, where were both the wine and corn land to the north of the port, and the wheat and mixed farming land to the north east of the port; the second was needed to develop the very sparse Karroo and also to have branches feeding the coast lands between the Karroo and the sea; the third was needed for the fertile grass land of the Eastern Province and to connect with the Veld in the Free State. On grounds of natural economy the first and the third of these were feasible ; the second, serving mainly the Karroo, could scarcely be expected to develop a paying traffic. The South Western Railway was undoubtedly the most needed, as it served agricultural and not pastural land. It had a thriving town to serve and a town which not only could consume great quantities of food-stuffs itself but which had excellent shipping connections both for export and for victualling trade. The need for a railway was considerable owing to the fact that the town was surrounded by a belt of shifting sand which only in the fifties and sixties was being fixed by the planting of shrubs. Even these shrubs, when they became plentiful, did not afford pasture to the animals which dragged the wagons. Pasturage for draught animals was then one of the chief factors in transport economics. The cultivation of the south western regions was eminently capable of being developed. Cheap transport to market might be expected to cause farmers to bring a considerably increased proportion of their lands under cultivation.

A railway was proposed in the early fifties. Finance, by the good offices of Cape Town, was forthcoming. The farmers in the districts to be served had offered to accept part of the responsibility by means of local sub-guarantees. This was not felt to be necessary and the line was built and opened for traffic in 1854. It consisted in some 65 miles and was built and worked by a company with headquarters in England under a guarantee from the Cape government. Its financial life was never a happy one, but actual loss was avoided, and the benefits of railway communication to responsive agricultural land were realised. While this railway was being built, the Eastern Province was demanding similar services. Here also was a fair prospect of ultimate success. Two ports competed for the serving of this area, Port Elizabeth, which was in touch with

# DEVELOPMENT PRIOR TO 1892

the best grassland on the eastern end of the Karroo, as well as with good agricultural land nearer the coast; and East London, which was in immediate touch with a belt of grass-land not then suitable for farming but possible for opening-up, and also with the sheep farming district leading up to the southern end of Basutoland and thence to the grass-land of the Free State. There were great differences, however, between this area and the Cape South-West. In the first place, costs of railway building threatened to be much higher; indeed it was found impossible throughout the fifties and the sixties to find contractors in England who would even make the necessary surveys on the spot preliminary to offering tenders. The distances were much greater; the routes for railways were much less definitely marked; the gradients encountered as one left the coastal belt were very stiff. In addition to these physical drawbacks the financing of the line would be much more difficult owing to the fact that the ports would not co-operate with each other and were a great distance from Cape Town, the financial centre of the colony. The traffic also was problematical. The enterprise would have been much more in the nature of "building a line to nowhere" and the nowhere consisted of a mixture of lands which were not at all certain to become productive. There was only one reliable product, wool, and this was not a product which would repay rapid carrying. It was brought to port fairly satisfactorily by ox-wagons, which though slow had the advantage of reaching every farm. Difficulty was encountered only when drought affected the grass lands and so made transit by ox-wagon difficult. In years of drought the traffic might go to the railway, but then the traffic itself was likely to be small. Even if one or two through lines were built, and this was all that could be hoped for, nearly all the farmers would have to travel considerable distances to reach the railway. There would be a distinct danger that since they had in any case to maintain their draught animals and wagons, and since the distance direct to the port might be only slightly greater than the distance to the railway line, they might save railway fares altogether. Had it been possible to build only one line, either from Port Elizabeth or from East London, it seems possible that the Cape Colony government might have made some attempt to do so ; but the rivalry between these two ports was such that for purely political reasons, to satisfy them both and possibly even to prevent the cession of the Eastern Province from Cape Colony, about twice the length of line economically justifiable would have had to be built. Actually the whole of Cape Colony was in a kind of prolonged depression during the sixties and neither of the lines were proceeded with. No attempt was made either to provide the Karroo with a railway system.

The depression was abruptly ended by the diamond discoveries. The customs revenue of Cape Colony was greatly increased, and Port Elizabeth and East London became busy as ports of entry of goods for the diamond district. These two ports now enjoyed a considerable advantage over Cape Town in that they were much nearer to the diamond regions. A scheme of railway building was at once drawn up and rapidly proceeded with. This scheme had to fulfil the two objects of connecting Griqualand West with the ports in the most economic manner, and, much more difficult, of providing each of these ports with its " fair " share of the traffic. The most economic method would doubtless have been a single line, either from Port Elizabeth or from East London. The most rapid line on the other hand for mails and passengers would be a continuation of the existing south west line from Cape Town across the Karroo. Actually all lines were built. The Cape Town line stretched across the Karroo into the high Karroo plateau and stopped some little distance short of Kimberley. A line was built also from Port Elizabeth to within about the same distance from Kimberley, and yet another was built from East London with the same object. The total mileage was some 2,000 miles.

## DEVELOPMENT PRIOR TO 1892

The costs of working were very high and the difficulties of management also very considerable. To deal first with management, we find that each of the lines was regarded as a quite separate unit under a manager who was responsible only to the political Minister in Cape Town. Each of the three systems kept its own accounts and was completely responsible for the buying of its own stores, the engagement of its staff, and most important of all, the determination of the rates at which it would carry goods and passengers. All three lines were now owned and run by the Cape Colony Government. The original sixty-nine miles of line in the south west had been acquired by the State to complete the system. The whole of the lines were working by 1876, and the next ten years saw Cape Colony struggling to maintain a railway mileage some three times as great as for most purposes it needed.

The history of this railway period gives instructive examples of the various problems which were to beset South African railways right up to the time of Union, and which indeed are inherent in the system for all time. These examples are all the more instructive in that they have to do only with natural conditions and not with the inter-state political complications which developed later. In the first place we see the influence of political conditions causing mileages to be built merely in order to keep the balance between certain districts. In the second place we see the difficulties in political management. In the third place, not unconnected with this political management, we have the difficulties in evolving a satisfactory rate policy. In the fourth place we have a group of problems arising out of the management of a considerable mileage stretched out nearly all its distance across sparsely inhabited land. The first problem has already been sufficiently indicated. The second problem, that of political management, was one which appeared to be entirely beyond solution in the period with which we deal. The ordinary difficulties of this kind of management were intensified by the fact that there was no communication whatever excepting by road or by a long sea journey between the administrative capital and two of the railway systems (for it must be emphasized that the two lines from Port Elizabeth and from East London inland were each a separate system). The means of administration as evolved by Parliament were the appointment of a Minister of Railways as a member of the Cabinet and the entrusting of everything to him subject to questions and criticism in the House. He was expected to hand all railway profits over to the general revenue, and no very clear definition was ever arrived at to show what were to be regarded as profits. Ministers never arrived at a uniform practice in regard to the provision of new capital expenditure out of railway revenue and out of funds voted by the House. No book-keeping system was ever successfully worked out to show which of the proceeds of railway activities ought to be put at the disposal of capital account and which to be regarded as profit to be handed over to the general revenue. Years afterwards, while rail unification was being discussed, it was found that the Cape railway accounts for past years were valueless on this question. It is clear that the House and a Ministry anxious to keep the support of the House, desired as much as possible to be handed over annually by the railways as profit for the State revenue. It was a perfectly open and unblushing system of taxation by means of railway. It was justified by the argument that it was not taxation at all but only profit made out of one particular industry, the mining industry, which was taxed only very slightly in other ways.

The determination of rates was effected by each general manager drawing up a rate schedule for his own system and then submitting this schedule to the Minister for confirmation. In practise the managers were in touch with the needs of their districts and their proposals were nearly always accepted, with the result, however, that districts which were not satisfied would get their

## DEVELOPMENT PRIOR TO 1892

members to bait the Minister in the House with questions. The Minister, in response to the expressions of opinion in the House, would consult the managers as to whether alterations in rate would be advisable. Within a very short time of the opening of the diamond lines it became clear that a system of preferential rates on Cape Colony agricultural produce on its way to market was to develop. In the next ten years this system had become an accepted policy and one which could not be changed. It was, indeed, confirmed by the customs tariff of 1889.

Apart from this preferential system the rate policies of the three lines developed differently. They had, however, one factor in common, which was that their inland working expenses were much higher than those near the coast. Thus the system of reduced rates for long distances found in railway systems all over the world was not brought into practice. The inland stretches had first of all to encounter heavy gradients and then to journey for hundreds of miles across land where water was scarce, where coal was unobtainable, and where labour and replacements were generally costly. The Western system encountered most difficulties in these respects. Its first hundred miles ran through good agricultural land, but all the rest of its length lay across the Karroo and the Karroid Plateau for a much greater distance than the total length of the Port Elizabeth line. In this case, however, the question of reducing rates for long distances can scarcely be said to have arisen. The traffic was almost entirely, after passing the coastal ranges, in one direction, and, indeed, to one destination. The rates applying to this traffic really had the nature of "destination" rates. The agricultural produce collected on the way was a very slight amount and received preferential rates, being carried more cheaply than similar food stuffs which had been imported. The colonial-produce rate, as it was called, was designed to give the most distant farmers an equal chance in the Kimberley market along with the nearest.

Apart from these Cape Colony lines there was only some twenty miles of line in the whole of South Africa. It is one of the main objects of this study to trace the development, both of railway lines and of railway policy from Cape Colony outward.

### REFERENCES

Reports and evidence of various select committees from 1854 onwards, chiefly one held in 1875 on the subject of Railway Expenditure and Administration, while another held in 1868 also printed a great deal of interesting evidence; its terms of reference were "To take into consideration the subject of railways—first with reference to the existing railways, and secondly with reference to railway extension." Report and Evidence of Commission on Railways, 1878, and of the Commission of Railway Rates, 1883.

### (f) *Agricultural Development*

It remains for us to deal with what was after all the most important feature in the economic growth in the whole of South Africa, namely agriculture. We have already indicated the main geographical features. It remains for us to trace the way in which those features became related by the agricultural methods of the Colonists, and the dominating influence of market connections, to the actual agricultural production of the soil.

In the first place we must mention certain conditions which prevailed over the whole of the sub-continent. One of the chief of these features was a sparsity of population due partly to the fact that only a small number of people ever undertook to pioneer in the hope of settling the land, but partly also to the fact that those who did settle laid claim to very large holdings so that the land was eventually monopolised by a small number of people. One of the necessities of intensive development, a necessity not faced until the twentieth century, was that the size of holdings should be reduced in order to induce more intensive cultivation. Over the whole of the area, excepting in a very few coastal districts, it was the custom for each settler to lay claim to at least 3,000 acres. This was carried out in different part of South Africa under different legal systems but the economic results were very similar. In some parts it was necessitated by the nature of the soil; for example, a small holding on the Karroo would have been impossible, but in other parts, as for example in the well watered regions of the Transvaal, the same system held, the fortunate first-comers taking their stand at the head-waters of a river and establishing their claim to a great distance around. Two factors were necessary to lead to a more intensive cultivation. In the first place, if more people came into the district in the hope of finding a living, then they might be accommodated somehow on the lands of other farmers. Natural increase of population would lead to the same result provided that there was no other outlet for the sons of farmers. In the second place, coast connection with markets, either by nearness to the sea-coast or by the building of a railway line, would cause land values to rise, so that a new and more commercial type of farmer would bid for the land. We find in fact that the first of these causes was at work in the inland parts of South Africa and the second in the more fertile coastal regions.

Another consideration applying to the whole region, was the nature of its water supply. Almost the whole of the sub-continent excepting the coastal regions, and in many cases them also, depends for its rainfall upon a very small actual amount of rain and for the rest upon the water brought down by the rivers from its mountain systems. The High Veld of the Transvaal, for example, prior to the building of railway lines, was scattered with patches of green. Each of these patches was a district where water either had overflowed from some river head or had been successfully taken out by means of crude irrigation. Later, railway lines made agriculture possible without the direct assistance of river water. This was done by scientific cultivation which made use of the small amount of moisture available from rainfall by

applying it to carefully selected soil. Much of the
soil, indeed, was excellent, but with crude methods of
agriculture it could be cultivated only by means of river
water. Each of the large holdings of the early pioneers
consisted of a very small portion of land under arable
crops, generally yielding, without any effort on the part
of the farmer, all the food stuffs required. On the
veld of the Orange Free State, as well as in the interior
of Basutoland, rainfall was slightly better, so that the soil
was really good for sheep farming and this determined
the economy of the district. In both of these districts,
however, in the high veld north of the Vaal and in that
south of it, water was distinctly scarce except within
half a mile of the river, and the ability of the soil to
support population depended upon its being kept in good
condition so as to be able to retain and to benefit from
every drop of rain. Over-stocking, with its consequent
trampling of the soil by sheep, would tend to harden the
soil and so to lessen its ability to respond to rainfall.
It would appear that in the Orange Free State, the sheep
farmers enjoying apparently good conditions to start
with, had not let overstocking become a serious evil.
On the other hand, neither did their sheep farming ever
become scientific. Their land was never paddocked;
they seldom grew winter fodder; they never sorted the
wool, and they generally sold in bulk to the nearest
store-keeper. Wool production was thus more a matter
of weight than of quality. But the natural conditions
seem to have prevented actual deterioration. North of
the river Vaal the conditions were somewhat less favourable. The absence of winter fodder necessitated the
trekking of sheep to the low veld for the winter months.
Each colonist owned not only his farm on the high veld,
but also grazing land nearer the coast. This trekking
kept the wool-producing industry in a very primitive
stage. The trekking of the sheep meant that they had
to be big-boned animals of little value either for wool or
mutton. The farmer himself probably wasted a quarter
of the year in travelling to and fro with his flocks. The

## DEVELOPMENT PRIOR TO 1892

growing of winter fodder would in some cases have been easy, in other cases almost impossible, but the absence of markets and the semi-barbarous life led by the farmers meant that in fact it never was grown. The trekking, however, did mean that the land was given several months in the year in which to recuperate. The system was only possible when land was plentiful and population scarce, but it did prevent the dangers of over-stocking. The only other part of South Africa in which similar conditions are found is in the great Karroo lands of Cape Colony. These, however, although superficially similar, really present a different group of problems and different types of agriculture. The soil is different in nature from that of the high veld. It is more sandy, but beneath this sand is a type of soil extremely well suited to drought conditions. The Karroo in the twentieth century has several flood rivers, that is to say, rivers which have a great deal of water frequently overflowing their banks during two or three months in the year and which are dry river beds for the rest of the year. Prior to about 1880, however, the existence of these rivers was a subject for comment. It appears that most of them are a recent creation. There is unquestionable evidence that the first settlers in the Karroo found that the land had a very small amount of rainfall, but that its natural vegetation retained and made good use of the amount of moisture available. The district had accommodated itself to scanty water supply. The soil was covered with drought-resisting shrubs and grasses. These sprang up after every fall of rain and provided excellent food for wandering herds of game. It appears that little or none of the water was allowed to enter river beds and run uselessly to the sea. On this land also the practice of the first settlers was to claim very large stretches of land. Here, however, trekking was impossible, for no reserve lands were available. Also, the region was nearer to the coast, so that cultivation of wool for export was always at least kept in mind by the farmers. The result was that a kind of intensive cultivation of sheep took place. It became the aim of the farmer to own as many head of stock as possible with a view to increasing the weight of wool which he could take to the store-keeper. This intensive cultivation led to what appears to have been a fairly rapid shifting of the balance between drought and non-drought conditions. As soon as sheep were kept closely stocked the more succulent grasses were eaten, thus depriving the soil of its best natural covering. In time these grasses almost disappeared over large areas and their place was taken by less valuable shrubs not liked by the sheep. Deprived of a large part of its covering, the soil was less able to retain moisture and this tendency was rendered still worse by the fact that the sheep were allowed to wander indiscriminately across the soil in search of food. The only control to which they were subjected was that they were driven into enclosures, known as kraals, for the night. This was necessary owing to the fact that the land was infested with jackals and other vermin. This daily rounding up and driving of the sheep had almost the same effect upon their physique as had the trekking in the Transvaal. It made selective improvement of the wool almost impossible. But an even more important result was that it hardened the soil in the paths in which they were usually driven, so that hardening and denudation was the inevitable consequence of this unscientific sheep farming. The flood waters of the Karroo became available for irrigation in the coastal districts through which they flowed, but they were lost to the Karroo itself. Cereal cultivation was almost unknown, excepting of course the minimum necessary for food. Some parts of the Karroo were better than others, and toward the eastern end the Karroo land merged into grass-land and here ideal conditions were found for the breeding of good sheep, and first-class Angora goats were kept successfully, an achievement which stands to the credit of no other part of the world outside their original home in Turkey. The success of the mohair industry may be

## DEVELOPMENT PRIOR TO 1892      45

taken to indicate the great value of Karroo land provided it is kept out of actual drought conditions. It is even possible that, given very careful tending and use of water, the great bulk of the Karroo land could be induced to grow cereal crops. While some of the Karroo is good, it must be remembered that that which lies about more than 300 miles inland is so little supplied with water that it is merely a vast region of semi-desert land. On the banks of the Orange River, which flows through the north-eastern corner of this region, a good deal of cultivation is possible. But the rest of the plateau, many hundreds of square miles, has been a heart-breaking region for generations of colonists. Despite many efforts, it has never been able to support more than a few sheep to the square mile and has been the refuge of broken-down colonists from other parts of South Africa who have virtually lost their civilisation while living in the wastes. In all of these regions, from the north of the Transvaal High Veld down to the south-western end of the Cape Colony Karroo, the same lack of water is evident, the same land settlement policy was originally pursued, and the primitive or speculative cultivation of foodstuffs exists. The differences between the Karroo and the High Veld we have seen. It is important to remember, however, that by about 1890 all of these lands were known only to colonists. They had not been scientifically cultivated in any way. Pressure of population had occurred in parts, but this, as we shall see later, had led to poverty rather than to scientific cultivation.

In the coastal regions, both of the south-west and of the east coast, we find a very different type of agriculture. The south-west of Cape Colony enjoys a Mediterranean type of climate with winter rainfall and with a good average quantity. Add to this its easy access to markets from the date of its first settlement, and it will be seen that it should stand apart from the inland regions. Actually, however, some of the same problems are found. The system of settlement, while not the same as further inland, was similar in principle. Various settlements of soldiers and of refugees from Europe were made in the course of the seventeenth and eighteenth centuries. The tendency was to give each settler sufficient land not merely to give him a living but to guarantee him against any possible loss. The result was that in 1895 it could be said that within 200 miles of Cape Town over 50 per cent. of the land was totally uncultivated. Laymen could see no reason for this. And indeed it is difficult to account for, since other regions apparently similar in all respects had by that date been successfully sub-divided and intensively cultivated. This, it may be noted, is one of the puzzles which we find throughout South African agriculture. Similar stretches of land lying next door to each other will be treated in very different ways, and one can only account for it by accidents in ownership and various other circumstances. Nevertheless, sub-division had in the greater part of the Cape Western Province successfully changed the methods under which wheat and wine were produced. The sub-division had not been entirely successful as regards its social effects, and it is possible that it had led to over-cultivation of wheat lands. The estimates of yield per acre support this supposition by showing a decrease about this period. But another equally possible supposition is that a great deal more land had been brought under wheat under the stimulus of the new Witwatersrand market. The wine industry was a very old-established one, and up to the date of the repeal of the British preferences by Gladstone (1865) a small but steady export had been maintained. It is possible that the repeal had not been entirely to blame for the decline of the export trade. Only a few rare wines such as Sweet Constantia had ever been exported, and they only in small quantities. In the decade before 1865 the British demand was very great owing to the ravages of the phyloxera in the French vine-yards. This increased demand had led to the Cape producers exporting somewhat beyond their real productive capacities. A reduction in quality had resulted, and with the recovery of French production the Cape article had fallen into disfavour. Be that as it may, the main products of the wine industry were light wines and brandies which had never been successfully exported. This was the fault of their chemical composition and not of any economic circumstances. The loss of the British market, however, had undoubtedly brought depression to the Cape wine farmers, and this depression was emphasized by the fact that the Cape market itself was not progressive. Even the diamond discoveries appeared to have brought no great improvement. The south-west district as a whole appeared to be a settled one oxcept for the fact that it was enjoying a natural increase in population, that this increase could find no outlet in trades or professions and only a slight outlet by buying Karroo land, and that in consequence the sub-division which we have mentioned was taking place and was preparing the district to meet the larger demands which would arise when inland markets were opened up by railway building. The district to which this applies was a belt of land running north-west to south-east, parallel to the coast. The same agricultural conditions are found in another belt of land somewhat separated from the former and running west to east, parallel to the south coast. This second region, as regards its western end, also produced wine and corn, though of slightly different kinds, but as it stretched to the east it came under different influences. The winter rains ceased. Their place was taken by scant summer rains which left the surface of the soil almost dry. Their water supply came almost entirely from rivers running down from the coastal ranges which separated the region from the Karroo. These rivers were dry for some eight months in the year but generally had plenty of water in the wet seasons. The development of the district obviously depended upon irrigation, and we find that the earliest concern of the Cape government with agriculture is to assist in the conservation of river waters in this district. The taking out of water, however, was an expensive and technically difficult process and was never actually achieved until the fortunate appearance of a highly profitable industry which depended upon it. This industry was ostrich farming. By the eighties it had been established that this southern belt could produce very valuable ostrich feathers and that fashions in England yielded a very profitable market for them. The soil devoted to ostrich farming was dry and soft. It was ideal for the growing of lucerne. The birds could be kept in paddocks on dry land where there was no danger of their feathers being soiled, while water led out of the rivers was growing excellent lucerne to feed them. Land values grew in the case of really suitable land by leaps and bounds until in 1913 a catastrophic change of fashion took place in England and America and the industry was plunged into ruin. The land was suitable for various kinds of mixed farming involving the growing of tobacco, possibly cotton, and, most important, dairy produce. But this mixed farming had been neglected while ostrich feathers paid. In the ostrich district the effect of profitable agriculture upon the size of land holdings had been made visible. Land had been settled extensively, as it had in all other districts, and unlike the neighbouring Western Province, it had never had regular agriculture to induce an increase in population. As a result, when the land became profitable large holdings were still the rule but were no longer necessary. Commercial capital was attracted. The settled farmers were in nearly every case tempted to sell out at very high prices, for they themselves usually had a predilection for more primitive types of farming. With the high prices which they got for their land they were able to buy more congenial large areas in the Karroo and Eastern Province, or even in the Orange Free State. A new type of farmer came into the Oudtshoorn district, almost the only case in South Africa of the progressive farmer displacing the primitive.

# DEVELOPMENT PRIOR TO 1892

The other coastal agriculture was that of the east coast. This has to be divided into two parts. In the more southern of these parts we have Native agriculture, and in the more northern the tropical agriculture of the Natal colonists. The former is easily described in outline and need not be fully dealt with now. The districts between the Ciskei and Natal were thickly populated with Natives. By 1890, and almost to the present day, their agricultural methods were traditional, consisting in the growth of enough food stuffs for their own needs and in the accumulation of cattle, which were regarded as the real sign of wealth. Commercially this agriculture was almost insignificant. Even before the beginning of our period individual traders had penetrated into the Transkei and were gradually teaching the natives that maize could be sold and more cattle obtained in exchange. But this teaching was very slow in its effect and had to be supplemented later by all kinds of other influences before any noticeable change in agricultural methods was brought about. To the south of this region was similar land which had passed into the hands of white colonists. It was excellent grass land, especially nearer the coast. The more inland region was also good for agriculture, but it is a noticeable fact that the land in possession of the whites had developed only slightly more favourably than the neighbouring land still inhabited by blacks.

The reasons for this are not by any means simple. One or two outstanding facts may be mentioned. In the first place, the grass belt near the coast was unbroken land infested by ticks, which rendered the economic holding of European flocks impossible. In the second place, the more inland region, while essentially fertile, yet required somewhat laborious cultivation to give results. It was essentially a grain growing district, while the white farmers were much more inclined toward pastural farming. Also, the district, although taken from the Natives, was still the home of many of them. Each white farmer, therefore, found himself in possession of land which he himself was not inclined to cultivate but which numbers of Natives were. The easy course was for the farmer to allow the Natives, either by tenancy or by share-farming, or by what was known as Kaffir-farming, to leave the land more under Native influence than European. It was a district neither essentially white nor essentially black. Many of the white farmers were absentee owners.

To the south of this district again was the coastal Eastern Province around Port Elizabeth. This had been settled as early as 1820 by settlers who had aimed at a small holding system for arable cultivation. The settlement had, on the whole, been successful, many of the descendants of the original settlers are there to this day, and others have sold out to English settlers, only to carry their careful German methods further north. In this piece of coastal belt, the portion from East London up to the boundary of Natal, and, of course, for some distance beyond that, has its agriculture practically entirely in the hands of natives.

The Natal colonists, as a result of their wars in the earlier part of the nineteenth century, succeeded in clearing a substantial stretch of land of native tribes. Most of these tribes were driven toward the south or toward the Drakensbergs, where they congregated thickly. The rest of the land was held by the whites. The land came within the zone of summer rainfall and was soon seen to be ideal for tropical agriculture. By the middle of the century, coffee and tea plants had been imported from India, and though the early imports fell victims to local diseases the tea plants were successfully established, and sugar followed. A difficulty, not unaccountable, in persuading the natives to undertake plantation work, was overcome by importing labour as well as plants from India. Tropical agriculture was thoroughly and safely established before the seventies. As every reader of the various biographies of Cecil Rhodes will know, efforts were also being made to grow cotton. These readers will also know that the growing

# DEVELOPMENT PRIOR TO 1892

of cotton had barely got out of its experimental stage when the diamond fields offered an alternative attraction to some of the more industrious as well as all the more adventurous colonists. Whether or not this coastal agriculture really received a set back from the opposition of the mineral discoveries we can never know. There were too many other speculative factors in the extension of tea and sugar and cotton. Capital was scarce, labour supply uncertain, central factories for sugar were built only in the nineties, native troubles were by no means over, and it was only after 1906 that Zululand was opened up for sugar cultivation. Natal between the inner edge of the coastal belt and the Drakensbergs passed from tropical near the coast to wheat growing regions further inland. Fruit was possible in the interior and was grown after railways had been built. It was in 1906 that maize was suddenly found to be exportable in large quantities and this led to the opening up of the interior of Natal.

### REFERENCES

Historical Sections of the Transvaal Indigency Commission Report.
Report and Evidence of the Imperial Commission on Land Settlement in South Africa, 1901.
Report of the Drought Investigation Commission, 1923.
Leppan, *Agriculture in Arid and Semi-Arid Regions.*
Reports of the Hydraulic Engineer of Cape Colony from 1887.
Reports of various Select Committees to Enquire into the Working of the Cape Colony Irrigation Acts, chiefly those of 1879, 1892, and 1896.
Report and Evidence of the Cape Colony Irrigation Commission of 1896.
Minutes of the South African Irrigation Congress, 1906.
Report on Wheat Growing in Australia. Issued by the Cape Agricultural Department in 1895. Throws valuable light on Cape Agriculture by comparison.

### (g) *Early Land Settlement Policy*

In this description of agricultural conditions references to land settlement have been inevitable. Early land settlement policy indeed is one of the chief factors in the development of South African agriculture throughout the whole of our period. In essentials that policy was the same whether in the Cape Colony or in Natal or in the Inland States, with the exception of those early settlements of soldiers and immigrants around Cape Town and Port Elizabeth. The Cape in its early days had tried more than one system of granting title to land. One specific form of tenure had been tried with a view to enabling farmers to settle temporarily on land as pasturalists and then to move on to new regions. This loan system, as it was called, had suited the needs ideally of a farming population in the process of trekking. It might equally have suited the needs of the Dutch farmers penetrating northward into the Transvaal. It is possible that some such system was tried by them. But by about 1840, when the actual trek movement was in progress, the need arose for a system of tenure which would give pastoral farmers permanent title to land which presumably they would use simply for pastoral purposes and which would be sufficient to support them and their descendants. The need for this kind of tenure was the same from the south of the Karroo to the north of the Transvaal. Actually it was applied to other districts as well, for the agricultural districts of the Cape southwest and other coast lands both of the Cape and of Natal were given out on the same system. Legally the Cape system was not the same as that of the two Republics. Its essential feature was the granting of permanent right to farmers either in a form known as perpetual quit-rent or in freehold. Natal adopted this Cape system and with it almost the whole of the Cape land settlement policy. The Boer Republic quite simply gave each settler permanent possession of as much land as he could ride round in one day. This generally amounted to some six or eight thousand acres, while if the land did not have natural winter pasturage the settler would also be given another holding on land which had. In the original settlement of the country, excepting in the Cape south-

## DEVELOPMENT PRIOR TO 1892

west and one or two other selected areas, the whole of the land in South Africa was alienated to settlers simply with a view to attracting the original colonists and attaching them to the soil by means of offering them undisputed possession of large tracts. Almost every new country has been settled in the same way. The Dutch and English Colonists, but especially the former, were certainly led to penetrate the interior of South Africa by the lodestone of individual possession of land. The difficulties of trekking into unknown South Africa could have been compensated by no less a reward.

Given the similarity of the first terms of settlement, the needs and policies of different parts of South Africa soon begin to create differences. Indeed the only part whose land problem remained at all simple by the time of which we write appears to have been the Orange Free State, a district which was happily situated as regards both quality and quantity of land and which also has an access to markets which rendered it possible to support an increasing population. Add to this the fact that a great deal of transport was passing through the Free State and so both giving employment to young Burghers and also letting them see that there were other means of life than permanent settlement on their fathers' farms. In these circumstances the original and primitive allotment of land seems to have sufficed and not to have been changed either by increasing population or by changes in economic circumstances.

In the Transvaal matters were very different. We have seen that the original farms were granted on the basis of giving to each man a wide area centring on a water head. In some parts of the Transvaal, as in the agricultural areas of Middelburg, Zeerust, and Heidelberg, the land, although given out in great areas for pastural uses, was yet capable of being used agriculturally so as to support many more people. In almost every part of the Transvaal, except in the Bush and the Low Velds, there was some possibility of each farm receiving arable attention. For the land was patchy in nature and few

settlers did not have some kind of arable soil. Perhaps
it was this, perhaps other causes which we cannot see,
which led to a steady inflow of immigrant Dutch into the
Transvaal long after all its good land had been claimed
by the original settlers. It is difficult to fix dates to
these stages but we may say with some accuracy that all
good land was taken up before 1860, and that the influx
of settlers continued steadily up to the date of which we
write when the discovery of gold radically altered land
settlement conditions along with all others. After the
Anglo Boer War fresh land was made available for
occupation by scientific work. But in our early period
that was unknown. There was no fresh outlet for
population other than trekking afresh into Bechuanaland
and Mashonaland. It was the desire to preserve free
scope for such trekking that was in the mind of President
Kruger in his dealing with Rhodes. The land expansion
of the Dutch was a vital ideal and also, as we shall see,
an economic necessity. For the land of the Transvaal
was becoming overcrowded and the Burghers demanded
access to new areas where they could live the only kind
of agricultural life which they understood. But this
desire to expand outside the borders of the Transvaal
did not prevent important developments taking place
inside the State. Let us imagine the development.
New arrivals, often the relatives of the farmers, were
coming in from Cape Colony during the fifties, the sixties,
and the seventies. At the same time the farmer's
families were growing. Ten or twelve children was not
an unusually high number. Land had to be found for
all of them. It would seem to be inevitable that the
original farms would have to be divided up to allow each
part to receive more intensive cultivation. The new
arrivals might be settled as tenant farmers. But both of
these solutions were quite foreign equally to the minds
of the people and to the conditions under which they
lived. Tenant farming implied a commercial rent which,
however, could scarcely be paid where coin was almost
unknown. Sub-division meant that farms which had

been selected carefully as economic units would be broken up.

It is necessary to appreciate the force of circumstances opposing both commercial tenancy and sub-division. The former was impossible where money economy did not exist. The second was impossible without losing the essential design of the Transvaal farms. Compromises were reached for a considerable time. The new arrivals were simply given rights to occupy parts of the farm for which the farmer had no use. Every farm had a considerable area of this nature. The right to occupy meant that the newcomer would be able to cultivate sufficient soil to feed himself and his family and he would have the right to graze his animals, probably mixed in with those of the farmer. Sometimes he would pay tribute to the farmer by giving him a proportion of his crop. This system brought gain rather than loss to the owner of the soil, and in its early stages appears to have been quite secure for the bywoner. Its advantages to the farmer were sometimes considerable. If he happened to be troubled by Natives he was very glad to have more white people on his land. Sometimes the bywoners would be given land which they had to clear of Natives before they could occupy. It would always lead to a more widespread cultivation of the farm lands, a cultivation which the farmer himself would most likely not undertake, and so to an insurance against drought. The more commercially minded of the farmers would be able to improve their farm homestead and to increase the number of their cattle by means of the shares which they took from the bywoner. The bywoner himself appears to have been quite happily situated until actual pressure of population began to be felt. Perhaps it was only then that he realised that he had no rights whatever.

While this settlement of bywoners was proceeding we should keep in mind that the policy of the Transvaal State was still to find free land for all white settlers. The newcomers could regard their status merely as a temporary one. They were living on the farms of their relatives until the State could find land for them. The State's obligation to do this was never called in question until in the late nineties when the Transvaal had been surrounded by spheres of British influence, when it had to be seen that it was impossible. Prior to that, we may suppose that almost every bywoner was waiting for the day when he would find his own farm. We do not know how many of them spent long periods on single farms or how many of them stayed for only short periods and then explored in the hope of finding land in some other region. The strong probability is that in the earlier parts of our period, say in the forties and fifties, and possibly in the sixties, the residence of bywoners was quite temporary. Later it is certain that they were only too glad to be able to cling to their holdings and not to be ejected.

A tenant class was never created, but sub-division was a process which could not be resisted. It was the one means of adjusting the land system to the needs of a larger population. In fertile parts of the world, with markets at their doors, sub-division of land may be a perfectly economic adjustment, but in inland regions it may be otherwise. In the Transvaal it was a process of sheer distress. In the first place, the Burghers were under the disadvantage of living under a legal system which regarded sub-division as a normal and advantageous process. The Roman-Dutch Law had been imported from parts of Europe where agricultural economics were the reverse in all respects of those of the Transvaal. Its most important provision for the disposal of land at death was that in the absence of testamentary disposal the land of the deceased person would be divided equally among his heirs. Such an inapt law could easily have been overcome had the farmers so desired and provided against it by will. Actually a good number did do this. But by a singular piece of bad luck the Roman-Dutch Law fitted in with the strongest prejudices of the farmers. A farmer reckoned himself bound to provide land for each son.

# DEVELOPMENT PRIOR TO 1892

He had no other way of providing for his children. In consequence the farms as their owners died came to be split up among the heirs. In the case of a few of the most advanced farmers it was possible to arrange for some of the sons to take money value in lieu of their shares. But when no other land was available this naturally was unwelcome. Each farm split into little shares. In an example which I have before me we find the most elaborate calculations entered into to give each legatee his rights. We find one establishing a claim to 1/freeeee of the original farm and 37 such claims being marked out. This stage of elaborateness was of course reached only after several generations of sub-division and after much bargaining. But it indicates the way in which farms could be reduced till all vestiges of usefulness were lost. The owner of each share would claim a section of the farm with one end in the arable portion so that this portion would be split up into a number of very small sections, and these would then extend away into pastural land widening as they radiated outwards, and in the outlying parts of the farm there would be one or more commonages on the least valuable soil.

It will be seen that the whole of the economic advantages or drawbacks of sub-division would depend upon the extent to which population became crowded and to which the land remained without contact with outside influences. The opening up of the diamond fields doubtless staved off ruinous sub-division both in the Free State and in the Transvaal for a considerable time. The sub-division appeared to have reached breaking point when in 1886 the Witwatersrand was discovered and then its effects were once again postponed owing to the fact that other activities now became available to the young Burghers.

Cape Colony had experience of the process of subdivision before the Transvaal. But it was only in the agricultural south-west. Such problems scarcely seem to have affected the Karroo, doubtless owing to the fact that in the first place its land was not agricultural and suitable for sub-division since it did not have the fertile patches of the Transvaal. In the second place, however, the Karroo has never been completely out of touch with markets. In the third place, its population has always been a comparatively shifting one, attracted sometimes even to the south coast for speculative ostrich farming, and always to the north where gold and diamonds offered prizes such as the Karroo did not have to offer. In the Cape South West, a sub-division process very similar to that known on the continent of Europe appears to have been well advanced by 1860. Some farmers appeared to have avoided the process, and to have kept large farms intact by making other provision for their sons. They were unable to make this provision by means of commercial connection. Other farms had been sub-divided to the furthest limits. It appears to have been a matter of family preference. The bywoner was by no means unknown both in the Karroo and in the coastal lands. He appears very often to have become a person of some wealth with a title strongly established by custom and economically advantageous to the land owner as well as to himself since he would very often be a kind of farm manager. It appears to have been the depression in the wine industry after 1865, which lasted into the twentieth century, which caused uneasiness as to the results of sub-division. We hear of loud complaints of the " poor white population " in the vine districts. During the eighties, people in the Transvaal pointed to this problem in the Cape as what would undoubtedly happen to themselves in time. How serious the problem really was we do not know. It is probable that its really only unfortunate effect lay in persuading some bywoners to try their fortune in the Cape North West, where civilised life was certainly very difficult. On the whole we must conclude that the process of sub-division led to better farming and was as beneficial in the Cape South-West, as it was harmful in the Transvaal.

Before 1886, the Cape Colony had been the only State

## DEVELOPMENT PRIOR TO 1892

in South Africa whose land settlement policy had attained to any complexity. With its early developments, say prior to the Great Trek, we are not here concerned. The process of alienation of lands also had been a simple one until by about 1860 all the good agricultural land in Cape Colony was in private hands given out to colonists on terms similar to those in the Transvaal. But other lands remained. The lands to the north-west, while they were known to be semi-desert, were always regarded as a possible future area of expansion for farmers who would take the risk of facing some years of drought in the hope that year in, year out, the land would support enough sheep to give them a reasonable livelihood. In addition, there were patches of land in between farms which the original settlers had either been unaware of or had not thought worth claiming. As farms gradually came to be surveyed the existence of these unclaimed pieces of land was made known. In addition, farms would sometimes revert to the State in the ordinary course of intestacy. It is true that the Transvaal had a greater quantity of such lands than had the Cape, but the Cape had an active government and formulated a policy to deal with them. A study of this policy betrays the extent to which the pioneer farmers' attitude and outlook dominated Cape governments. In none of the land laws was any provision made for beneficial settlement, or for the giving out of land to people who were qualified to use it. In dealing with all types of unalienated land, the government's policy was simply to achieve the maximum of financial gain from their disposal. It may be suspected indeed that it was only the fact that the Cape government was involved in financial enterprises which taxed its resources which led it to take any notice of the unowned land. With regard to that on the outskirts of the Colony, the policy was one of sale. The land was sold on a small first payment to be completed within some forty years. During the period of payment, the settler was given no right in the land or in his improvements. No system of State tenancy was ever adopted. In the case of lands inside the Colony an even more frankly commercial policy was pursued. The land was set up to auction with the upset price fixed previously by the government. The idea behind this policy apparently was that the surrounding farmers would bid for the land in order to round off their farms. This very often was done, though it is noticeable that in these cases the farmers would almost invariably form a ring to prevent prices rising. In many cases, however, outsiders were attracted with considerable gain to the government, and loss to themselves and those to whom they succeeded in re-selling the land. The existence of land hunger was sometimes clearly evidenced as a result of these auctions. Sometimes speculators would bid fabulous sums, doubtless with a view to selling again to would-be small farmers. In other cases new settlers with capital would bid for the land and would be ruined in consequence. If a bad season happened to follow, even the government might lose since it would have to reduce the quit-rents which the purchasers had agreed to pay. As a rule none but the neighbouring farmers would be accurately informed of the true value of the land or able to use it, so that the government policy might be taken as a good one in so far as it would enable farmers to round off their land, but as a very bad one in so far as it applied to new settlers. The policy of the sale of land received its real test when Bechuanaland was annexed in 1895. The Bechuanaland farms were then available to settlers under the Cape government, and it was an opportunity for the State to allot the land scientifically, to grant good terms and secure tenancy to men with small capital. But the existing landed interest was too strong and syndicates were waiting to buy the land. People in Cape Colony were not all unaware of the drawbacks of the State land policy. It was evident that new settlers were not invited to the colony and that existing farms were so large that the holders were quite

## DEVELOPMENT PRIOR TO 1892

unable, even if they had been willing, to attempt their cultivation. Political prejudices, however, on the part of the Dutch population, were against attracting immigrants from oversea, and were opposed to a reduction in the size of farms except by the natural process of sub-division. Amendments providing beneficial terms for new settlers were moved in the House to each land act, and also providing for the right of the States to take back land and to re-allot it. But these amendments were invariably lost, being opposed equally by the Dutch, who feared an influx of European population and by the English, who were interested in land syndicates.

The Colony of Natal took its land policy ready-made from the Cape. Lands were given out in true colonial fashion to first comers and only in the twentieth century, as in the Cape, were serious efforts made to reclaim them and to re-allot them more economically. The lands near the coast, however, became quite commercialised early in the history of Natal.

To sum up the characteristics of early land settlement in South Africa, there was first of all the giving of ownership of large tracks to the first settlers; there was then the disposal of other less valuable lands which were ignored by the Transvaal government, but which were the centre of the only land policy which the Cape could be said to have; there was then the process of sub-division, very uncertain in its results; and finally there was the absence of any kind of good tenancy, sometimes compensated for by the success of the bywoner system but always acting to prevent the immigration of whites without capital of their own to live on the land; there followed the difficulty of any new-comer, especially if his capital was limited, in obtaining a footing in South African agriculture; there was speculation in the land generally to the detriment of the new-comer also; there was the Roman-Dutch Law fostering tendencies totally unsuited at least to the inland regions. and finally, a factor which we have not yet mentioned, the presence of native labour which was soon recognised as having a monopoly of the manual work of the farms, so inducing the colonists to lose their own physical skill and making it impossible for new-comers to obtain a footing in the country by beginning as farm workers

### REFERENCES

Annual Reports of the Surveyor-General for Cape Colony from 1876 onward.

Reports of the Registrar of Deeds of the South African Republic, 1893 and 1894.

Report and Evidence of the Transvaal Indigency Commission. The report is extremely valuable in this connection.

The Report of the Select Committee upon Agricultural Distress in Cape Colony, June, 1898, and the much more full report and evidence of another select committee held in October in the same year.

Report and Evidence of a Select Committee (Cape Colony), 1889, to enquire into the operation of the Land Act of 1887.

Report of Select Committee (Cape Colony) held in 1890 to enquire into the Utilization of Waterless Crown Lands.

Report and Evidence Cape Colony Select Committee (1895) on Crown Lands Bill.

The First Report of the Union Lands Department, 1911, summaried the History of Land Settlement in the Orange Free State as well as in other parts of the Union.

Reports of the Commissioner of Lands in the Transvaal from 1904 to 1907 are very valuable.

### (h) *Early Native Economic Policy*

The contact of white colonists with the natives of South Africa and with peoples of mixed breed constitutes one of the chief economic problems of South Africa throughout the whole of its history, and we shall try here to describe the development of the economic influences of contact between black and white prior to the discovery of gold in the Witwatersrand.

We should first point out that the original natives of South Africa, known to have been there for long periods before the white man ever arrived, were the Hottentots and the Bushmen of Cape Colony. These, however, occupied a very small territory and soon betrayed an inability to continue to live in a pure-bred

## DEVELOPMENT PRIOR TO 1892

state. They either fled into the desert to the north of Cape Town or mixed with the white settlers. Those who fled are now almost extinct; those who mixed with the white are now represented by some hundreds of thousands of coloured people living almost entirely in the Western Province of the Cape and providing that district both with agricultural and with manufacturing labour. The natives of South Africa so called, are the Bantu, who migrated from the North some time since the Portuguese first penetrated into Africa. Thus both European and Bantu may be regarded as colonists simultaneously establishing rights in a new country. The numerous wars and migrations by which the Bantu came to be settled in the parts of South Africa which they now occupy, belong to the history of an earlier period, and were, to all intents and purposes, completed by the seventies or eighties of the nineteenth century.

The settlements arrived at then, have turned out to be more or less permanent. The political happenings which culminated in the annexation of Pondoland and Bechuanaland in 1895 made no real difference to the lands actually held by natives and by Europeans. These native land holdings can be quite simply described. Going round the map from Bechuanaland we find first of all that great territory very sparsely settled, then no more actual native land until we come round the coast to East London. There the Transkeian territories begin. These territories comprised the whole area between the great Kei river, the border land of Natal, and the Drakensberg as their inland boundary. Inside of these provinces there is only a little land held by whites, most of the whites there being traders, medical men, and administrators. The boundary with Natal does not correspond to any natural boundary, and the native populations continue to occupy the same type of land until, when about a hundred miles inside the Natal boundary, the land begins to be held by white farmers. Natal has a very large native population, living in this continuation of the Transkeian lands, and

on the high lands approaching the Drakensbergs. To
the north, both of the Transkei and of the Natal native
areas, is Basutoland, which, however, will be regarded
for the purposes of our study as a district apart, since it
did not come within the boundaries of the South African
Union in 1910. It is also geographically separate from
the surrounding districts, being almost entirely enclosed
by mountain ranges, and having a different economy
partly on that account, partly on account of the fact
that its land is high and especially suited to native
pastoral life, and partly owing to the fact that a great
native leader, Moshesh, had succeeded in establishing
a coherent native tribe or nation there. Moving along
the coast we next find native land in Zululand to the
north of Natal. This district has a considerable population of natives who occupy lands near the coast and
to the north, and also circling Natal in the north districts
of Vryheid and Newcastle, so that Natal is practically
surrounded by native lands. All these lands are in the
possession of natives, with the exception of the coastal
lands of Zululand, which in 1906 were given out to
sugar planters. Going northward along the coast we
come to the territories of Portugal, which, as is well
known, are thickly inhabited by natives. The Transvaal
has most of its native population in its less settled
areas to the north. These are very considerable, with
a large population thinly spread. The Orange Free
State is the only area without a large native population
of its own. This statement may seem to be belied
by census figures, but these figures give merely the
number of natives residing within the State at the date
of the census. Actually there are only two small native
reserves, accounting for some 4,000 natives, in the Orange
Free State ; the large number appearing in the census
is accounted for entirely by Basutoland natives who
move into the Free State to do agricultural work for
the white farmers. Some of those may be considered
entitled to be reckoned as residents of the Free State,
since they may spend two-thirds of the year within its

boundaries, but the vast majority spend less time there, and all of them, with only a few exceptions, retain their tribal holdings in Basutoland and keep their families there.

This difficulty of relying on the census is to be found all over South Africa. In some parts the natives are quite a steady population, as in the interior of the Transkei ; but in other parts they move great distances in response to harvest demands or droughts in their home areas, or mere rumours that good living is to be obtained in some particular part of the country. It is with populations such as these that any census is, by its very nature, unable to deal.

We shall now attempt to describe the ways in which the natives actually lived in the various parts of South Africa. Our starting point, and one of the most important points, will be the Transkei. This area had been gradually coming under the rule of Cape Colony from the early forties and, by the date of which we speak, that rule had by no means become complete. We may say that white rule there was not consolidated until the annexation of Pondoland and the passing of the Glen Grey Act in 1894. The district consists of semi-tropical grassland some of which, however, is thorn bush-land. All of it is capable of supporting natives living their simple tribal lives. Much of it is coveted by the whites since it would be excellent for maize growing and as pasture for sheep and cattle. The area came to be reserved for natives by various treaties contracted in the earlier part of the nineteenth century. The main tenor of these was that the lands should be reserved to the natives for all time excepting in case of rebellion. This applied only to the occupation of the soil, however, for the government of the native territories came more and more into white hands. The general system of government was to appoint administrators for convenient areas and to give them a free hand to influence the natives in peaceable ways. Fortunately the natives were, excepting for a few outbreaks, a very peaceable people. The administrators were able to establish positions for themselves as magistrates, courts of appeal, often as doctors, and always as the final authorities in case of disputes between tribes. The nature of their functions was really very complex and no attempt is made here to analyse its real nature. The important point is that the natives of the Transkei had more or less lost their original tribal formation in the course of earlier wars and migrations. They now had their families and their kraals intact as political units and in vague ways aggregations of kraals recognised certain native leaders as chiefs. But these chiefs had neither the permanence nor the power of the real hereditary chiefs of the Bantu. It was here that the white administrators were able to come in and to use their influence. This influence was generally very great.

The natives of the Transkei had an economic system which had grown up in the course of their migrations and which consequently was a great deal less definite than the systems of primitive peoples generally tend to be. The centre of the system was the conditions on which natives had the right to use land. This right lay in the hands of the chiefs or recognised leaders. There was no individual ownership of land; this may have been due partly to the inherent attitude of the native mind which regards land as we regard air, or the sea, that is, as something which is essential to life and to which everyone has right of access but to which no one is able to establish a claim of ownership. Or it may have been due partly to the fact that for one or more centuries the natives now settled in the Transkei, had lived as nomadic peoples gradually travelling southward from central Africa into their present abode. It was the function of the chief to share out land so that each member of his tribe would have the use of as much as he needed or was entitled to under the custom of the tribe. Cultivation was entirely primitive, the general practice being for the natives to grow, by means of the cultivation done by their women-folk, as much food as they would need over the winter, and not to think of growing any surplus whatever. The real concern of the natives was to be able to increase the numbers of their cattle. Land for cultivation was merely a secondary consideration. For their cattle they did not demand individual lands, for pasturage was in common. Nevertheless the real political power in each tribe rested with the authority who could give natives the right to land ; either an individual right to cultivate certain lands or a right to the tribe as a whole to pasture its cattle and to protect them against the claims of other tribes. In the course of the migrations it had doubtless been the duty of the men to hunt, to scout for other land, and to protect the herds of cattle as they grazed from the raids of neighbouring tribes. As conditions became more settled these functions had become less important, and it was now the duty of the men merely to supervise the tending of the cattle, and they had little else to do. During the migrations it had naturally fallen to the women to cultivate the land in so far as the shallow scratching of the soil could be called cultivation. This function had been retained by the women and they were now the cultivators. It would appear that it was still the practice to abandon pieces of land when they began to give a diminishing return. This did not mean that the abandoned land was really left for other tribes to occupy, it was really only the equivalent of leaving the soil fallow, and it would be returned to in the course of another season. Later in this study, when we come to deal with the Glen Grey Act and its meaning, we shall attempt to describe more fully the economic system of the various native tribes. Our present object is to describe the relations of the tribes to the neighbouring white colonists and their government. The point is that the native men had a tendency to move great distances from their tribal homes, and this made them available as labourers for mining industries and the farms of the white people. The

whole of the agriculture of Cape Colony, excepting that
of the extreme south west, depended upon native labour
for the shearing of the sheep and for the sowing and
reaping of crops, so that natives were constantly
moving about between the Transkeian territories and
the various parts of Cape Colony. It was this moving
about which constituted the essence of the "labour
problem" of Cape Colony, for the farmers found themselves depending upon a totally incalculable labour
supply. Those in the south west were fortunate in
having the Cape coloured people, while those in the
extreme east were more doubtfully fortunate in being
very close to the source of the labour supply. The
farmers of the centre of Cape Colony, from Oudtshoorn
up to Beaufort West, were constantly complaining of
labour shortage, and frequently attributed the smallness
of their arable cultivation to this shortage. Its effect
upon the Colony's agriculture was certainly felt to be
very great and was no doubt considerable. The State's
native policy consisted in attempts to regulate the labour
supply and to render it more amenable to control. In
the first place were the Master and Servant laws. These
had not been passed specially to deal with natives, for
they were part of the Roman-Dutch Law regulating
the relationship between apprentices and other articled
workers, and their employers. They were applied to
the natives, however, and farmers would enter into some
kind of agreement with natives who arrived on their
farms, whereby the native was bound to stay for a
certain period. Actually these agreements were of the
rudimentary kind; they were never reduced to writing
and it is very doubtful whether they could ever have
been enforced in any ordinary court of law. But they
were recognised by the local magistrates, who, of course,
were the farmers themselves, and in this way the freedom
of movement of the natives would be to some degree
reduced to enable the farmer to be more certain of having
sufficient labour for his next sowing or harvest. Another
body of law with the same object was the Location Law.

## DEVELOPMENT PRIOR TO 1892

The aim of this was to enable each farmer to settle a certain number of natives, not only the men, but their families as well, on their farms, so that they would have a more permanent source of labour on their farms than they could have by relying on wandering natives. But a further aim of the law was to prevent other farmers from settling too many natives in this way. Each of those aims came into force according to the area in which the farmer lived, and to his methods. In the extreme east of the colony the latter aim of the law was the more important for there the trouble was an excess rather than a shortage of native labour. It should be explained that the river Kei by no means had the whole of the native population on its northern bank, for although it roughly delimited the land which was reserved for natives from that which was made available for white ownership, there were still considerable numbers of natives on the white land, and these outnumbered the whites very considerably, at least as far south as the Great Fish River, and in many other parts of the Eastern Province. In these parts there was such an excess of native labour available, while the land also was of such a nature that it was more valuable to the natives than to the whites, that it was the general practice for white farmers to indulge in what was known as Kaffir farming. This practice took many forms, but its essential feature was that it enabled a farmer to have more natives on his farm than were necessary to enable him to cultivate in a European manner. He would enable whole families of natives to have permanent holdings on his lands and to pay him a kind of rent either in money or in shares of their produce. The practice was obnoxious to the farmers further west, who held that this Kaffir farming, apart from leading to bad farming on the part of the white farmers, caused a great deal of labour to be held up in the Eastern Province when it should have been available all over the colony. The law attempted to limit the numbers of families which each farmer could establish on his farm. As we shall see later, the law has not to this day been effective.

The native policy of Cape Colony thus consisted of two parts, one of which applied to natives in their own reserved lands, and the other of which applied to the natives in the Colony Proper. The former was simply a means of administration of primitive natives, while the second was a means of controlling natives on white land and of making their labour available in as advantageous a manner as possible.

The native policy of the other states in South Africa had much in common with that of Cape Colony. Natal was in the position of having an even larger number of natives living on their tribal lands with of course a much smaller white population from which to draw administrators. In consequence her administrative policy in native territories, while having the same aims as that of Cape Colony, was much more rudimentary and consisted in recognising the power of chiefs and in leaving all matters of administration, so far as possible, to the chief. In consequence her natives were much less influenced by European civilization, and whether rich or poor chose to keep themselves to themselves and to live on their tribal land. Probably owing to the fact that these lands were mostly mountainous and that communication between them and the lands of the whites was not easy, the natives did not have the migratory habits of those of Cape Colony. Numbers were always available as domestic servants in the Natal towns and as farm servants over nearly the whole of Natal, but when tropical industries were established near the coast it was quite impossible to induce a supply of native labour. Natal had the same apparatus of Location laws, Master and Servant laws and Pass laws as had Cape Colony. Her problems, while much less defined, were very similar. The farmers with an excess of native labour were also to be found, and as in Cape Colony, they were those who had settled lands on the outskirts of the native reserves. Their method was to indulge in Kaffir farming just as was done in the Eastern Province of the Cape, and the same laws were applied

# DEVELOPMENT PRIOR TO 1892

to them. There is the difference that there was not in Natal, apart from the coastal regions where a strange type of agriculture was developed, which repelled the native, the same great area of land which was actually short of native labour for ordinary farming purposes.

The inland republics are generally claimed to have quite different native policies though, as we shall see, the differences were superficial rather than essential. One main difference was, that whereas the Cape and Natal had definitely reserved lands to natives by means of treaty, this had not been done in the Northern States. The problem had scarcely arisen in the Orange Free State excepting in the case of two small remnants of tribes which had been allowed to hold land as their own without the formality of treaty in two small locations or reserves. In the Transvaal the problem of native lands had certainly been present but had never developed into the stage in which legislation was possible. Right up to the time of the Anglo Boer War constant friction and wars had been the rule in the north of the Transvaal. Hardy Dutch colonists were constantly attempting to claim and occupy lands which were peopled by natives. The lands themselves were not by any European standard suitable for white farming. But they were suitable for the crude pastoral methods of the Dutch. A kind of continuous war for land had proceeded ever since the Dutch had first settled the Transvaal. A white colonist would establish his claim to a farm according to Roman-Dutch law. His claim would be recognised by the government, and then it would become evident that the farm was occupied by natives. The farmer would call upon his neighbours to help to clear the land of natives, and possibly the government also would be called in. It was a very primitive state of affairs. The only government policy was to assist the colonists generally in their struggle for land, and the only government official was the Veld Cornet, whose duty it was to collect taxes from natives whenever possible, which was done with surprising success, and to assist the colonists. Complaints of shortage of labour were constantly made by farmers in the more central parts whence, of course, the natives had been successfully driven. A Pass law was in force which forbade natives to travel about the countryside unless they were in possession of a pass signed either by the Veld Cornet or their latest employer, thus giving the farmer a certain hold on the natives by being able to refuse a signature. But it is certain that this Pass law was more of an irritant than of a successful measure. Location laws had not been resorted to in our early period. The nearest equivalent to them was the system of apprenticeship to farms. Under this system native children, either who had been born on the farm or who were orphans, were entered into an agreement whereby they were to stay on the farm until reaching the age of nineteen, and in this way the farmers had a more or less permanent labour supply guaranteed to them.

To sum up the native policy of South Africa as a whole, we may say that its first object had been to secure as much good land as possible for white occupation. This had been achieved in the Cape by a series of native wars and annexations which were not at an end; almost the same stage had been reached in Natal excepting for the coastal land of Zululand which was given out to white sugar planters in the early twentieth century; in the Orange Free State the question had scarcely arisen excepting on a very small part of the boundary of Basutoland, where a portion of the Basutos' territory had been annexed after a war during the sixties, but otherwise the boundaries of the Free State were naturally well marked; in the Transvaal the primitive stage of disputing land with natives was still in process. The second aim in native policy was the elementary one of preserving the peace. This was achieved so far as the native territories were concerned by a comparatively simple system of administration, whether the advanced system of the Cape or the mere tax-collecting of the Transvaal. In the lands outside of the native reserves

# DEVELOPMENT PRIOR TO 1892

this aim was achieved by means of Pass Laws and by one or two similar measures in addition to the ordinary system of justice. The third aim was the comprehensive one of making use of natives in the economic scheme, that is to say, of selling goods to them and so making use of their purchasing power ; of inducing them to cultivate their lands so that the food production of the whole country would be increased ; and of inducing them to give their labour to white colonists in exchange either for monetary consideration or other advantages. In our early period the last of these was by far the most important, but it was already beginning to be seen that all three of them were inter-dependent. This, however, was less true before the nineties than it was afterwards. After the nineties the demand of the gold mines for labour was a new factor of a very great importance. It took natives by the thousand away from their homes for several months in the year. No more intimate means of contact between the two races could well be imagined, for the natives thus leaving their homes were the young people who would otherwise have been absorbing tribal traditions but who were now obtaining quite different experiences. In the eighties this wholesale exodus from the territories did not exist. Only very few of the natives in districts such as the Transkei looked to money wages as part of their income. They still farmed for their own subsistence and only some few of the young males looked ever to employment with white farmers as a means of obtaining cash. There were few inducements to them to travel long distances from their own lands to earn wages. Their idea was, if they could not live with their own families and tribes in the reserves, to live in as similar a way as possible outside the reserves. With this end in view they would attempt to settle on land which was owned by white colonists just as if its ownership made no difference whatever. The nearest to tribal conditions in this respect was Crown land, nearly always worthless and not yet given out to white settlers. On this land, wherever it was found, natives would nearly always tend to settle, overflowing from their own reserved land Land of this type was a comparatively small problem in Cape Colony, but in Natal was much more serious, while in the Transvaal it applied to millions of acres. It has been one of the constant problems in South African economic policy to decide on what terms natives might occupy this type of land. In general, it had not been the practice of the government to collect any rent, and they had satisfied themselves with collecting the ordinary hut-tax, which applied to natives on all other types of land. When natives could not settle on Crown land, they next chose, as we have already indicated, land which was owned by white colonists, but which yet was available for use of natives. Of this land there was a good deal in nearly all parts of South Africa at the time of which we speak. In the first place was land owned by whites but left quite uncultivated. Of this type were the coastal lands in Cape Colony just south of the Transkei which were unsuitable for grain growing and which had proved very dangerous for stock raising owing to the presence of animal diseases. The owners of this land could make no agricultural use of it. Another example was land in the Transvaal of an unbroken and uncleared character which might be owned by Dutch colonists or not owned at all, or, very soon after the date of which we speak, by mineral companies which bought up large tracks in the hope of discovering future values. In land of this kind it was generally found that its only value lay in its use for native occupation, and the owners invariably allowed natives to occupy it in exchange for rent. Very often it appears that this renting to natives was very profitable. We hear of examples of larger amounts per acre being received from natives than could ever have been obtained from white farmers. The explanation for this is that land was let to natives in small quantities and they could often by their cultivation make good use of it, and could often make a certain additional income by going out to work for farmers, and also were in the position of being willing to pay very

## DEVELOPMENT PRIOR TO 1892

heavily rather than to give up their holdings. This letting out to natives was very often a very profitable concern. So much so that it appears that the certain profits to be derived from this may frequently have deprived the white owners of any incentive to cultivating the land in their own ways.

Apart from this absentee ownership nearly all South African farms, as we have seen, allowed a generous margin over what the farmer could actually cultivate. So that on every farm there were areas available for the settlement of natives. There was no hard and fast line between the totally absentee farmers and the ordinary farmers of the colony. In nearly every case farmers could make more profit by renting part of their land to natives than they could by treating it as agricultural land. Thus considerable numbers of natives came to be settled on white farms. While this had the effect of rendering their labour available to the farmer, it had very little effect upon their actual tribal economy. Those who lived in this way lived almost exactly as did their kinsmen in the tribal reserves. True, they were not under any chiefs, and the part of the chief in the allotting of land was in some sense taken by the white farmer. But the use made of the land by the natives would be almost exactly similar to the use they would have made of it in their reserves. The only difference would be that they would now have to cultivate a slightly larger area in order to pay their rent. They might also have more difficulty in accumulating cattle, since the farmer would put a limit to the number of native's cattle which he would have on his land.

This keeping of natives on white farms has gone under various names. It may be called Kaffir farming, or squatting, or share-farming. These terms are used almost indiscriminately though really somewhat different meanings should be attached to them. Squatting should be taken to mean simply the settling of natives anywhere on undefined terms, as on Crown lands where they pay no rent and may be ejected at any moment, and also on the less valuable of private lands where almost the same conditions may be found. Kaffir farming should mean the actual giving out of land to be occupied entirely by natives who pay rent so that the landowners' profit will come from this rent instead of from his own farming enterprise. Share-farming should describe the conditions under which natives are allowed to occupy land on farms actually worked by white farmers on condition of their paying rent in the form of part of their crops. But these three systems naturally ran into each other. It is often impossible to say whether natives on private lands are merely squatting there with the tacit consent of the owner or whether they are actually paying rent; it is often very difficult to draw a line, at any rate as regards economic consequences, between natives being found on unoccupied land and those on the other side of a boundary occupying land on a farm the rest of which is being worked by the white farmer. Share-farming may be a very indefinite or quite a definite concern. It was applied not only to natives but to white bywoners, at least in the Orange Free State and in the Transvaal. In the case of these whites, share-farming would be a perfectly definite arrangement, and it frequently appears to have been equally so in the case of natives, especially of those natives who could adopt more or less advanced systems of agriculture. The system shaded off, however, into mere Kaffir farming, and on the same farm there would be found some natives giving definite shares of their produce to the farmer while others possibly on more outlying parts of the farm would pay a money rent whenever they could. One difference, however, would appear to have been found between Kaffir farming on unoccupied farms and any system on occupied farms; in the latter case the natives would be required to give labour to the farmer when called upon to do so.

It is impossible to say how important this labour provision was. In some cases it would appear that farmers retained native families on their lands simply

# DEVELOPMENT PRIOR TO 1892

with a view to ensuring a supply of labour at sowing and harvest times. It is certain that this ensuring of labour was always a consideration of some importance. Those farmers who were situated in parts of Cape Colony or the other states, so far away from native reserves that they could not find native families to occupy parts of their land, frequently complained loudly that their efforts were frustrated by the lack of labour. It would appear that these farmers, if they could, would all have devoted a certain part of their land to native occupation. Their complaint was that all systems of Kaffir farming and share-farming with natives had the effect of locking up labour, so that it was not available for the general agricultural development of the country.

The case against these various systems of keeping natives on white lands was, however, a wide one. Apart from locking up labour they had distinctive effects upon the cultivation of the soil. We have already mentioned that farmers who could draw rents from natives would have less incentive to experiment with real agriculture. This applied on all farms. The keeping of natives would sometimes have the effect of bringing land under cultivation which otherwise would have been barren, but it would also have the effect of preventing the application of European methods to this land. Yet another consideration was that farmers who chose to keep more natives on their land than they actually needed to do might be preventing neighbouring farmers of more energetic disposition from obtaining the necessary labour for extending their cultivation. For different practices were to be found between neighbouring farmers. It would appear that one backward farmer, by monopolising the labour supply of a district, might set the pace to all the other farmers in that district. In addition the natives living on the farm would always have stock of their own which in unfenced country would run wild and mix with the stock of other farmers, thus making scientific breeding very difficult. Finally, the natives had views on property, not only landed property but animals as well, which by no means agreed with European ideas. So that the stock of white farmers found mingling with the cattle and sheep of the natives would frequently be taken possession of by the natives; stock-thieving was thus one of the evils contingent upon the residence of any number of natives in any neighbourhood.

The native policy of the colonists thus had to deal with a very mixed set of conditions. The provision of labour was mixed up with a very intricate land question. The Location Acts were the methods resorted to in the period of which we speak in Cape Colony and Natal. Under these Acts it was lawful for a farmer to keep about five families of natives on his farm, and these five families were registered with the local magistrate and constituted what was known as a location. It was illegal to keep more. But conditions were much too unfavourable for the enforcement of any such law. Many efforts were made to spread the native population and consequently the labour supply in this way, but repeated efforts left matters only as they had been found.

To conclude, before the opening up of the Witwatersrand, no fundamental influences existed actually to change the natives' economic system. The one exception to this, the diamond mines at Kimberley, were very much a proof of the rule, for they drew their labour supply mainly from a quite exceptional country, Basutoland. Otherwise, although labour was needed for farming it was got only by enabling the natives to live according to their tribal ideas and not by inducing them to change their ways of life excepting in certain quite superficial ways as for example in forcing them to pay some rent which imposed no great strain on their resources. The exploitation of the purchasing power of the natives was still in the hands of pioneer traders.

### REFERENCES

Natal Native Commission, 1853. Mainly valuable for the Report and the Evidence of Mr. Theophilus Shepstone.

# DEVELOPMENT PRIOR TO 1892

Cape Colony Commission on Native Laws and Customs. Also valuable for the Report and such Evidence as that given by King Cetywayo and Sir Theophilus Shepstone.
Report of Cape Colony Commission on Labour Supply, 1893—statement of farmers' view points.
Report and Evidence of the Glen Grey Commission, 1892.
The following are the indispensable Cape Colony Select Committees—that of 1889 on the Masters and Servants Act, that of 1892 on the Location Act, that of 1899 on the Location Act.
Divisional Reports of the Natal Native Affairs Department from 1879 onwards.
Annual Reports of the Cape Colony Native Affairs Department.
Files of the *Transvaal Times, Transvaal Advertiser, Cape Times,* and *Natal Witness.*

# SECTION II

## CHAPTER I

### EARLY RAILWAY AGREEMENTS

PRIOR to 1887 there had been two colonial railway systems in South Africa, those of Cape Colony and of Natal. The inland areas within the boundaries of the Orange Free State and of the South African Republic were quite unserved. The necessity for any agreement between States, as to the passing of railway lines over the territory of more than one State, had been obviated by the inclusion of the diamond territory within Cape Colony. It now happened that gold was discovered much further inland. By 1889 it was clear that the Witwatersrand gold fields were of a much more permanent nature than such earlier discoveries as those of Lydenburg and Barberton, and the building of the new railway lines was eagerly discussed. Railways had been projected in earlier times to serve the South African Republic. The Republic, although inland, was not great distances from natural harbours; it was its misfortune to be cut off from these harbours by other political units established along the coast-line. Actually the distance between Johannesburg and the Port of Delagoa Bay was less than the distance between Kimberley and the nearest Cape Port. While distances generally in the Transvaal, as well as other geographical conditions, were comparatively favourable to the building of lines. Much of the Transvaal was more accessible to the coast than was much of Cape Colony. There were no high coastal ranges to be climbed. These geographical advantages became much more evident when gold was located in the Witwatersrand, near the centre of the Transvaal high veld. Distances and other geographical conditions now favoured the Transvaal very greatly as opposed to Cape Colony. As against some 300 miles between Delagoa Bay and Johannesburg, there was 1,000 miles between Cape Town and Johannesburg. Not only were the distances greatly different; the paying conditions were almost as favourable to the Transvaal. The short distance between Johannesburg and the coast could easily be made to pay by gold traffic alone, but actually there was good coal on the spot as well, and it could reasonably be hoped that the country through which the lines would travel would nearly all develop agriculturally. There were also natives to be carried from the coastal regions, which in the Portuguese territory were dense native reserves. As against this, the Cape Colony had the advantage of already having a railway system, or rather as we have seen, three separate railway systems, actually in working order. These systems were too elaborate for the existing traffic of Cape Colony, and from the point of view of revenue it was becoming difficult to do something to make them pay. It happened also, that the three lines were geographically perfect in that they pointed toward the Witwatersrand and merely needed to be extended in order to connect that district with the three chief ports of Cape Colony. Natal was in an intermediate condition. She already had a short line connecting Durban with Pietermaritzburg, so that she had the advantage of possessing railway works and experience. This line also pointed directly toward the Witwatersrand, and as regards distance, while Durban was almost twice as far from the gold fields as was Delagoa Bay, it was much nearer than the nearest of the Cape ports.

But in order that the gold fields should be reached by any railway system, it was necessary for inter-State agreements to be made  The making of these agreements marks a new period in the development of South

## EARLY RAILWAY AGREEMENTS 83

Africa, for Colonies and States which previously had felt only slight disadvantages from being independent, and from blocking each others' ways to the coast or to the interior, as the case might be, now found that it was economically impossible to exist without the closest agreements as to everything concerned with the transport of goods. It was the necessity for the smooth working of these agreements that ultimately led to the unification of the whole territory, and we must now begin to trace their history

Cape Colony was in the position of having to cross the territory of two other States in order to reach the gold fields. The first of these was the Orange Free State, and here few difficulties existed. This State had only a very elementary economic development of its own, and consequently it had no conflicting interests to consult when approached by Cape Colony for permission to build a line through its territory. Not only was the line built without a hitch, but a customs union was entered into. Under the terms of a railway agreement Cape Colony undertook to find the whole of the capital and to do the whole of the building. When constructed, the line was to be the possession, however, of both States, and for this purpose the Cape made a loan to the Free State. This loan was redeemable at five years' notice, and the Free State was also entitled to expropriate the Cape from the remainder of its share in the line. Actually the Free State did take over the whole of its own mileage in 1896, but up to that date the line was run and managed exclusively by Cape Colony. In the agreement it was provided that the rates on agricultural produce from the Free State, travelling in either direction, were to be no higher than the most favourable rates granted to Cape Colony farmers. There was thus a kind of economic union of the Orange Free State and Cape Colony as an immediate result of gold discoveries. The extension of the line into Transvaal territory was achieved with almost equal ease but with certain reservations. Here matters were not facilitated by a customs union ; on the contrary, a stiff customs barrier was erected on the Transvaal-Free State border. It has also provided for, that the line, which was only some forty miles in length, should be taken over at an early date by the Transvaal government or by any railway company which it should choose to nominate. The Transvaal government was thus setting out to control its own railway affairs.

The economic system of Cape Colony now found itself in command of a much larger sphere of activity than it had ever had before. Its three separate railway systems were now linked up in joining on to the line through the Free State. All of its railways were now directed to serving both the diamond and the gold fields. There were no other branch or agricultural lines. These were yet to come. The whole of the financial resources of the Colony were invested in the railway system, depending for its main traffic upon an industry far from the northern border of the Colony. As was to be expected, the Colony made energetic efforts to exploit this traffic to the full, keeping in mind the fact that now, in 1890, she had a monopoly of the gold fields traffic, but that two rivals were planning to build lines to compete for the same traffic. Within Cape Colony there was competition for the gold fields traffic between Port Elizabeth, East London, and Cape Town. The two former of these had almost a monopoly between them of the goods traffic, for Cape Town, while quicker for purposes of mails and passengers was at a great disadvantage as regards all other kinds of traffic. Later, after competition from Durban and Delagoa Bay had set in, Cape Colony tried to decide whether it was more economic to divert the main bulk of the goods traffic to Port Elizabeth, or to East London, but at first the government in Cape Town fixed rates which gave these two ports approximately equal advantages, although it would have been more strictly economic to concentrate on one of them. The Cape Railway system was now running as a whole and not in three separate parts as

## EARLY RAILWAY AGREEMENTS 85

previously. Accounts were kept for the system as a whole, and it was no longer possible to say how each individual line was paid. The aim was to make the maximum profit from the whole railway enterprise and to devote the profit to the general revenue of the colony. These profits were very considerable during the first three or four years of the nineties, while the Cape still had the monopoly for all practicable purposes, since, although the Delagoa Bay line was opened in 1892, it was not economically successful until the Port accommodation in Delagoa Bay was developed. Railway profits actually accounted for some two-fifths of the total revenue of the Cape Colony. The practice of handing over to the general revenue profits which should have been devoted to capital expenditure was continued, and new capital, either for the improvement of the existing lines or for the building of branch lines, had to be found by Parliament. The using of the railway as an instrument of taxation was thus carried to the furthest possible point. It was regarded as a taxation of the foreigner.

To turn next to Natal, we find that this colony was in one respect more fortunate than Cape Colony in that it could reach the Witwatersrand without having to pass through the territory of an intermediate state. It proceeded at once to build a line to the Transvaal border, some two-thirds of the way to the gold field. From this point on the border the traffic could be carried by ox wagon the rest of the distance to the gold field. The railway was held up at the border for some three years on account of a failure to get the permission of the Transvaal government to proceed. The fact was that that government had now given a contract to a Dutch company to build the Transvaal's own line to Delagoa Bay, for which permission had been given with great readiness by the Portuguese government. The facts of competition for the gold fields trade were now beginning to show. The President of the South African Republic found himself under no necessity to concede to the request of Natal, and he wished to make sure, first of all, that there would be ample traffic for the Delagoa Bay line. The gold fields had shown themselves quite able to develop with the assistance of the Cape Colony line alone, and it was not clear at first that there would be sufficient traffic to make both Natal and the Delagoa Bay lines payable propositions. The Dutch line itself would obviously compete easily with the Cape line, but Natal was a more difficult proposition. In 1895 the permission was given, but only on the understanding that Natal would never carry goods at a lower rate for the whole distance than they would be carried from Delagoa Bay. Natal was also obliged to agree to reduce the custom's duty charge on goods in transit to the Transvaal. We thus see the second of the inter-State agreements. Its main feature was to show the powerful position which the Transvaal occupied by reason of the fact that it was able to offset the various people who were now beginning to compete for its traffic.

We must now look at the various railway systems which were springing into existence and compare their main characteristics while tracing, so far as possible, their effects upon the several states. The system of Cape Colony, as we know, had its main lines marked out some fifteen or twenty years before the other states began seriously to build. The system of management by means of managers, each responsible for a stretch of line and answering only to the Minister in Cape Town, was continued. The control of railway policy was entirely a political one. The building of new lines had to be sanctioned by Parliament without any other advice than might be given by a select committee. The fixing of rates was done by the Minister of Railways, and he was answerable only to the House. The determination of what new lines should be built was a matter of extreme importance now that the main line system was yielding good profits, and all the agricultural districts were beginning to demand branch lines, to be financed through an admitted non-paying stage out of general revenue. The Minister of Railways was, in fact, the only executive chief of the whole colonial system, being advised by the departmental managers, but being able to determine the whole of the day to day policy of the railways without answering to anyone except in Parliament, should its interest be aroused, The amount of money invested in the Cape lines between 1874 and 1894 was as follows :—

|      | (000 omitted) £ |      | (000 omitted) £ |
|------|-----------------|------|-----------------|
| 1874 | 1,008           | 1885 | 13,407          |
| 1875 | 1,482           | 1886 | 14,130          |
| 1876 | 2,395           | 1887 | 14,186          |
| 1877 | 4,481           | 1888 | 14,214          |
| 1878 | 5,435           | 1889 | 14,282          |
| 1879 | 7,146           | 1890 | 14,665          |
| 1880 | 7,990           | 1891 | 16,686          |
| 1881 | 8,611           | 1892 | 18,557          |
| 1882 | 9,275           | 1893 | 19,557          |
| 1883 | 10,487          | 1894 | 20,092          |
| 1884 | 12,407          |      |                 |

In 1874 this was 40 per cent. of the total public debt of the Colony, and in 1894 it was 72 per cent. The railway debt per head of the population was £12 to £13 at the later date. The railway profits handed over to revenue were as follows :—

|      | (000 omitted throughout) | | | | | |
|------|Railway Revenue £|Total Revenue £|   |        | Railway Revenue £ | Total Revenue £ |
|------|-----------------|---------------|---|--------|-------------------|-----------------|
| 1874 | 82              | 1,518         | .. | 1884  | 964               | 2,949           |
| 1875 | 110             | 1,602         | .. | 1885  | 1,037             | 3,317           |
| 1876 | 163             | 827           | .. | 1886  | 1,048             | 3,039           |
| 1877 | 216             | 1,318         | .. | 1887  | 1,271             | 3,159           |
| 1878 | 326             | 1,586         | .. | 1888  | 1,451             | 3,426           |
| 1879 | 477             | 2,082         | .. | 1889  | 1,759             | 3,836           |
| 1880 | 641             | 2,522         | .. | 1890  | 1,896             | 4,430           |
| 1881 | 878             | 3,009         | .. | 1891–2 | 1,896            | 4,495           |
| 1882 | 968             | 3,524         | .. | 1892–3 | 2,248            | 4,971           |
| 1883 | 915             | 3,299         | .. | 1893–4 | 2,559            | 5,321           |
|      |                 |               |    | 1894   | 2,713            | 5,390           |

It will thus be seen that, by 1894, 50.3 per cent. of the total revenue of the colonies was derived from railway profits, after the paying of interest on the railway debt. Unfortunately, although the three lines still kept profit and loss accounts, there is nothing in the statistics to deferentiate the contributions of the various parts of the system. All that we know is the goods tonnage carried on each of the lines, and we give this in the following table.

(ooo omitted throughout)

| Year | Tonnage | | |
|---|---|---|---|
| | Western | Midland | Eastern |
| 1885 | 145 | 138 | 91 |
| 1886 | 141 | 106 | 64 |
| 1887 | 146 | 131 | 81 |
| 1888 | 165 | 163 | 85 |
| 1889 | 203 | 227 | 111 |
| 1890 | 217 | 279 | 122 |
| 1891 | 239 | 296 | 136 |
| 1892 | 255 | 277 | 157 |
| 1893 | 299 | 267 | 224 |
| 1894 | 296 | 279 | 257 |

It will be seen that the tonnage of Port Elizabeth and East London together rapidly overtake that of Cape Town. By 1894 they are each carrying a tonnage only slightly smaller than that of the older port, which in 1885 had been approached only by Port Elizabeth.

In the case of Natal the total public debt from 1880, when the first piece of line is built, to 1896, by when the railway line to Johannesburg had begun to work, and the railway debt in that period will be seen from this table:—

(ooo omitted)

| Year | Public Debt | Railway Debt | Year | Public Debt | Railway Debt |
|---|---|---|---|---|---|
| 1881 | 1,631 | 1,204 | 1889 | 5,035 | 3,000 |
| 1882 | 2,101 | 1,369 | 1890 | 3,060 | 3,650 |
| 1883 | 2,554 | 1,867 | 1891 | 7,170 | 4,528 |
| 1884 | 3,215 | 2,345 | 1892 | 7,170 | 5,820 |
| 1885 | 3,762 | 2,594 | 1893 | 7,170 | 6,060 |
| 1886 | 3,972 | 2,679 | 1894 | 8,066 | 6,078 |
| 1887 | 4,035 | 2,700 | 1895 | 8,054 | 6,117 |
| 1888 | 4,535 | 2,765 | 1896 | 8,019 | 6,236 |

# EARLY RAILWAY AGREEMENTS

It will be seen that the railway debt constitutes an even greater proportion of the total public debt than in the case of Cape Colony. The debt per head of the population was also considerably greater, being £98 in 1891. The Transvaal Government was unable to finance its own railway system. It contracted with a Holland company to undertake the whole of the work. This railway company was floated with a nominal capital of £4½ millions which, however, cannot be compared to the total national debt of the republic, since this was insignificant.

The cost of building the lines was fortunately low in all three states. Land did not have to be bought, and single lines sufficed. It happened that the first cost was lower in the Transvaal than in either of the other states. This was largely accounted for by the fact that both the Cape and Natal had to surmount difficult gradients and also to build through almost uninhabited and waterless land for hundreds of miles. The return per cent. on capital invested from 1886 to 1899 was as follows:—

|      | Cape Colony (per £100) | | | | | Natal | | |
|------|---|---|---|---|---|---|---|---|
|      | £ | s. | d. | | | £ | s. | d. |
| 1886 | 2 | 16 | 11 | .. | .. | 5 | 10 | 0 |
| 1887 | 4 | 3 | 1 | .. | .. | 9 | 12 | 0 |
| 1888 | 4 | 17 | 10 | .. | .. | 12 | 10 | 0 |
| 1889 | 5 | 15 | 1 | .. | .. | 17 | 16 | 0 |
| 1890 | 5 | 15 | 10 | .. | .. | 16 | 12 | 0 |
| 1891 | 4 | 13 | 4 | .. | .. | 12 | 12 | 0 |
| 1892 | 4 | 14 | 8 | .. | .. | 9 | 2 | 0 |
| 1893 | 4 | 16 | 11 | .. | .. | 6 | 16 | 0 |
| 1894 | 5 | 6 | 5* | .. | .. | 7 | 12 | 0 |
| 1895 | 7 | 9 | 0* | .. | .. | 8 | 10 | 0 |
| 1896 | 8 | 19 | 7* | .. | .. | 18 | 4 | 0 |
| 1897 | 6 | 2 | 6 | .. | .. | 15 | 18 | 0 |
| 1898 | 4 | 13 | 11 | .. | .. | 14 | 2 | 0 |
| 1899 | 4 | 12 | 9 | .. | .. | 12 | 18 | 0 |

*Excluding Orange Free State share which would give a much higher rate.

It will be seen that the returns for the last four of these years show a marked decline in both colonies, but whereas the Cape percentage is reduced to under five, that of Natal is maintained at nearly thirteen. Natal is stronger than in the years 1892, 3 and 4, while the Cape profits are back to the level of these years. Since the Transvaal had a very different system of bookkeeping, its returns cannot be given for comparison.

When in 1895 the railways of all three states were in working order it became clear either that there must be cut-throat competition between them or that some form of treaty or agreement must be entered into. The initiative was taken, as was to be expected, by Cape Colony. This Colony stood to lose most in every way by unrestricted competition, for she had much the greatest amount of capital sunk in the railway lines, on which a profit must be made or state bankruptcy ensue, and she was in some danger of losing, not merely a small proportion, but possibly almost the whole of her goods traffic, to the railways of Natal and the Transvaal. At her invitation a conference of railway managers from all of the states was held in Cape Town in 1895. In the discussions of this conference all the main features of later South African railway problems are found in every detail. The Cape representatives argued for an arrangement whereby certain proportions of the total import traffic into the Transvaal would be allotted to each of the three competitors. They were able to argue that such an arrangement would leave ample traffic to return a good profit on all of the lines. They argued further that in the event of cut throat competition ensuing the Transvaal might be the worst loser. Also an attempt was made to prove that Cape Colony, by concentrating the whole of its efforts on one of its lines, would be able to economise to such an extent that Natal at least would feel the competition. The strongest point in the Cape case was that if all four of the states engaged in a war of rates then whatever other results might ensue the bankruptcy of each state would be certain. This was a view which, in later years, came to be accepted, but in 1895 other circumstances dominated the situation. Cape Colony had had a monopoly and was accused, not without justice, of having bled the inland states. The South African Republic now found itself in a dramatically changed position and was not inclined to bargain. It was much more important for the statesmen of the Republic to secure the maximum of tonnage for their own line, and secondly for the Natal line, one-third of which lay within their territory, than it was to consider the public finances of the other states. Natal, having secured an agreement with the Transvaal, was neutral in the dispute. The conference broke up without arriving at any agreement and a rate war followed.

The results of this war were scarcely less serious than could have been expected. Cape Colony at once entered into a period of depression, mitigated at first by the opening up of the deep level mines, but nevertheless very noticeable, and getting steadily worse toward the outbreak of the Anglo-Boer War. The progress of this depression may be seen by taking the tonnage figures for the Cape, Natal, and Delagoa Bay ports. As will be seen from the following table the geographical factors now took full effect.

Value and Tonnage carried by each competing Administration. Through Goods Traffic to the Transvaal.
(ooo omitted throughout)

| Year | Cape Govt. Railways | | Natal Govt. Railways | | Portuguese Railway | |
|---|---|---|---|---|---|---|
| | £ | tons | £ | tons | £ | tons |
| 1897 | 843 | 313 | 869 | | | |
| 1897 | 618 | | 532 | | 138 | |
| 1898 | 541 | | 377 | | 118 | |
| 1904 | 843 | 313 | 869 | 477 | 207 | 342 |
| 1905 | 756 | 297 | 894 | 525 | 272 | 390 |
| 1906 | 675 | 257 | 692 | 435 | 244 | 365 |

It should be noticed that by geographical factors we do not mean simply the actual economic advantage that the shorter lines enjoyed, but also the advantage of the Transvaal railway system, in that owing to its central position its managers were able to concentrate traffic on to its lines by quite artificially charging higher rates on those parts of the Cape and Natal lines which lay within its territory.

The effect of this transfer of traffic was to reduce the amount paid over to the Cape general revenue. In each of these years the Cape Government experienced financial difficulties resulting, of course, not only from the reduction of railway revenue, but from a corresponding reduction in customs revenue, which was largely bound up with the other. Cape Colony was the only loser, for Natal had no previous railway workings on which a loss could be incurred. At the worst her profits from railway enterprise might turn out to be slightly less than were expected, but the only question really was whether she got enough traffic to enable the line to pay and, in fact, this was obtained. The Transvaal line was in the same happy position. Here also good profits were made for the Holland company and for the Transvaal Government. It is impossible to say what would have happened had the South African War not broken out.

The period from the first building of the gold lines to the outbreak of the war may be said to be the period in which the various inter-state problems of South Africa, problems of railways and of customs as well as of shipping and agricultural and native administration, first became clearly defined and showed themselves to be insoluble excepting by united effort. We have outlined the railway development of this period and we have seen that the first and most certain effect of unrestricted competition was to threaten the oldest state in South Africa with financial ruin. Customs problems were not far behind. It is quite impossible to say which of these was the more immediately important, for they worked completely in conjunction with each other. The other problems were certainly less vital from an immediate standpoint, but with the growth of communications the spread of animal diseases over the whole of South Africa became a pressing problem which alone would have necessitated a certain amount of co-operation between the states, and the increased movement of natives between the various parts of South Africa was also raising pressing problems of control. It was the railway and customs problems which had to be solved immediately, however, and one can only liken them to two blades of one pair of scissors, without being able to say which was the sharper.

## REFERENCES

Annual Reports of the Cape and Natal Managers of Railways. and of the N.Z.S.A.M. Railway.

Select Committee, Cape Colony, 1893, To Enquire into the Entire System of Railway Management in this Colony.

Memorandum, 1894, on the Comparison of the Cape Colony Midland and Eastern Railway Routes.

Files of the *Transvaal Advertiser* from 1893 to 1896.

Article on the Colonial Lands of Natal, with references to the Railway System, in the proceedings of the Royal Colonial Institute, 1895 to 1896.

A series of articles on South African Railways in the *Transvaal Times and Observer* during June, 1892.

A paper on the Development and Working of Railways in the Colony of Natal, by Sir David Hunter, in the Proceedings of the British Association for the Advancement of Science, 1905.

Minutes of Railway Conference held at Cape Town, 1895.

Minutes of the South African Railway Officers' Conference, 1898.

Report and Evidence of the Transvaal Industrial Commission, 1896.

Annual Reports of the Transvaal Chamber of Mines.

Text of the Railway Conventions of 1891 and 1895 between the Orange Free State and the Cape Colony.

Text of the Agreement between Cape Colony and the Netherland South African Railway Company regarding the completion and working of the Line from the Vaal River to Johannesburg, 1892.

Text of the Conditions of Concession for the Building and Working of a Railway Line in the South African Republic from the Portuguese Frontier to Pretoria. Barberton, Johannesburg and Vaal River, printed as an annexure to the Report of the Imperial Concessions Commission, 1900.

# SECTION II

## CHAPTER II

### CUSTOMS AND TRADE IN THE GOLD DISCOVERY PERIOD

#### (a) *Inter-Colonial Tariff Relations*

WE have seen that the first customs agreement of this period followed upon the railway agreement of the Cape Colony with the Orange Free State. As the railway systems developed so did customs systems. The customs policies, both of the Cape and of Natal, were from this time onward run in full concurrence with their railway policies. Natal also had the advantage of her newness in this respect, for with the exception of protection given to her tropical industries, her customs policy was able to be an entirely commercial one. Both the Cape and Natal had to collect not only their own customs duties, but also duties in some form or other on goods passing through to the inland States. The customs policy of each may be said to have been twofold. Both of them had in previous years pursued a policy of ignoring the claims of the inland states, and of collecting duties on all of the goods entering their ports according to their own tariffs. This had been inevitable in the days before railway connections, since it had been impossible to know what goods had been destined for the interior. The best that could have been done was to make an estimate and to pay over moneys collected according to this estimate. The coastal states had always refused on principal to admit obligation to pay over more than a certain proportion of the duties collected, the remainder being claimed in consideration of services rendered at the ports. With the building of the railways it became possible to know with some definiteness the amount of traffic which was to go through to the interior. Agreements had to be arrived at, especially as it became known that the Transvaal, if not the Orange Free State, intended to enforce a customs policy on its own borders. The repayment of duties now became one of the bargaining factors in the situation; the Cape at first claimed to retain twenty-five per cent. as transit duties, but by the end of the century this was down to three per cent. In this way all goods entering the Cape ports paid ordinary duties, and those that went through into the Transvaal also paid the Transvaal duties, but the Transvaal government got not only all of the money collected on its own border, but also ninety-seven per cent. of the money collected on the same goods at the Cape port. In the case of Natal, a further step was taken. Here all goods for the Transvaal were admitted free of duty excepting for a transit duty of three per cent. The Transvaal was able to set up a customs boundary with a general level slightly lower than that of the Cape.

The policy of the Cape was to get a customs agreement at least with Natal, and, if possible, including the Transvaal as well. Discussions on this point, however, followed the lines of those on the railway question. Natal stood to lose by adjusting her tariff to meet that of the Cape, while the Transvaal was now able to draw profit from its central position. Imported goods destined for the Witwatersrand were not the only factor, however, in the customs policy. South African produce affecting the farmers and the local merchants also had to be considered, and was of great importance to the various governments. The Transvaal was able to confer real benefits both on the Orange Free State and on the Portuguese territory by admitting their home

produce free of duty. The farming interest in the
Free State objected to the customs union with the Cape
since it exposed some of its farmers to the competition
of grain sent in from the Cape. The same farmers
opposed even more strongly the admission of Basutoland into the customs union on the grounds that the
natives of that territory would be able to send grain
into the Orange Free State. They did not object, so
they said, to the admission of any civilised state into
the customs union, but they did object to the admission
of a barbarous state, which merely had a civilised
government. Basutoland, however, was included in
the customs union for reasons of state. The farmers
of the uplands of Natal also objected to customs unions
with the Orange Free State on the grounds that they
had nothing to gain from it, and might encounter
opposition. These considerations of internal produce,
however, do appear to have been minor ones in the
actual forming of policies.

### (b) *Foreign Trade*

Leaving the subject of customs policy, we come to
deal with the foreign trade of South Africa. It is
commonly said that at this time South Africa was a
vast agricultural and pastoral area importing nearly all
its own food stuffs, wheat from Europe, tinned and
frozen meat from Australia, and preserved fruit. This,
of course, is true, but an important qualification must
be made. It must be remembered that South Africa
had been a self-supporting country as near as any country
can be until two sudden and new demands had been
made upon her resources, the demands of the diamond
industry in the early seventies, and of the gold industry
in the late eighties. Food stuffs had had to be imported to feed those two areas, and since these areas
were connected by railway with the ports, and by good
shipping routes with highly-developed food-exporting
countries, it is not surprising that they drew their food

## CUSTOMS AND TRADE

along these lines of communication. Nor is it surprising that South African agriculture had not succeeded in increasing its output at once to meet the new demands. Johannesburg was nearer to Australia by railway and steamship than she was to many parts of the Transvaal. The key to South Africa's apparent failure to feed herself is to be found in the fact that the chief consuming areas were connected with Cape ports and not with South Africa's producing areas. The railway lines when once built collected all possible food supplies from the lands which happened to lie along their routes, and these lands received all the stimulus that is given to an agricultural district when mechanical transport is applied to it for the first time, but it is noteworthy that scarcely any of the land through which the trunk lines ran, has developed agriculturally to this day, thus showing that it was not agricultural land. One wonders whether if the trunk lines had been built less directly to reach their objective they might incidentally have led to a far more rapid development of the country and so saved much later expenditure on branch lines. For the country was one of great distances and of few points of consumption. It was also a country of a very mixed quality of land which would become productive only where a happy conjunction of land and water and skilful farming was to be found. Its points of successful production are even to-day points rather than great areas; each point probably lies many miles from it nearest neighbour. And in 1890 this was very much more so, for the very lack of transport had meant that the soil had only in one or two places been really tested for development; the Transvaal was known to have fertile areas, but it had been settled by farmers whose total lack of contact with any market, or with any outside influences, had made them quite forget whatever they might have known about arable cultivation. The building of branch lines after the South African War, although these lines seldom paid their way at once, turned the balance and made South Africa begin to be an exporting, and less an importing, country.

We have already looked at both the foreign trade of South Africa and the interchange of its various states with each other in the period prior to the gold discoveries. During the nineties the general character of the inter-colonial South African trade appears to have remained unaltered so far as the few very scanty statistics show excepting that a slightly increased amount of food stuffs produced in the Free State and the coastal colonies were imported into the Transvaal. That this increase was so slight is explained by the considerations which we have mentioned in the previous paragraph. All the produce so sent to the Transvaal had to be carried the greater part of the distance by ox-wagon, and it happened that other circumstances prevented even the ox-wagon from being used to the full for agricultural transport. The first of these was that up to 1895, all those farmers who were within reach of the Transvaal found it much more profitable to employ their ox-wagons in the carrying of miscellaneous produce from the rail heads to Johannesburg than to collect food stuffs from the agricultural countryside and carry them to the town. In the second place, after 1896, the whole of the ox-wagon transport was paralysed by an outbreak of an epidemic of cattle plague known as rinderpest, which spread from the north right through the Transvaal and the Orange Free State, penetrating even into the coastal districts of the south-east, and, apart from killing cattle by the thousand, made it necessary for the movement of the others to be stopped. These causes alone, added to the fact that the railway lines were not built to feed the agricultural districts, would account for the imports of food-stuffs during the nineties.

Apart from food-stuffs, the imports into South Africa from oversea consisted almost entirely of the materials needed for the equipment of the goldmining industry, and for the building of its contingent towns and railways.

The machinery imports fell off in 1893 and 1894 as compared with the two previous years. This would appear to indicate the presence of two factors : in the first place, the mining industry had come to a stage in which it appeared that the development of the surface reefs had been carried as far as circumstances warranted. The question of deep levels was being enquired into, and imports were waiting upon the result of these enquiries. In the second place, the mining industry was waiting for the completion of the railway lines which would compete with those of the Cape and so cheapen import. With the successful proving of the deep levels in 1895 imports at once show an upward tendency both as regards machinery and building materials. Political troubles, however, did not begin only with the outbreak of war in 1899. Three years previous to that the Jameson raid took place, and we can only suppose that this accounts for the failure of the improvement in 1895 to continue. Imports in nearly all classes of goods, declined from that year onwards.

In the total of goods used by the mining industry and its accessory population, it would appear that produce of South Africa was almost negligible. The one exception to this was coal, which very fortunately was found in excellent supplies within easy reach of the Witwatersrand ; much of it indeed actually on the Rand. The failure of South Africa in the supply of raw materials for building was quite as definite and more fundamental than its failure in the supply of foodstuffs. We find large imports of all secondary and raw materials, such as leather, in all its stages of manufacture, timber, candles and grease, and many other materials which were, of course, produced on nearly every farm in South Africa, but of which this production does not appear to have satisfied the needs even of the farmers themselves.

During the nineties an alarm was raised to the effect that South Africa was rapidly increasing the percentage of her imports from non-British countries.

That this was true, will soon be seen from the following table :—

British South Africa Imports from
(000 omitted)

|  | United Kingdom | Germany | Holland | Belgium | France | United States |
|---|---|---|---|---|---|---|
| 1890 | 12,043 | 245 | 153 | 3 | 68 | 489 |
| 1891 | 9,820 | 185 | 87 | 5 | 24 | 431 |
| 1892 | 10,119 | 281 | 166 | 18 | 31 | 418 |
| 1893 | 11,075 | 300 | 129 | 40 | 33 | 605 |
| 1894 | 10,730 | 498 | 163 | 53 | 3 | 621 |
| 1895 | 17,537 | 825 | 234 | 132 | 45 | 999 |
| 1896 | 17,383 | 1,264 | 226 | 374 | 147 | 2,412 |
| 1897 | 17,089 | 1,054 | 282 | 301 | 147 | 2,412 |
| 1898 | 15,256 | 981 | 208 | 312 | 71 | 2,767 |

But it should also be noticed that although the percentages from foreign countries were increasing rapidly, the totals were so small that the percentages had very little significance. They can nearly all be explained by the fact that England on account of her Cape Colony connections had been first in the field when the gold mines had been opened. At first, English goods had had almost a monopoly, then other countries stepped in and made connections. The trade of such a country as Belgium increased very rapidly during the nineties for the simple reason that it began from almost nothing. The only serious competition was found in specialities for use in the mines, which could be turned out by America, which already had within her own territory gold and other mines very similar to those of the Transvaal. This was an undoubted advantage. Not only mining machinery, but also mining engineers were imported largely from America, and the engineers naturally preferred the machinery to which they had been accustomed. So far as agricultural machinery was imported, the same applies. America already used exactly the type of agricultural machine which was suitable in the few districts in which South African agriculture wanted machinery. We hear all the usual criticisms of British products from the Transvaal miners; the machines were too heavy; they were built to last for ever, and the conditions were constantly requiring new experiments; spare parts were not available, but owing to the roughness of the work, they were frequently needed; the machines were expensive in consumption of power as well as in their original cost; finally, the Americans and the Germans did not disdain to employ commercial travellers, and these travellers came armed not only with illustrated catalogues, but with well-stocked warehouses, which they made it their first business to set up in Johannesburg. These criticisms of British trade are known the world over, and it certainly appears that in the case of the Transvaal, there was much substance in them.

On the other hand Great Britain had almost the whole of the textile trade, excepting very rough cottons, and blankets for use by Kaffirs. Most of the food-stuffs imported were from various parts of the British Empire. The whole of the wheat coming from Australia and Canada, while articles such as tea and coffee were re-exported from British ports. South Africa's balance of trade with Australia was a particularly one-sided one since she took large supplies of butter and frozen meat and sent virtually nothing in exchange.

It would be quite useless in the case of South Africa to give details of the exports per head of the population, for those exports depended not upon the population as a whole, but upon some thirty thousand people in and around Johannesburg. Imports per head of population, have little more significance, consequently we do not give them in this study. We mention this point only because sensational conclusions have been drawn from mischievous uses made of these figures.

As compared with other "new" countries, South Africa still stood out as a country of low tariffs. The duty on the import of wheat was much lower than the same duty in Australia and Canada, although it must be kept in mind that its effect upon South Africa was greater since South Africa was a wheat importing country, whereas the two others were exporters. In respect of textiles the countries are more comparable since all of them imported these. In this case the South African duties are higher than those of Australia and Canada, the aim evidently being to secure the largest possible revenue. As regards mining machinery, we find that the South African importer had to pay a much higher duty than the Canadian or Australian importer, this being due not to the tariffs of Cape Colony or Natal, who were obliged by competition to keep them low, but to the Transvaal tariff being added to one of the others. On the whole, the South African tariff wall remained throughout the nineties, and, indeed, well into the present century, a purely revenue concern.

### REFERENCES

The Files of the *British and South African Export Gazette*.
The Reports of the Customs Departments of Cape Colony and Natal.
The Report of the Special Commissioner on British South African Trade, 1903.
The Files of the South African Newspapers already referred to.
The Cape Colony and Natal Government Gazettes for the period.

## SECTION II

## CHAPTER III

### AGRICULTURE IN THE MINING DEVELOPMENT PERIOD, 1887 TO 1899

(a) *Types of Land and Farming Methods in Cape Colony*

THE foreign trade of South Africa, like that of any other country, can be fully explained only by means of a survey of the whole of its internal economy both as regards productive industry and its consuming population. We now, therefore, shall attempt to give the story of South African agricultural development between the time at which the gold industry began to give new values to agriculture, as well as to everything else in South Africa, and the time when, after a devastating war, systematic reorganization was attempted. As we have already seen, practically the whole of such land as was desired by primitive colonists had been taken up before the eighties. The land was now occupied by these first settlers. Most of it was not in touch with any market and agricultural practice was in consequence predominantly non-commercial. One of the main facts to keep in mind is that another consequence of these conditions, and by far the most important one, was that the value of nearly all the land was unknown. No agricultural survey had ever been made. The land had never been traversed by skilled farmers of the type which was to be found in Australia or Canada. No official stimulus by way of education, or scientific research, or financial assistance, or scientific land settlement, had ever been applied excepting in a very few minor cases, with which we hope to deal. In the case of nearly all farms the land was not surveyed but was marked off in the primitive parts by means of beacons, and in other parts by boundaries recognized by custom. In the decade under review the first efforts were made to supply these wants. An uneasiness set in at the import of foodstuffs for the Transvaal. Cape Colony became keenly aware of her subsistence upon the carrying trade to the north, and as this trade suffered in competition with better situated countries her determination to improve her agriculture developed. In the Transvaal most of the land, both on the high veld and in the less valuable regions, passed out of the hands of the Dutch colonists and into the hands of land companies who held it for speculative purposes. In Natal the coastal semi-tropical industries were able to aim at selling their goods in Johannesburg to be sent up there by means of the trunk line. The Orange Free State found itself with free access to the Johannesburg market. Around Johannesburg itself garden farming grew up rapidly to supply the new population with fruit and vegetables. In the Cape and Natal a new type of farmer, organized mainly in syndicates, began to buy land, and both these syndicates and the older fashioned farmers began to agitate for the building of agricultural lines and other state assistance. The dependence of the members of the Cape Parliament upon the votes of farmers rendered all parties only too eager to render this assistance whenever possible.

The large size of South African farms is common knowledge. Five thousand acres was a common size, and it was not unusual for prosperous farmers to buy up more than one farm. General Botha, before he entered politics, was the owner of some thirty thousand acres, and he appears to have been only a slightly exceptional farmer. The greater number of farmers, however, lacked his business instincts and lived only on one holding, except where summer pasture was held separately. We have already seen that in the south-west corner of Cape Colony farms began to be sub-divided by the sixties, and our present point is that this subdivision was confined to the south-west corner. In all the remainder of Cape Colony the average size of farms was scarcely reduced at all even during the nineties, and

# AGRICULTURE, 1887 TO 1899

remain for the most part at the pioneer size to this day. Let us look first of all at the farm lands of the Karroo. This land is composed of limestone worn down to a fertile condition in the course of centuries. The average rainfall is some three inches per annum. This is not supplemented by any supplies of river water. It has a tendency to vary from five inches in a good year to a mere one inch in drought years, three or four of which commonly come together. The vegetation is entirely a drought resisting one consisting of shrubs and Karroo bushes, which in their natural state spring to maturity after each fall of rain and thus quickly provide the surface with a vegetal covering which prevents too rapid evaporation under the terrific sun. When the ground loses its moisture the grasses and shrubs at once wither up and the surface is left desolate. Before the land was occupied by colonists it was uninhabited excepting by tribes of wandering natives who imposed no strain upon its resources and by herds of antelopes which ate the grasses and shrubs and moved instinctively to regions where rainfall was good. The accounts of early travellers leave no doubt that it was common to see grass land dotted about over the Karroo; that in many parts the grasses and shrubs had grown to such profusion that they were able to retain moisture in the soil almost permanently despite drought. It is probable that the travellers' accounts put too rosy a complexion upon the matter. But it does appear that in its natural state the Karroo had been able to develop resources of soil as a result of the action of the water upon the surface, and by means of vegetation had been able to retain this soil and to strike a balance between desert conditions on the one hand and agricultural fertility on the other. Had this land been settled in its natural state by scientific farmers these resources would have been supplemented by devices to improve the vegetation and to conserve still further the water supply. In this way the land would have been made to produce crops of wheat and other cereals. Actually, however, the mode of settlement was very different and had very different results. The farmers who took up the land marked it out for their three thousand acre farms and proceeded to treat it by agricultural methods as primitive as the size. Each farmer proceeded to put as many sheep upon the land as it would carry. He cultivated only a small home-garden to provide food for himself and his family. He did not produce winter fodder for the sheep because he already had as many as he could look after, and owing to market conditions he had no inducement to improve the quality of the wool or to breed the sheep for mutton. The favourite type of animal was the fat-tailed Africander sheep which gave a good deal of heavy coarse wool, and of which the chief virtue was that it could pick up its food by roaming over the Karroo. Each farmer kept his sheep in one flock and did not fence off any parts of the farm. The sheep thus ran free over the land, eating the best grasses that they could find, first of all the more succulent ones and then those that were coarser. Toward evening the sheep were all collected and driven back into one kraal where they spent the night. The reason for this proceeding was the existence of jackals, which killed the sheep during the night and which, while they could be kept down by hunting, could never be exterminated on these great open farms. The sheep were thus allowed to denude the land of its vegetal covering by eating the grasses in an unregulated way. This in itself was fatal under Karroo conditions, for once the vegetal covering was interfered with the sun could reach the bare soil, any moisture that fell would quickly be lost either by evaporation or by running off, and the balance between fertility and drought was lost. Add to this the fact that the sheep were habitually driven to and from their kraals along paths which became well marked and they also trampled over all the rest of the land in their search for food, moving more and trampling more as vegetation became more scarce. The surface became hard and was baked by the sun, the run-off from the rainfall took the course of the sheep paths which became small streams

# AGRICULTURE, 1887 TO 1899

causing the water to run away in floods after each fall of rain. The only compensation which the soil received was the manure of the sheep and this was much less than it should have been owing to the fact of the sheep being kept in the kraal during the night. The attitude of the farmers was one of resignation. They formed fixed impressions that the climate was changing. They said that the old steady soaking rains no longer fell but that instead the rain fell in storms and so was lost to the soil. A good example of malobservation.

The karroo proper was only an extreme example of what was happening in the more fertile Eastern Province. This region, excepting the part near the coast, was Karroo land, but with much better rainfall. It was here chiefly that efforts were made to improve the breed of the sheep, and in the course of the nineties Merino sheep were successfully introduced by some of the more successful farmers. The methods generally were the same. Cultivation was confined to the home farm and the sheep occupied all the remainder. Kraaling with its attendant evils was practised, but owing to the more favourable natural conditions it had much less serious effects. But one great improvement in method was in progress; the fencing of land was being more and more resorted to. The importance of fencing cannot be over estimated, and there is evidence that the farmers themselves and the officials in Cape Town realised this. For example, the Cape censuses of 1891 and of 1904 asked for returns of fenced land. They attempted to distinguish between rail fencing and the mere building of rough stone walls by asking for returns of these latter separately. At the two census dates the returns were as follows:

|  | MORGEN (000 omitted) | |
| --- | --- | --- |
|  | 1891 | 1904 |
| Wire | 4,100 | 12,451 |
| Stone | 309 | 189 |
| Clay or Mud | 66 | 54 |
| Other Fencing | 239 | 557 |

Without attaching too much importance to these figures, we may safely say that the practice was on the increase. Its first effect was to make selective breeding possible, thus having the same result as had the enclosing of common lands in European countries. This was probably the first object aimed at by farmers who fenced. But the practice was soon seen to have other scarcely less important results. It made possible the extermination of jackals since once these had been killed out in an enclosed camp that camp would be free from them so long as the fencing was kept in good condition. Stone walls and wooden fences did not keep the jackals out ; wire fences were necessary. But even stone walls made it possible to paddock the sheep, so that they could be directed on to one piece of land at a time, thus giving all of the land rest periods and allowing the vegetation to recuperate. A few farmers of whom the best known was a Mr. Southey, took land on the Karroo and carried out experiments upon it often with striking success. On the Southey farm the first step was to fill the water courses with rough dams made of bracken and pebbles, and these dams soon collected the soil which the water was carrying away so that an overflow of soil-laden water took place and the good soil was deposited around the original dam, and on these spots crops were soon successfully grown. Attention was given as well to the conservation of vegetation and to the stopping of all sluits. The Southey experiment, while successful, aimed at proving the land capable of agricultural crops rather than at merely increasing its sheep carrying capacity. Whether if the land was now taken in hand by scientific farmers and covered with good motor roads it would become a grain growing district is a question which may be decided in the far future. The Eastern Provinces of the Karroo got the benefit of the trunk lines built from Port Elizabeth and from East London. As a result of these lines the land through which they pass was able to develop in the direction of mixed farming. On every farm it was possible to increase the extent of

## AGRICULTURE, 1887 TO 1899

land devoted to arable cultivation. The cultivation carried on previously had aimed merely at feeding the farmers' families and only contact with markets was needed to bring increased land under the plough. The agricultural districts around Queenstown, Molteno, Bedford, Somerset East and Craddock, were all of them sufficiently good land to develop mixed farming. Wheat growing land had been established for some time at Craddock and Molteno, and in the other districts named. The emphasis came to be turned from pastoral farming pure and simple to the production of grain along with the improvement in the breed of cattle for dairy produce.

We have looked at the farming of the Karroo proper and of its Eastern end, where it merges into grass land. We may next turn our attention to the agriculture of the south-west corner of Cape Colony. This agricultural land stretches from Clanwilliam to the north to Riversdale to the south east. The whole of this area, bounded to the north east by Karroo mountain ranges, has winter rains and so can grow both wheat and fruit trees. It is a coherent arable district, the whole of the land for hundreds of square miles being cultivable, and thus differing from the land in almost every other part of South Africa, where the most scientific efforts have, as a rule, succeeded only in putting small patches of green on the map. The Cape south west differed also from almost every part of South Africa in that its potentialities were fully explored before it was permanently settled. Trade with passing ships in the seventeenth and eighteenth centuries led to the agricultural regions being systematically colonised by immigrants who were both expected and induced to produce foods for sale. It was this process of colonisation coupled with the inherent fertility of the soil, which had led finally to the size of the farms being very much less than in any other part of the sub-continent. Cattle and sheep received very little attention, the former being kept only for incidental dairy produce, and the latter being kept only on small patches of land which were lying fallow. Wine farming was much more widely spread than was wheat farming, for the latter was concentrated almost entirely around Malmsbury, while wine was produced both in the north and the south of the region. The wheat fields did not cover much territory. They had no resemblance to the wheat lands of Australia. They were cultivated intensively by the families of the farmers, and it was clear that there was no similar land available to be brought under this crop. It was clear, also, that the wheat production per acre could not be increased, indeed, there were signs that in response to the increased prices, resulting from the opening up of the Kimberley and Johannesburg markets, the yield per acre was falling. It was a well-established farming industry, but not one with a future. Wine growing, on the other hand, though equally old, was much more problematical. The types of vine grown had become well established before the sixties, when, as we have seen, an export trade to England in certain choice types of wine existed. But on the collapse of this export trade the whole of the industry was forced to become experimental once more. Indeed it is probable that one of the causes of the collapse was that in the effort to increase the production of the exportable wines the quality of these had been somewhat changed. Efforts were now made to produce wine in bulk; not only choice sweet wines, but also light wines which would be exportable in larger quantities. The efforts were not successful, for the chemical composition of all the wine that could be produced made it impossible for export excepting in a very spirituous condition. Its local market was assured and matters were somewhat improved by the opening up of the Kimberley market. Yet the industry as a whole never succeeded in making good regular use of all the land available for vine planting. It was still in this vague experimental stage when in the early nineties it was attacked by the phylloxera which finally made it necessary to change over to other vines of which the

## AGRICULTURE, 1887 TO 1899

stocks were imported from America. These stocks were grafted on to the existing vines and succeeded in rendering them immune to the disease. But in the meantime the market for the wines had been still further lost and the change over was made beneficial only by being used as an occasion for changing the emphasis of the whole industry from wine production to fruit growing. In 1895 a meeting between Cape Town merchants and neighbouring farmers was held, at which the merchants impressed upon the farmers the possibilities of developing a regular export of fruit. Ships were regularly sailing back to Europe with half-empty holds. Very favourable terms could be secured for an organized export. A trade commissioner was sent to London in order to introduce the fruit. The effects of this new opening upon the farming industry were very considerable. The farms were now of a size which made individual supervision of the fruit trees quite practicable. Fruit had for a long time been one of the by-products of the district's agriculture, for it had had a ready market in Cape Town, and some of it had even survived transport to Johannesburg, where it was always bought with eagerness. With a prospect of an oversea market much more attention was given to fruit cultivation. The produce so far had been most variable in quality, consisting of small specimens of such hard fruits as peaches and plums. But fruits of the highest quality had also been produced here and there. If the quality was to be raised and made uniform much of the good land which previously had been devoted to vines as well as much land of which no great use had been made, would now have to be given to scientific fruit cultivation. An example was set by Cecil Rhodes, who bought several farms near Cape Town and farmed on a large scale, employing expert managers from America, and so giving a lead to the neighbouring farmers. The success of this new cultivation was proved, although unfortunately it cannot be indicated by statistics, since only export figures were kept, and no indication given of the internal consumption of fruit in South Africa, which must have risen considerably in addition.

The success of this new fruit cultivation had at least one important result for South Africa as a whole; it showed the possibilities, both of government assistance and of the advantages of applying more capital to the soil. The government and the Rhodes farms in conjunction had discovered the types which could best be cultivated. The government agricultural department which had existed in a desultory way since the seventies was almost for the first time able to show definite results for its experiments. And the farmers in changing over from one type of crop to another had been under the necessity of finding capital, which they had been able to do owing to their farms having been of a manageable size and fertile and consequently mortgageable.

Another part of Cape Colony which was showing signs of activity was the Oudtshoorn region, situated south of the Karroo, between the coastal mountains and the sea. Oudtshoorn had neither the winter rains of the south west, nor the summer rains of the south east. Its rainfall was actually less than that of some parts of the Karroo. But it had a water supply in the form of rivers running down from the coastal ranges. These rivers were dry for about eight months in the year and, as might have been expected, the early settlers had attached but slight importance to their agricultural possibilities. The soil, however, was excellent, being rich, black, dry, and finely powdered. It had been found that wherever the river waters were held up by dams the land was very good for such crops as lucerne and tobacco. The growing of lucerne was at first undertaken for sale to sheep farmers as winter fodder, while tobacco was grown in an unsystematic way and made up and sold locally. Its nicotine content was so high that it was said to have an excellent future as a sheep wash. During the eighties, however, attention had been drawn to the value of ostrich feathers and Oudtshoorn in common with many parts of South Africa

## AGRICULTURE, 1887 TO 1899

had considerable numbers of wild ostriches. Farmers everywhere began to shoot the ostriches in order to secure their feathers. But others tried to keep the birds and, if possible, to domesticate them. The success of these attempts in one district has given a wide impression that it was an easy process everywhere. Actually, it was successful to a reasonable degree only in Oudtshoorn. There, a most fortunate collection of favourable conditions was found to exist. In the first place, lucerne could be grown of excellent quality and with certainty by irrigation from the river waters. In the second place, the complete absence of rainfall which made the feeding of ostriches impossible in almost all other parts of South Africa meant that the air in Oudtshoorn was very dry and consequently that it tended to produce feathers of first-class quality. In the third place, absence of rain combined with the excellent quality of the soil enabled the birds to be kept without injuring their feathers when they lay down. These natural advantages soon marked Oudtshoorn as the best ostrich district. The farmers began to establish ostrich camps. They devised ways of incubating the eggs, and scientific breeding was established. Land in Oudtshoorn which was really suitable for ostriches rose by 1910 to be sold at £500 an acre. We do not know what its price increases were during the nineties, but judging by the market prices of ostrich feathers and by the steady increase in the quantities exported, the land must have risen in value to an extent parallelled only in the Transvaal. Much of the land changed hands and new farmers with capital at their disposal entered the district. During the nineties there was no railway service and mixed farming in consequence did not develop. Later, cattle became more important than ostriches, but at first and until after 1910, nearly all attention was concentrated on what was by far the best paying, although the most speculative agricultural industry in the country. It has been frequently stated that this development of ostrich farming was really a

set back for South African agriculture ; that it gave
fictitious values to land ; that it caused an influx of
speculators who aimed not at agricultural development
but merely at reaping profits from one luxury article
whose market was as fickle as that for diamonds.
However this may be it seems to the present writer
incontestable that at least three important results were
achieved. In the first place the possibilities of artificial
irrigation were explored. In the second place the
importance of the fencing of the land for all stock farming
was demonstrated. In the third place the lucerne
feeding of ostriches demonstrated the value of winter
fodder for all stock. And, we may add in the fourth
place, the final collapse of the ostrich industry demonstrated the advisability of cultivating a variety of crops.
(The ostrich industry, although it neglected mixed
farming, yet had by-products in the form of a more
intensive experimentation with tobacco and cotton,
since these crops were grown to clean the land while
it was resting.)

### (b) *Irrigation*

Dealing first with irrigation, this subject has now
assumed such importance in South Africa, as was
natural in a country of limited rainfall, that there is a
tendency to forget its limited nature. In countries
which are short of water supply it is probable, not only
that irrigation would be highly beneficial, but also that
it would have very limited possibilities. Its true
importance may be realised by calling to mind that it
was first adopted and discussed in South Africa by the
Oudtshoorn farmers. It was much later, not until the
twentieth century indeed, that the possibilities of
conserving river and rain water over the whole of South
Africa were first discussed. The coastal strip of
agricultural land of which Oudtshoorn is the most
important part, was seen to be a district which could
really benefit by irrigation, and which would be almost
useless without it. It was during the seventies that

# AGRICULTURE, 1887 TO 1899

the Oudtshoorn farmers first became known to be practising irrigation. It was almost unthought of in any other part of South Africa excepting the south west of the Cape, where natural irrigation as opposed to artificial was practised as a matter of course. The farmers of the Karroo would sometimes build small dams in order to hold water up to cultivate their home gardens when this was the only way of extracting a food supply from the soil. It was only in Oudtshoorn that actual conservation and furrow irrigation were introduced. During the seventies the commercial possibilities of the agriculture there were beginning to be realised and crops were being grown by farmers who extracted water from the rivers when they were in flood and conserved it in rough ways. The practice became known to the public when in 1876 an irrigation act was passed by the Cape Parliament. The farmers were experiencing difficulties in carrying out irrigation works, and they asked for assistance from the government chiefly with the object of enabling them to obtain the necessary capital. The Irrigation Act of 1876 was the first of a series passed in Cape Colony with a view to popularising irrigation among farmers, largely in the hope of discovering new grain-growing districts. The principle of all of these acts was to give the farmers the advantage of technical advice supplied at specially low rates by government engineers, to advertise irrigation by means of lectures by these engineers and by notices of the Acts published in the newspapers, and finally to grant loans to farmers to enable them to carry out irrigation works approved by engineers. The repeated passing of these Acts and the enquiries held into them makes it clear that they were not generally successful. The farmers in most parts of Cape Colony were not in a financial position to experiment with irrigation works, even assisted by a government loan. And in most parts, including all of those afflicted by drought, the evidence goes to show that the Acts were a dead letter. The administration of the law was to be carried out by the formation of irrigation associations among the farmers. These associations were to unite all of the farmers who would benefit from each irrigation scheme, and were to supervise the sharing out of the water from each scheme. But not a single association was formed until 1886, and by the end of the century only some half dozen more. The acts were a failure so far as their direct efforts go. The farmers who suffered from drought were unable to take up government loans, even on terms which were made more and more favourable as the acts were revised. On the other hand the farmers in Outdshoorn who had been expected to benefit from the acts were now enjoying a commercial prosperity which enabled them to progress without mortgaging their land to the State, although they did make use of the advice of government engineers. Irrigation in Oudtshoorn by the nineties was commercially established, although we have no figures as to the number of schemes carried through or even as to the extent of land under irrigation. The farmers were solving the problems themselves and were accumulating experience which later was to be used in the drawing up of legislation for United South Africa. In this respect, as in others, agriculture suffered from a code of law taken over from a country with very different natural conditions. In Holland the conservation of water was a positive evil and the Roman-Dutch law on water questions aimed at making the building of dams and weirs as difficult as possible. This law now applied to South Africa. It is certain that no general scheme of irrigation could be successful until the general law of water rights was amended. This was done in Cape Colony in 1908 and was embodied in the Union Irrigation Law of 1911. Under the Roman-Dutch law the upper holder, that is to say the holder of land nearer to the source of a river, was entitled to take as much water out of the river as suited his own purpose. The next holder could do likewise with what remained, and so on. In South Africa it was necessary that the upper holder should be enabled to take only so much water as he was entitled to by reason of the amount of land which he habitually had under cultivation and with due respect for the uses which lower holders could make of a water supply. With this object in view it was necessary to change the law so that every holder would be entitled to build a weir but also to leave an overflow of which the other holders would be ensured. In Oudtshoorn the disadvantages of the law were felt very strongly, but they were gradually got over by the making of agreements and by the fighting of legal cases by the farmers. It became customary to sell water rights along with the farms, and in this way irrigation developed, doubtless at a considerable cost for litigation, but with satisfactory practical results.

The other features of the Oudtshoorn farming need less attention from us. It is enough to say that the growing of lucerne especially set an example which could be, and was, followed in many parts of South Africa, while the advantages of fencing the land and paddocking the stock were almost equally applicable to stock farming in general.

### (c) *Marketing Methods of South African Farmers*

It may be advisable at this stage to describe the marketing methods of the South African farmers. These, as one might expect, were very simple until the nineties, and even then no very great changes are to be reported. In all districts except those very near to towns, produce was disposed of through the agency of the storekeeper. The storekeeper was the sole commercial agent in all up-country and in most coastal regions. The wool and hides were brought to the storekeeper and entered to the account of the farmer at a ruling price generally accepted for the season in the district. The farmer would then take his household requirements, and whatever farming implements he might need, in exchange. Money was seldom used in the period of which we speak. In good years the value of wool sold would exceed the value of the requirements of the farmer, and in bad years the reverse would be the case. Always, however, each farmer would have an account with one storekeeper, and most frequently he would rely upon the storekeeper to grant him credits during drought periods. In this way each farmer felt himself to be tied to his storekeeper, and it was undoubtedly common for the farmers to be in debt and for the trader to accept mortgages on the farms. The general belief was, probably correctly, that in districts such as the Karroo, the storekeepers were more often than not the real owners of the land, and that this applied to the Free State and to the Transvaal almost equally, for there also, even where the land was more grassy than in the Karroo, droughts were common and all produce was disposed of to the local storekeeper. The storekeeper would then undertake, having bought the wool, to transport it to the ports, or to one of the few inland wool sale towns. South Africa wool for export was classified only as good merino, and as ordinary. It was not until the twentieth century that finer classifications were made. The chief cause of this rough classification was undoubtedly the storekeeper system, under which wool was disposed of by farmers to general tradesmen who had no expert knowledge and who in their turn sold to other tradesmen until, when the wool finally reached the wholesalers, any merchants who might have been prepared to offer better prices for finer wools, found that they could not make this willingness known to the farmers. The storekeepers really held the key to the position in that it was they who actually received the wool from the farmer and who disposed of it to the next agent. A farmer who happened to turn out finer wool might find his efforts rendered worthless since on taking the wool to the storekeeper, he would get no more than the standard price for it. The storekeepers had played their part in introducing commerce to the agricultural regions; they were now ceasing to act beneficially by acting as a vested interest when the farmers needed a more complex commercial service. It was impossible for most farmers to sell their wool to new storekeepers or other agents, and only the most prosperous of them could afford to take the wool to market themselves. Wool buying under the storekeeper system was done simply by the bale, and the bale was a collection of wool and dirt and possibly even stones, which was the conventional standard. The sheep farming districts were not yet highly developed enough to demand a more complex commercial system than that of the storekeepers, and on the other hand, wool producing methods could not hope to improve until some better commercial service was obtained. It was this problem which caused farmers to look for help to co-operative societies, land banks, and other associations by which the farmers themselves would be able to do the marketing and the financing now in the hands of the old-fashioned storekeepers. Actually the problem came to be solved by private enterprise which, in the earliest part of the twentieth century, ventured to establish wool sales at some of the more important inland centres.

(d) *Agriculture in Native Areas*

The next agricultural region with which we may deal is that known as the Ciskei. This land lies between the Kei and the Great Fish River, and is almost of a piece with the Transkeian land occupied by natives. It gets the summer rains of the east coast, and consequently its vegetation consists of tropical grass-land and bush. It is land which has a considerable native population, although it is almost all owned by whites. The presence of this population, combined with the tropical nature of the vegetation, have dominated the agricultural development. It was practically impossible to grow any cereals, excepting maize, and prior to the development of a maize export in 1907, this was grown only for household purposes, and on very small patches of land, practically as the natives grew it themselves. The grass-lands near the coast were potentially excellent for cattle, but before the nineties the keeping of cattle had been rendered impossible owing to the presence of tick-born diseases. Cattle dipping was introduced from Australia after the turn of the century and almost at once it was proved to be effective against the tick. Its adoption, however, was slow. One reason for this was that some of the most progressive farmers had suffered severe loss through importing good cattle, and those losses had spread fear among all the farmers. Another reason was, that cattle themselves, even if successfully kept, are of comparatively little value unless a dairy industry is developed and a market established for meat ; both of these conditions were absent in the Ciskei up to the nineties, and were being only gradually acquired. A third reason and a very powerful one, was the presence of the native population, which acted in ways we have already described. It was much easier to draw rents from natives than it was to turn them off the land (a very difficult proceeding) and to engage in cattle farming, which was really very speculative. The discussion of the Ciskei leads us naturally to the Transkei, and we may describe its agriculture here, although this might be done equally well under the heading of " Native Ways of Life " when dealing with the native populations. In the Transkei, the land was essentially the same as that we have described in the foregoing paragraph. It was semi-tropical with luxuriant grass-lands alternating with tropical bush and wood-land. The grass-land was generally in its natural state too luxuriant for cultivation, and had to be cleared before maize, the staple crop, could be grown upon it. The natives had many resemblances to the European cultivators of South Africa in their general outlook. Their arable cultivation was done only with a view to providing each family with foodstuffs, and their main idea of wealth was the accumulation of cattle and other stock, which, however, did not lead to scientific stock-farming. The resemblance, however, goes no further. The individual holding of land adhered to by the Dutch and English

## AGRICULTURE, 1887 TO 1899

alike, found no counterpart among the natives who knew no ownership in land. Land among them was owned by no one; neither by individual nor by family, nor by tribe. It was the duty of the chief to procure the use of land to the natives, who, as members of his tribe, were entitled to ask his protection. Although there was no ownership, an elaborate system of rights in land had grown up, which aimed at insuring to each family certain occupation of any land which they had brought under cultivation so long as they wished to use it, and to preserve their right to it while they might be away hunting or fighting, or, later, working on the mines. Provisions were also made to ensure the right of inheritance of land cultivated by the father to all his children. A given piece of land would be occupied by a tribe or by a collection of families recognizing one leader. Within this land each man would pick out pieces of land which he thought fit for cultivation, and on the principle of "first come first served," the chief would allot these lands. Each man was entitled not merely to one piece of land, but to one piece for each of his wives. The family then became the unit for cultivation; each wife was responsible for her own garden as regards its cultivation, while the man looked after the cattle. The cattle were grazed on land common to the whole tribe. The aim of each wife was to produce enough food for her own children, and to make a general contribution to the well being of the family of which she was a part. The methods of cultivation were extremely primitive. The only implements used were shall hoes, which the women could work; cattle were never used for cultivation, nor did the men take any part. Even fallow was almost unknown, for when any piece of ground showed signs of exhaustion, it was allowed to go back into its natural state, and another piece was claimed for the family. These statements cannot be taken to apply with equal accuracy to the whole of the Transkei. Some parts were much more advanced than others, such, for example, as Fingoland, at the extreme south-western end, had been settled in the early part of the nineteenth century by a peaceable tribe, who took refuge under the British from some of their more warlike neighbours. These people showed an aptitude for trade, which soon changed their agricultural methods. It was common for the young men of the tribe to add to the family income by doing transport riding for white farmers. This accustomed them to the use of money, and brought about a somewhat revolutionary change, in that their cattle became instruments for the production of wealth instead of being themselves symbols of wealth. The Fingos were known as the Jews of the Bantu. They showed an aptitude for commerce found only exceptionally among natives of other tribes. In earlier times, it appears that they had acted as the commissariat to other tribes on the warpath. Their lands were situated within easy reach of such market towns as Kingwilliams Town and Queenstown. They were served also by the usual white traders who penetrated into the native territories. As a result, they soon came to grasp the idea of the production of a surplus for sale, and this led to changes in their agricultural methods. The first change was a gradual one; it consisted in the natives holding on for longer periods to the garden lands which had been allotted to them. They came to regard their tenures as almost permanent, and gradually proceeded to improve their cultivation by means of a simple use of fallow. The second change, whether more rapid or not, was more noticeable and attracted more attention from the outside observers. This was the use of the plough drawn by cattle, which had the further effect of causing the men to tend the fields as well as the women, for cattle were greatly respected, and no native would allow the women to drive them. A steady export of maize grew up, sold by the natives mostly to the traders, and in exchange European products, such as ploughs and blankets, began to be taken. It was in this way that tribal tenure of land began to be changed into something approaching individual tenure for life, though not individual ownership. At the other end of the scale to the Fingos were such tribes as the Pondos, who had scarcely come under European influence by the early nineties, and where the general practice was merely for families to scratch the soil and to eat the resulting crops, using the land completely as a free good, and allowing it to go back into general circulation as soon as each crop had been reaped. It would appear, however, that by the beginning of the nineties most of the Transkeian natives were approaching the practice of the Fingos rather than that of the Pondos. This was doubtless due partly to the influence of white traders, but more definitely to the fact that an increasing population upon a limited amount of land inevitably led to more fixity of tenure which, if it did not have immediate results in better methods of cultivation, at least prepared the way for this in the future. It would be wrong to assume that the agriculture of the Transkei was of no importance to South Africa as a whole. The prosperity of Queenstown and Kingwilliams Town contributed materially to that of East London, and the possibility of increased production by the native was always a factor to be reckoned with in discussing the future of South Africa. In 1894, a definite step was taken by the Cape Government, which had as one of its aims the stabilising of land tenure among the natives, and the modernization of their agriculture. This was the famous Glen Grey Act, which, in addition to undertaking to give natives, in certain districts, permanent individual rights to their cultivated lands, undertook to set up in all parts of the Transkei native councils, which were to have the benefits of advice from agricultural experts. The results of this measure were slow in coming, and it is difficult to see that up to the time of the South African War, anything more definite than the education of some of the more advanced natives in the use of the plough, and in the inoculation of their animals, had been achieved.

The boundary on the northern side of Pondoland between Cape Colony and Natal, cut what was essentially one region of native occupation into two parts. One natural difference, however, existed, namely, that the natives of Natal lived less on the coastal tropical land and more on the high lands approaching the Drakensburgs. This difference in land appears to have made the tribes more pastoral in their outlook than even the least advanced of the Transkei peoples. No approach to permanent individual tenure was noticeable, and the agriculture, apart from this comment, needs no description.

### (e) *Natal*

We must next describe the agriculture of Natal in the nineties. To deal first with the coastal tropical products we find that steady progress is shown by the establishment of sugar mills and the steady employment of the imported Indian population. There are no actual reliable figures for production here, any more than in most other parts of South Africa. Imports of sugar continued during the nineties and have been quoted as showing Natal's inability to supply herself. But what they really show is rather the amount of sugar sent via Durban to the Transvaal. Yet this process was not direct. For Natal's fiscal policy was to impose a duty upon imported sugar which rendered it more expensive at the coast than that locally grown, so that the local sugar was sent to the Transvaal while the imported, being unable to stand the additional high cost of transport to the Transvaal, tended to be kept for consumption in Durban. But although this was the tendency it must be made clear than the amount of sugar entering Durban was certainly greater than the total amount consumable by Natal. Thus import and export figures give us little or no indication of the development of the sugar industry, and the same applies to tea. The census returns for 1891 and 1904 show a substantial increase both in the acreage and the yield per acre, but it cannot be taken as

## AGRICULTURE, 1887 TO 1899

giving any indication whatsoever of the course of development in the nineties. It represents a post war boom. In Natal the land had been originally settled on the same pioneering principles as the rest of South Africa and her actual land system was taken over from Cape Colony. All of her lands excepting those at the coast remained as large farms often owned by absentee farmers, but those at the coast were early submitted to a process, not of sub-division, as had happened in the Cape south west, and as might have been expected here, but to a process of commercialization and conversion into estates. The coastal industries, after an experimental time during the sixties, were developed by companies which produced on a large scale. This large scale production held sway throughout the eighties and the nineties, but after that a certain tendency grew up for sugar to be grown by small planters served by milling companies with sugar mills. These several mills, however, were not built until the twentieth century, and in the period of which we now speak both the original farmers and new settlers with limited amounts of capital found little or no place in the production of tea and sugar. One of the chief reasons for this large scale farming appears to have been the original difficulty in importing and adapting seeds and plants from India. Although the land was similar to that used for tea and sugar growing in the East, these plants were quite unknown until they were introduced by the colonists first of all in the fifties, and on a larger scale, and with more security in the following decade. The early importations were very largely lost and a coffee industry which appeared to have been successfully established from seeds imported from Ceylon died out very quickly and with great loss in the fifties. Attention was thus turned to tea and sugar, and the importation of seeds was proceeded with, but the expense was considerable, and it appears that the poorer planters fell out of the running and only some three firms with sufficient capital resources were able to carry on until the crops were finally established. These planters were able to reap the benefits of their enterprise by securing control of the bulk of the suitable land. Another factor in the concentration of the industries was the difficulty in obtaining a supply of labour. These industries indeed give us the first example of a South African industry which was quite unable to persuade the indigenous natives to perform wage labour. The Natal natives did not live on the land on which tea and sugar were being cultivated. They lived to the north in the hilly regions, and found their tribal lands quite satisfying. Later on they took to mining with some success but, in the early days, they were unacquainted with any outside employment, and it is noteworthy that they have never to this day consented to do plantation work, which is doubtless to be accounted for by the natives' firm belief that such work as field cultivation is beneath the dignity of a man. By 1865 it had become clear that not only the seeds, but the labour as well, would have to be imported from India. For this, however, government assistance was needed, and this could only be obtained by the industry giving certain guarantees of employment, which again it was difficult for small planters to do. The Indian coolies were imported on the enterprise of one or two big firms which were sure of being able to employ them on their estates. The number of Indians in Natal is shown in the following table :—

(ooo omitted)

| Year | Population |
|---|---|
| 1876 | 10 |
| 1880 | 20 |
| 1885 | 30 |
| 1890 | 33 |
| 1895 | 46 |
| 1900 | 65 |

From this it will be seen that the number of coolies was greater in the nineties than in any previous period, and this may be taken as indicating a steady development of the planting industries. A further sign of growth, however, was the establishment of sugar mills, and of tea factories during the nineties, and these increased very considerably.

In the upland regions of Natal the land was generally more rough and better suited to maize than any of the land in, for example, Cape Colony. It had the tropical summer rains from moisture-laden west winds condensing on the Drakensburgs. After 1906 this land was to become highly productive of maize. But in the nineties it was largely uncleared land, cut up into very large farms unsuitable for settlers and largely occupied by natives. Its development was held up partly by the great size of the farms, which rendered the owners unable to afford to clear the land, without the stimulus of a direct market for any crop that might result; and also by the native occupation, which made absentee ownership often necessary and, whenever rent could be collected, very profitable. Here, as in various parts of Cape Colony the natives were able to make a more immediately profitable use of the land than were the whites, and when they were under the necessity of finding about twenty shillings per annum per family to pay the rent, they contrived to find this.

### (f) *The Orange Free State*

To continue our survey of South African agriculture during the nineties we may look next at the Orange Free State, and we shall find this to be perhaps the most happily situated of all parts of the sub-continent as regards its agriculture. The shrub and bush of the Karroo changed, as one went northward into the Free State, into grass-land. The presence of the Drakensbergs caused a higher rainfall, which lifted the land out of the desert category. A sheep-farming industry had become well established over the whole of the area excepting in certain small districts, chiefly around the market towns, which had been agriculturally developed with some success. The sheep farming resembled that of Cape Colony in the size of the farms and in the general methods, but methods which were destructive of Karroo land were fairly suitable for this grass land, and although a shortage of grass would generally be experienced in winter the land would recuperate with each summer rain, and, while the industry was not progressive, neither did it show any signs of exhausting the soil. It was almost as well situated for market purposes as were the Karroo lands, for transport down to the Cape Colony ports was easy, excepting in times of drought, when there would be no grass on the road to support the oxen dragging the wool. There was the same tendency for the wool to be unclassed on account of its all being sold to general storekeepers. This was unavoidable in such an inland district in which the producers were scattered so widely. But there was evidence by the early nineties of attempts to hold wool sales at Bloemfontein, the capital of the state. The arable cultivation in the Free State was governed mainly by the needs of the population, although one wheat-growing district existed and sold its product in other parts of the Free State; this was the land of high altitude, on the borders of Basutoland, which had been taken from the Basutos and thoroughly cleared of them in 1865 and the following years. This wheat area clamoured for railway connection as soon as the Cape line passed through the Free State, and this was soon obtained. To the north of the Free State, within reach of the gold fields by ox-wagon, clear signs of an agricultural stimulus were to be seen, for the prices, both of mutton and of all other food stuffs, rose enormously, and especially around Kroonstad, which happened to be on the railway line, much land was put under crops. This land was not exceptional in quality; it was developed simply on account of the railway communications, and it was such examples as this which led farmers and farmer politicians to hope that the whole of the agriculture of the Free State could be changed by the building of development lines. It was only after the South African War that such lines were undertaken, with results which we shall see later. In the nineties no general agricultural developments took place beyond

# AGRICULTURE, 1887 TO 1899

that we have indicated, but this development and the increased employment found for the population in transport riding appears to have preserved a balance between the natural increase of population and the resources of the soil, which prevented the rise of a landless white bywoner class and the sub-division of farms, which were leading to endless difficulties in the Transvaal. The Free State was happy also in its supply of native labour. It was the one state which had no disputable or essentially native land within its borders. Its permanent native population was almost insignificant although the census returns might convey a different impression. These returns, however, include all natives working on white farms, and most of these were only temporary labourers travelling the countryside for shearing and harvesting seasons, and then returning to their own land in Basutoland. Basutoland indeed served all the purposes of a native reserve for the Free State with few of the disadvantages. It was definitely marked off from the Free State by natural boundaries, the only disputable land being that wheat land whose acquisition we have already mentioned. The natives of Basutoland were a very peaceful body of people, skilled in the handling of sheep and of crops in ways suiting the condition of the country and satisfying the Boer farmers. As soon as the natives learned that they could increase their wealth, that is, acquire extra cattle, by working for white farmers in the Free State, they did so, and became a fairly reliable supply of labour. We do find in the Free State what was known as Kaffir farming and share-farming with Kaffirs. We have complaints by neighbouring farmers of the bad results of this in the district where any one farmer practised it. But so far as can be seen the evil, if it was an evil, was on such a small scale that it cannot possibly be compared to that found in the Ciskei or in the uplands of Natal. It appears rather that some of the farmers, and in all probability some of the best ones, aimed at securing increased cultivation of their soil and a permanent labour supply for themselves as an insurance against the possible danger of their sheep not being clipped at the right time, or their harvesting having to wait too long until travelling labourers appeared, by inducing some natives to accept permanent residence on their farms. This is supported by the system under which this was generally done; this was that known as share-farming; so that the natives were really put on the same basis as white bywoners. It is more than possible that the objections of neighbouring farmers were made on the grounds that the natives in this way were treated almost as white men and were able to become prosperous. The present writer has met Free Staters who refused to believe that this system was ever resorted to, saying that it amounted to admitting the native into partnership, and thus behaving in an un-European way. This, however, was precisely the objection of other farmers and the evidence that the system was resorted to is quite clear. While the development of the Free State was probably held up to some extent by the large size of the farms we cannot find that even this was such a serious drawback as it was in other parts of South Africa. For the Free State land, being essentially pastoral, could be worked with a fair approach to maximum economic returns better in large areas than in small. This could not be said of the land in the more cultivable parts of Cape Colony, or in the more accessible uplands of Natal.

(g) *Farming Methods in the Transvaal, and Changes consequent on the Gold Discoveries*

It remains for us to deal with that agglomeration of lands known as the Transvaal. The soil here varies from the most fertile, capable of producing with only elementary treatment the highest quality fruit, to the most backward and irrecoverable bush veld. And between these two extremes are found almost all grades of land. It is not surprising that the Transvaal was a land of unknown capabilities until the establishment of scientific agricultural administration after the South African War. Prior to the opening up of the Witwatersrand the Transvaal had reached the stage of apparent overcrowding. The land had all been taken out in most liberal fashion by the firstcomers; later arrivals had been accommodated as bywoners; as families increased the bywoners were being made to feel unwelcome and were realising their position as tenants merely on sufferance. We must ask ourselves why this overcrowding was being felt in the Transvaal while it was scarcely, or only just, known in the Orange Free State. No single explanation appears to be satisfactory, but we may advance the suggestion that the Transvaal was a much wilder country than the Orange Free State and that this wildness both accustomed the Transvaalers to eke out their livelihood by hunting expeditions and by perpetual trekking in search of new land and to ignore steady cultivation of any kind owing to their being completely cut off from markets. Hunting was always to be had in the bush veld, and valuable skins and ivory were generally brought back from a hunting expedition. The grass land was more subject to winter drought than that of the Free State, and the farmers had at their disposal the low veld near the coast to which they would trek annually, thus spending about a third of their year away from their Transvaal farms altogether. These conditions alone would account for agriculture falling into decay. This neglect of agriculture resulting from wild conditions, coupled with lack of market, had brought about the result in the course of the seventies and eighties that agricultural skill had largely been lost while at the same time outlets for population were being stopped. The bush veld was denuded of game so that this source of subsistence was lost. The lands to the north were wild and inhabited by natives, so that there was no outlet for the population by new migration although efforts were constantly being made. The settlers in consequence found themselves confined to their present land, the skilful use of which they had largely forgotten. The sheep farming was primitive in the extreme, for winter fodder, never a part of the Dutch system, was quite unknown and long annual treks kept the sheep lean and muscular with hides more valuable than their wool. The population was thus driven in upon the land suitable for arable cultivation; and it was on this land around Rustenburg, Middelburg and similar regions that the extreme sub-division which we are considering had taken place. This sub-division took the form of providing every farmer's son either with an actual portion of the farm or with the right, when such portions became too small for further sub-division, to a share in the land along with his brothers for purposes of cultivation. This was the stage reached when the Rand goldfields were opened up. At first this appeared to have led to no new developments in Transvaal agriculture. For among other disturbing features of the past had been the fairly frequent discovery of goldfields which put money into the farmer's pocket for " options " and which gave them a temporary prosperity, but in all probability only distracted their attention still further from actual agriculture. When it was seen that the Witwatersrand was to be something different Transvaal agriculture became really stirred. Land was bought all over the state by prospecting companies. The farmers enjoyed this influx of wealth which immediately relieved them from anxieties as to whether the land would continue to support them. At the same time their bullock wagons became an exceptionally valuable asset in transporting goods across country to Johannesburg, while any produce which they could grow received high prices. Cultivation, however, was to the farmers in the state to which the developments of the last twenty years had reduced them the least attractive of the ways of making money. Transport riding suited their natures better. It became a commonplace, and a true commonplace, that the Transvaal scarcely responded at all to the demand for foodstuffs created by the new industry. The very creation of towns created an outlet for congested

## AGRICULTURE, 1887 TO 1899

agricultural regions such as the Transvaal had been looking for in vain. The country had existed too long without markets and without commerce to be able to respond instantly to the great market which appeared with such suddenness in its midst.

Although the disturbing influence of the gold industry dominated Transvaal agriculture throughout the nineties, we must yet attempt to indicate its main features, which existed beneath these disturbances. Cultivation was paralysed but the land remained to be used another time. It was certain that, given time, adjustments would be made and the land cultivated in accordance with its potentialities and its opportunities. It is absurd to give all the credit for this to the administration by Lord Milner after the South African War. The new values created about 1890 were bound to require time to make the necessary readjustment in such a large and variable country. Much of the land, estimated by contemporaries at about two-thirds of the whole of the Transvaal, was bought by land companies. This included the best agricultural land as well as the worst, for it happened that the Witwatersrand was situated in the midst of the agricultural high veld, thus causing the surrounding land to be acquired. This company land was largely taken out of cultivation *en bloc*, for while farmers were allowed to remain on it they were given no permanence of tenure and were indeed constantly liable to having their operations disturbed by prospecting. And all the other land of the Transvaal was in a similar state since even on farms not acquired by companies, prospecting was carried on equally energetically with the ready consent of the farmers. This wholesale withdrawal of land from cultivation was bound, however, to be only temporary. As soon as the mineral resources came to be accurately known the land would either be mined or abandoned by the prospectors and made available for cultivation once more. This was a question of time, and the time of uncertainty continued throughout the nineties, but would not in any case have seriously continued much longer excepting for desultory prospecting on a much smaller scale. In the northern parts of the Transvaal the company lands were made to yield a revenue by the collection of rent from natives and in other parts by the collection of rent from anyone who could live on them. There was naturally some variation in practice between companies; some of these were beginning in the course of the nineties to offer reasonable terms to settlers who would undertake to cultivate the land. One result of this wholesale change in the ownership of land was that it opened up a way for the redistribution of farms and for an escape from the too extensive settlement of the early pioneers; this was an advantage which was at the disposal of the British administration after 1902. With respect to native labour the more central parts of the Transvaal appear to have been almost as happily situated as was the Orange Free State, but in the northern parts the native labour situation was less favourable to development than almost in any other part of South Africa. The land was rough and unbroken, and white settlers who were determined to take up farms had either to clear the land of natives or to make a living by collecting rent from the natives. In other parts of the Transvaal there were the customary complaints of labour shortage which, however, were relative to the state of cultivation and were seldom well founded, while to the north Kaffir farming assumed its worst aspect.

(h) *Summary of Agricultural Development in South Africa as a whole*

We may now sum up the main characteristics of South African agriculture as a whole with reference to the stage of development at which it had arrived at the time of the discovery of the Witwatersrand and to developments which followed up to the time of the Anglo-Boer War. No advances had been made as regard land settlement policy in any of the states. The Cape was the only colony with a policy which showed signs of development, and this development was rather in the direction of enabling the state to make the largest possible revenue out of the sale of crown lands rather than to direct farming energies to the better cultivation of the soil. The opportunities afforded to the Cape by the annexation of Bechuanaland in 1894 were missed and the new lands were sold on the same terms as the old. While policies were not changing, the effects of the early extensive settlement were being overcome in certain parts, especially in the south west of the Cape, where subdivision had already achieved good economic results. Also in such lands as those of Oudtshoorn and Natal where commercial influences were at work leading not so much to sub-division as to the cultivation of the land in estates of economic size. Size of farms in the Transvaal was also being reduced, but from a variety of causes this reduction could not be said to be leading to economic progress. State activity in regard to agriculture was being encouraged in Cape Colony and in Natal; in the former by the development of a fruit export and by the lead in irrigation given by the Oudtshoorn farmers. In the latter case the State was called in to make possible the regulated immigration of Indian coolies. As land was brought under commercial influences its qualities were explored and the surveying of farms was gradually proceeding along with an increasing knowledge of the nature of the soils. The Cape government encouraged this increase of knowledge by supplying experts to discuss irrigation schemes and other matters with farmers and by enabling two enquiries to be made, one of them, by a committee of farmers who were sent to Australia to compare agricultural conditions there with those in Cape Colony and the other by Professor Wallace, of Edinburgh University, who published a full report on the agriculture of Cape Colony.

The Cape government was being pressed to take a more active interest in agriculture by the middle of the nineties, when it became to be realized that the monopoly of the carrying trade to the interior would inevitably be lost.

There is no evidence that any of the agriculture in the interior of South Africa showed any progress during the nineties with the exception of certain agricultural regions within easy reach of the Witwatersrand and of such wool-producing regions as the Eastern Province of the Cape and some parts of the Orange Free State which made steady but small improvements in the breed of the sheep and in quality of the wool. The Karroo sheep farming land had reached a stage at which its drought resisting qualities had been seriously impaired, while the Transvaal agriculture was temporarily weakened after having already reached a state of exhaustion by the influences described earlier. Nearly all of the interior, however, especially the Orange Free State and the Transvaal, had been subjected to disturbing commercial influences which were destined ultimately to lead to improvements.

The provisions for the marketing of produce remained elementary throughout the nineties on account of the continued dominance of the local storekeeper, whose lack of connection with the outside world made him unable to discriminate between various types of wool, while the local monopoly enjoyed by many storekeepers, and their function in financing as well as in trading with the farmers, prevented any except the most prosperous farmers from seeking other marketing arrangements. Up-country wool sales, however, were established in several centres before the close of the century. A sensational outbreak of cattle plague in 1896 forced all governments to make active enquiry into the nature of this disease, while farmers began to take measures against stock diseases which were to have the effect, after the turn of the century, of rendering lands suitable for cattle which previously it had been impossible to use.

The effects of the native population upon agricultural development became better understood during the nineties on account of the general disturbance of values. The importance of making the native reserves self-supporting, and also of improving their agriculture so as to enable them to contribute to the food supply of

# AGRICULTURE, 1887 TO 1899

South Africa, was realised and was expressed in the Glen Grey Act. The necessity of regulating the native peoples outside of the reserves so that they would not overcrowd any land which might be better used and so that they would be distributed among farmers wherever their labour was needed was recognized in the Location Acts passed by the two coastal colonies and in the Orange Free State and by the increased enquiry which was given to the whole subject and which found its first expression in the terms of the Glen Grey Act and later in the report of the Native Affairs Commission for the whole of South Africa which was made in 1903.

Finally, we may repeat that although South Africa failed during the nineties to supply the Johannesburg market with foodstuffs, that failure was in the nature of things only temporary; that the railways were so built that the Johannesburg market was actually nearer for economic purposes to Australia and England than it was to many parts of South Africa; and that in any case the new demands made on account of the gold mining industry and its attendant developments were so large and sudden that the agricultural regions required time to adjust themselves so as to achieve the necessary increase in output.

## REFERENCES

The Evidence collected by the Royal Commission on Empire Resources, 1914.
*The Conquest of the Desert*, by William MacDonald.
*The Agricultural and Pastoral Resources of South Africa*, by Owen Thomas.
The Annual Reports of the Dairy Expert of the Cape Colony Department of Agriculture.
The Reports and Evidence of two Select Committees (1892 and 1895) to enquire into the working of the Cape Colony Department of Agriculture.
Select Committees in Cape Colony also reported upon (between 1894 and 1898) the working of the Scab Act, the re-organization of agricultural schools, the administration of the Scab Act in the Transkei, and on means of preventing the spread of prickly pear.
Roper, *Land Banks in South Africa*.
Three articles on the Sources of Agricultural Credit in South Africa by Cyril Hall, in the *Journal of the Institute of Bankers*, 1923.

## SECTION II

## CHAPTER IV

### THE DEVELOPMENT OF ECONOMIC CONTACT BETWEEN EUROPEAN AND BANTU BETWEEN 1890 AND 1899

#### (a) *The Inter-action of Recruitment with Native Modes of Life*

THESE dates are taken to indicate the period during which the opening up of the Witwatersrand exercised a definite influence upon the relations between black and white. Up to the first of these dates the relationships between the advanced and the primitive peoples in South Africa had been almost entirely governed by agricultural development, and have largely been already described. Apart from this, however, some little experience of the management of black labour in manufacturing and in mining work had been obtained. Railways and towns had been built largely by means of Bantu labour, and the diamond mines of Kimberley had given regular employment to numbers of natives. These experiences had served to forecast the problems which were now to arrive on a large scale. The central problem was that of inducing natives, most of whom already had a satisfactory economic existence, to undertake entirely new modes of occupation. In other parts of the world this had been achieved by force, but in South Africa the native populations were too well entrenched, and the economic services required of them too complex, to enable this to be thought of. Most of the industrial labour secured from natives before this period had been got by offering tempting inducements

# CONTACT BETWEEN EUROPEAN & BANTU

to comparatively small numbers of the more adventurous. Work on railway construction had enabled young natives, away from their homes, to enjoy the pleasures of alcohol, and to return home dressed in gaudy uniforms. The diamond mines had at first obtained their labour supply through a desire of the Basutos for fire-arms, and only later had they realized the advantages of an extra source of income in enabling them to add to their flocks and herds. The masses of natives in the Transkei, in Natal, in the North Transvaal, and in the Portuguese coast lands, were yet quite uninitiated excepting for such small portions of them as those Fingos who had learned how to fetch and carry for the white man. After the problem of inducing the natives to come out to work, there followed the two-fold problem of regulating relationships between them and the whites, and between members of different tribes when they were out of their territories, and of regulating and guiding the changed development of the native reserves as a result of large numbers of their young people always being away for long periods and returning with money to spend. The developments must be studied from two points of view, first, from the point of view of the mines obtaining labour, and second, from the point of view of the native tribes supplying labour.

The means of obtaining supply were at first singularly crude, consisting in employing recruiters supplied with unlimited brandy, who went among the native kraals and persuaded groups of natives, by means of liberal presents and promises of more, to accompany them to the nearest railway line, where they were packed off toward Johannesburg. These, in addition to those who were found in the neighbourhood of the gold mines, formed the first labour supply. But this was not nearly sufficient for the amount of work, both development and producing, which the gold mines had to go through in their early stages. The deficiency was met by increasing the activities of the recruiters until this activity became a regular, and, from all accounts, an exceedingly profitable occupation for men who were skilled in the ways of the natives. Mines competed against each other, each outwitting the other to secure natives from the recruiters who had brought them in. They began to employ their own recruiters, who worked against each other in the native territories, causing distrust on the part of the native, but still persuading them to come to work by the very liberal presents which they were able to give. The mines found that the labour of the natives was generally very satisfactory although not permanent, and that it could be got for wages which were gratifyingly low. But although the wages were low, the cost of bringing the natives to the mines was exorbitant, being sometimes double the wage bill, or even more. The remedy against the high cost of recruiting was soon found in the amalgamation of the mining groups, first of all to reduce the competition among themselves for natives brought to Johannesburg by independent recruiters, and then to cause the recruiters, in the exclusive service of particular mines, to compete less against each other. A further development of this was the formation by the Chamber of Mines of an association of recruiters to work in the most profitable area, which was Portuguese East Africa. They were able by means of an agreement with the Portuguese government to secure the sole right to recruit natives in this territory. This accounted for about 80 per cent. of the total supply of labour, and when the natives were brought to Johannesburg by this Association, they were not competed for, but were allotted to the mines in accordance with an accepted list of requirements. In the other parts of South Africa, where it was not easy to secure a monopoly for any one body of recruiters, the old system continued, but efforts were made to organise the recruiters on a more liberal basis, and the bulk of them were soon included within the scope of a limited company, which worked for the benefit of the Chamber of Mines and not of individual mines. This organization of recruiting had the effect of reducing substantially the cost per native recruited. What was of no less importance, it guaranteed a larger and much more regular supply of labour, though it fell radically short of supplying the mines with the whole of the labour required. The native population of South Africa, including Portuguese East Africa, was some five million, of whom we may take it that about one million were men of a suitable age for manual work. The total number employed on farms, on railways, in other industries and on mines, was reckoned in 1903 to be only one third of that number. To account for this discrepancy at a time when the mines were making hard and very skilful efforts towards increasing their labour supply, as they undoubtedly were doing during the whole of the nineties, we must look at the other side of the problem and return to the native territories.

In the territories, as we know, the natives were living satisfactory lives according to their own ideas. There was no constant force impelling them to seek other modes of life. For there was no sign of over-population or of any approach to it; perhaps an occasional drought would render them uneasy, but this very uneasiness would make most of them sit tight at home and starve, rather than risk new dangers and leave their families to starve. Some ten years later, when mining work was more of a calculable factor in the native mind, a failure of their crops would almost certainly increase the exodus to work. But in the early nineties everything, excepting the adventurousness of some of the younger men, pointed to the natives remaining a tribal people, at any rate, until in the course of some generations their population should increase in numbers and over-tax their efforts to produce food from their lands. In Natal recruiting for the mines, after a short period of ineffectiveness, was actually prohibited by the government, nominally on account of its withdrawing labour which was required in Natal, but partly, at least, we may be sure, on account of its disturbing influence upon tribes of natives whom it was the policy of the Natal government to encourage to live in their own ways for the sake of peace. In the Transkei the efforts of recruiters appeared to have varied greatly from district to district. Unfortunately, here again there is a lamentable lack of accurate information. Attempts were made to issue passes to all natives leaving their own magisterial districts, and the number of passes issued has been taken to indicate the numbers of the natives proceeding to work. But many natives escaped the pass authorities, while others obtained passes merely to wander about in their own country. The reports of the Chamber of Mines also give but few details as to the operations of their recruiters in the interior of the Transkei. We do know, however, that the following numbers of natives are stated in the Chamber of Mines reports to have been received from Cape Colony in the years given :—

|  | Natives |
|---|---|
| Nov. 1896 to Dec, 1898 | 5,963 |
| Year 1902 | 3,031 |
| ,,     1903 | 7,082 |
| ,,     1904 | 10,405 |
| ,,     1905 | 10,620 |

The average time which each native stayed away from home appears to have been about seven months, so that these figures will include those natives who were recruited twice in one year, and must be reduced accordingly. On the other hand, these figures failed to include Transkei natives, who had found their way to the Transvaal without the assistance of recruiters, but still on account of the recruiters' work. It appears from what little we know of recruiting in the interior of the Transkei, that it was successful in direct ratio to the extent to which the natives had come under Western influence. In Pondoland recruiting appears to have been negligible until after the South African War, although the country was annexed in 1895, and so was opened up to recruiting then. Among the Fingoes, on the other hand it would appear that recruiting had almost equally little effect for the opposite reason that they were already advanced enough to

## CONTACT BETWEEN EUROPEAN & BANTU

promote their own economic welfare in ways of their own and were not to be influenced in the direction of manual labour, which incidentally they found distasteful. With the exception of the Fingoes, however, the rule just stated appears to hold good, and the natives who were most influenced by traders and by magistrates, were those who were most influenced by recruiters. The reasons for this were deep-rooted. But we shall be able to understand them better if we state first that the traders themselves almost invariably were also recruiters or worked in close conjunction with the recruiters. The influence of the traders was and had been for many years in the direction of accustoming the natives to the idea of increasing their wealth by means of exchange. Up to the beginning of our present period, this had been done by offering to buy from the natives whatever surplus crops they had to dispose of, and any wool and animal skins they might have, and by giving them in exchange ornaments and luxuries such as brown sugar, and even, when the crops were very large, an occasional much-valued cow. A trade in these articles had grown up steadily, but had been very limited and showed but little signs of expanding. The traders naturally seized upon the opportunity of increasing the natives' spending power by enabling them to earn cash wages. The first difficulty was to persuade the natives to leave their homes. The natives who were married, and most of them of working age married early, could not be persuaded to leave their homes on what was to them a dangerous quest. A beginning had to be made with the young natives aged about eighteen or twenty. But even these faced considerable risks in leaving the territories; it might be that they lost the certainty of obtaining the piece of land to which they were entitled, as members of the tribe, on coming of age; it might be that their families would share up their lands, especially if the father died in the meantime; in either case, the young native ran the risk of losing that title to land, which was his main security throughout life. Much depended upon the attitude of the chief or headman toward recruiting. If he was favourably inclined he would be able practicably to guarantee that lands would be reserved for the natives returning from the mines, as it already was for natives returning from war or from hunting expeditions.

The interest of the chief was torn in two directions. In one way he stood to gain by his young men going out to work, for if he assisted the recruiters he could be sure of being handsomely repaid by them. And if the boys came back able to buy many cows the wealth of the tribe or village would be increased. On the other hand, on a more far-sighted view, the chiefs felt that they stood to lose in the long run, for natives who earned regular incomes from the mines would cease to be dependent upon the power of the chief to provide them with land. In some cases, as we have seen, the tendency was already for the garden lands to be held on what was practically a permanent independent tenure, and in these cases the essential power of the chief was already undermined. The general practice undoubtedly had been that once a native family had established a claim to a garden land, their right to it would stand even although it was abandoned for quite long periods, either by reason of fallow, or while the man went out to hunt, or while the family as a whole might be away searching for new land. This right, however, could be interpreted in different ways and practice was not fixed.

The trader-recruiters soon discovered one way in which nearly all natives could be brought under the necessity of earning money and of spending it. This was to make advances in the form of goods or cattle and to tell the native that he could repay by going out to work. The advances system appears to have been the first effective instrument in introducing the new economy to the native minds. The traders sometimes found it profitable to advance even more to a native than he could possibly repay by bringing back the whole of his earnings from a period of work in the mines. The reason for this was that the trader in his other role of recruiter would get a capitation fee which would more than recoup him. Advances to natives, especially of cattle, were quite irresistible, and the system soon became one of wide-spread grievances. A native would accept a cow and rather than face the journey out to the mines would disappear and become a fugitive. He would receive frequently other articles of personal use for himself and his family, and he would be told that he would not need to leave for work until such time as suited himself; the articles would all be used up, and perhaps the native threatened with prosecution for debt before he went to Johannesburg. The natives again, in nearly all cases, but especially when drought was threatened, would strike an agreement with the trader that while they were away their families would receive all necessary supplies, the cost of which would be deducted from his wages when he should return. The native might then realize that he would return to find himself only deeper in debt than he had been when he went away. So great did the advances evil become that late in the nineties advances were limited by law, first to a total of £5 and then to a total of £2, being the amount necessary to provide the native with equipment for his journey. This, however, did not prevent the family from running into debt during the boy's absence, and the only real remedy for this was the improvement of native agriculture.

It must be understood that the economic unit in native life was the family. Lands were allotted to natives at the rate of one garden for each wife. The first land was obtained by each man upon his first marriage. Those who were not yet married were without responsibilities excepting a general one to assist their parents. The labour supply could thus be increased by obliging the parents to incur debt or to pay taxes which they could meet by sending their young men out to work. This was the idea behind the notorious labour tax in the Glen Grey Act, which had to be paid in respect of every young, able-bodied native who could not show to the magistrate that he had been actively engaged in some economic operation for a part of the year. Married natives could generally satisfy the conditions by indicating that they had been supervising the use of their lands at home. The unmarried natives could not show this. They were thereupon taxed to the extent of ten shillings each per annum. The responsibility for the payment of this tax fell upon the parents, who would find that it would probably run to several pounds a year. The parents were, in this way, according to the theory behind the tax, to send the young men out to work in order to avoid payment. The tax was never successfully enforced, but this appears to have been due to administrative difficulties arising out of the fact that the natives strongly objected to it as open compulsion, while the magistrates, themselves half-hearted, had not the necessary force behind them to collect the money. The theory of the tax appears to have been quite sound. It appears even that it fitted in with the best progressive tendency of the time, namely, that as land was becoming less easy of access, and more of an economic and less of a free good, each young native should acquire some economic resource before being entitled to his garden.

Having attempted to analyse the methods of the mines in obtaining labour and the conditions in the native territories supplying labour, it remains to describe the ways in which these re-acted upon each other. In the first place, no efforts could induce any supply of natives to become permanent workers on the mines. No families were taken to the Rand; it is not clear that the mines themselves desired this; compounds to accommodate families were seldom offered. Labour could only be obtained by contracting with individual natives to go to the mines and to stay a definite period. It was in the interest of the mines to ensure that this period, especially in the case of natives on their first visit, should be long enough to cover a training and acclimatization period of perhaps six weeks and that the remainder of the period during which the natives' work would be efficient should be long enough to pay for his wages, his cost of upkeep, and the cost of his recruitment. Attempts were made at first to contract natives for twelve months' service. The native, on the other hand, required to work for a sufficiently long period to enable him to pay his railway expenses to and from the mines and to take home a sum of money large enough to meet any obligations that might be awaiting him there, so that he would not be obliged, by finding himself still in debt, to return to work if he did not wish to do so. But while this might have pointed to a long contract favouring the native, he in practice felt quite unable to stay away from home and his family for more than about six months. This finally became the contract period. The rate of wages was the next consideration. It was a highly complex one, the factors in which cannot be reduced to accurate generalizations. Since the cost of labour to the mines was made up roughly of two parts to recruiting and one part to upkeep and wages, the economic wage which could be offered would not be an absolute factor but would be a function of the combined effective power to obtain supply of all the moneys spent. If increased wages would attract natives and so diminish recruiting costs, then the increase would very likely be highly economic. It is certain the good rates of pay did cause natives to feel that work on the mines was worth doing, and even more certain than if the natives found, as they too frequently did, that if the rates of pay were considerably less than had been indicated by the recruiters, they felt they had been defrauded and would not return to work another time excepting under some compulsion. On the other hand, the native did not regard wages as a continuous flow of income coming in at a particular rate, he regarded them rather as a lump sum reward for certain efforts on his part which he would be able to take home and exchange for satisfaction there.

His object was to secure as large a lump sum as possible, and in many cases the more he brought home the less soon he would think of going out to work again ; so that a high rate of wages might actually slow down the flow of labour and, in addition, as a consequence, throw an extra burden upon recruitment, thus increasing real labour costs very considerably.

### (b) *The Glen Grey Act*

At this stage we may attempt to fit the Glen Grey Act into its place in the development of economic relationships between the Europeans and natives in Cape Colony. This act was constructed with a view to guiding the whole development of the Transkeian territories toward an increased westernization, so that in the first place they would contribute labour toward the industrial development of the country ; in the second place so that the native land systems would develop permanence, thus enabling native agriculture to become more scientific ; in the third place so that this increased settling of the natives on their land would lead to their becoming self-supporting and so prevent any future overflow of native population into neighbouring white lands. Such a comprehensive aim as this could be achieved only by confirming existing tendencies. The Act really aimed at little more than this and it is chiefly for this reason that it enjoyed some measure of success and that it requires our attention. It concerned itself with practically every phase of native life ; with land tenure, with inheritance, with agricultural methods, with the conversion of the native into a wage earner, and even with his alcoholic habits. The native system of economic life had been a well established one. To take the chief as starting point, we find that one of his most important functions was to lead the tribe to good land. Having found the land, and the tribe having settled on it, the chief had to allot garden patches. Neither he nor the tribe had any conception of ownership in land but regarded themselves collectively as entitled

## CONTACT BETWEEN EUROPEAN & BANTU 149

to the use of land which they occupied, tribally and individually, and cultivated according to their needs. Heads of families, that is to say married men, picked out pieces of land for cultivation and, provided these lands had not been previously claimed, were confirmed in their occupation by the chief. They could be forfeited only by rebelling against the chief or by leaving the district for such a long time that it might be supposed that they were not to return. If the holder wished, he could abandon a piece of land, and in that case it returned to the disposal of the rest of the tribe. All of the land not occupied or claimed for cultivation was common land, on which the stock were pastured. The land, however, was not given out merely at the rate of one garden for each head of a family; the family heads did not themselves cultivate; they claimed and obtained one garden for each of their wives, and the size of the garden was regulated by the amount of land which the woman who was to be in charge of it could manage. The work of clearing the land in the first place was performed by the men, but after that the women were responsible for agriculture while the men were responsible for the stock, and especially for the cattle. A rough balance always appears to have been maintained between agricultural land, which was private, and pastoral land, which was common. The position of the women appears to have been an important one in that they managed the supply of food and had the last word in decisions as to the taking up or abandoning of lands and in the selection of new land. The men on the other hand regarded the tending of the cattle as work of the highest importance which, as we shall see, it was, on account of the part which it played in social life. The division of functions had important results in that it limited the extent of cultivation to what could be done without the assistance of draught animals by women; when the plough came to be introduced it involved the men becoming cultivators, since they refused to allow the women to manage the oxen. The garden lands would be separated from each other by strips of grass-land which were never interfered with excepting in times of the utmost necessity. In the wilder regions these strips would be of relatively less importance since there might be cultivation only on odd gardens scattered indiscriminately over wide areas. The methods of agriculture were of the crudest, the land being tended only by means of rough hoes, while rotation of crops was unknown except possibly in a quite unformulated way, since the cultivators appeared to have known that a change of crop would sometimes refresh the land and so postpone the time when it would have to be abandoned.

This land system fitted in with the native marriage system. The more wives a man had the more cultivated land was at his disposal. But wives could only be obtained by the making of an economic exchange in the form of cattle. When a man succeeded in increasing his stock of cattle he was able to go to the father of a girl and bargain with him for the right to marry her in return for the payment to the father of a number of cattle. In this way cattle were a most important form of currency. This necessity of paying out cattle in return for each wife ensured that polygamy was socially controlled. Only the more energetic and skilful herdsmen were able to build up families, while a young man could not marry for the first time either until he had secured cattle in some way, or, and this leads us to the next important point, had inherited land.

The native system of inheritance was a mixture of primogeniture and of sub-division well suited to maintain the economic system. The lands left by a man at death were left in the charge of the widows. The widows, however, were under an obligation to support the sons until they should be able to get lands of their own. Frequently the widow would hand over during her lifetime her land either to her eldest son, whose wife would then cultivate it, or to any other son who had not already obtained land. The widow, being old, was thus relieved of the labour of cultivation while the land was still in the family in its original form. The chief power over the various lands left by a man was vested in the wife, who, during his lifetime, had been given a position of superiority within the family and was known as the "Great Wife." The power of the "Great Wife" over the estate of the deceased, however, was controlled by custom and was used to supervise the disposal of the land in the way which we have described. The estate was treated as a whole but its various parts were shared out among the children entitled to them.

The working of this system presupposed an excess, though not necessarily a great excess, of the number of males over the number of females. It provided for the development of the wealth of a tribe in accordance with the number of cattle possessed by the members and the number of garden lands at the disposal of the chief for allotment among members. The second factor appears, however, to have been the predominating one since a shortage of land would bring about a change in the number of cattle to be given in exchange for each wife. Contact with white colonists had for its first effect the limiting of the amount of land available. While the tribe had been able to be semi-nomadic it had been able to regard land as a completely free good. With the limitation in the supply of land following upon the confinement of the tribe to definite areas a change in this outlook, in practice if not avowed, was inevitable. This change might be postponed by the natives overflowing into land owned by whites as they did into the Ciskei and continuing their tribal mode of life as best they could. But the change was inevitable and we have described in an earlier part the main direction which it took as regards the land system. Wherever pressure was felt lands were clung to by the holders and treated more and more as permanent holdings which it became difficult to distinguish from actual possessions.

Most of the native land in Cape Colony had been successfully demarcated by treaty in the early part of the nineteenth century. But cases still occurred of land which was neither European nor native. A case in point was the Glen Grey district lying just outside of the Transkei. The land here was of poor quality and subject to drought. It was clear that it could be occupied beneficially only by natives. Considerable numbers of these were settled on it and were being added to by immigrants from neighbouring districts. Some permanent settlement was sought and was undertaken by the Rhodes Ministry in 1894. The Bill prepared for the purpose, however, aimed not merely at giving the land to the native population but at settling its present population in such a way that they should not become overcrowded and also in such a way that they should serve as the material for an experiment. This experiment consisted in giving the natives permanent individual title to garden lands, in providing that the common land should not be encroached upon in charging rent for the holdings and in addition in bringing the natives under a new form of local self government for the upkeep of which they would be taxed and which would receive the assistance of white administrators mainly in order to promote advanced methods of cultivation. In the Glen Grey district itself this was an artificial scheme, but it was intended to extend it to districts in the Transkei where it would conform to tendencies already in operation.

As extraneous provisions a labour tax was included, and a building site was provided for each land holder, so that instead of living on or near their lands as was the custom, the natives could be induced to live in a village and so be more amenable to administration.

This was by no means the first time that attempts had been made to give natives individual tenure to land. It had long been a cure-all for native problems to give them land of their own for which they would have to pay rent like a white man. It was a suggestion which naturally came from colonists jealous of the natives for their good land resources and annoyed at not being able to secure a plentiful supply of native labour. Actual early experiments, however, may be said to have all been carried out under special conditions. On mission stations individual tenure had been given, and on other pieces of land on which it was desired to settle small numbers of natives. The Glen Grey district might be classed as another of these special cases, but the act was at once applied to three other districts within the Transkei. These were all in Fingoland, where, as we know, the practice of the natives themselves had already been carried to its furthest point in treating land as a private concern. The Act worked very differently in its two main spheres of operation, Glen Grey and the Fingo districts. But certain features were found alike in both places. One of these was the minor one that the natives saw no advantage in living in villages away from their land; the building site provisions remained inoperative. The labour tax was equally resented in both cases and applied with equally little results. A more fundamental feature in which both cases showed difficulties was the necessity for a survey of the land prior to its being allotted to the natives. Survey was an operation none too much resorted to among the white settlers and totally foreign to the natives. The lands in the districts, both the Glen Grey and the other districts, were on soil which was uneven as regards both quality and surface features; it was divided up in the Transkei by winding rivers and in the Glen Grey district by uncultivatable ridges. The natives had marked their lands out in accordance with these natural features, but the surveyors, whose time and patience were limited, thought to provide the natives with more or less neatly divided rectangular fields. These surveys were carried out, but left much dissatisfaction, for the natives were torn between accepting the artificial boundaries which they were told the government would support, and the natural boundaries which were no less insistent. The natives arrived at working compromises, although in the Glen Grey district the uncertain effectiveness of the surveyors' boundaries enabled newcomers to take up lands to which they were not entitled and also facilitated encroachment upon the common land. But what the natives could not get over was the high cost of the survey. Before title could be obtained these costs had to be paid by the future tenant. In many cases they were two or three times the probable market value of the land. An instalment plan was adopted and the lands were taken up. The Fingos were able to meet the costs, but payment in the Glen Grey area was very slow. On this point of survey, which had been regarded as merely incidental, the whole of the Glen Grey attempt came almost to a standstill. For the matter was really fundamental; the cost was prohibitive and prevented extension of the Act; the operation was unbeneficial, for the natives were quite able when they wished and when circumstances were favourable to arrive at a working system of individual tenure which met all the needs of the case.

It cannot be over-emphasized that the Glen Grey Act, ambitious and far-seeing as it was, introduced little that was new. The tendency in the territories was already toward individual tenure, while in the outside lands both in the Ciskei and in the unoccupied Crown land natives still lived practically according to tribal ideas. In the Glen Grey district immigrant natives were still able to settle with the connivance of the residents, over-running the survey lines and encroaching on the common land. In the Transkei the native economy was already adapting itself to changing conditions. The provisions of the Act with regard to inheritance had to be changed by an amending Act in 1903 whereby the native practice was conformed to in its entirety. The original Act it would appear had had no definite intentions of changing native practice in this matter, but had merely by a mistake failed to conform to it.

We may now attempt to sum up the changes in tribal economy which followed the change in the attitude to the land. The scarcity of land, which manifested itself in the tendency to adopt individual tenure, was accompanied by increased opportunities to dispose of any marketable surplus that might be produced. The natives in this way had an incentive to improve their methods of cultivation and at the same time were supplied with advice as to how to set about this improvement. This was speeded up by the traders, who, in addition to offering ready cash for natives' maize crops, sold ploughs to the natives to assist in the growing of these crops and to be paid for out of the money got for them. The introduction of the plough not merely made possible the improvement of agriculture in an ordinary way, but by necessitating cattle for the dragging work gave a new value to these symbols of wealth and further led the men to turn their attention to cultivation, for it was only men who could be trusted with the cattle. In part this increase of tendency for the men to work on the land diminished the outside supply of labour. But on a long period view this was certainly less significant than might have been thought. Both increased cultivation and going out to work led to a modern habit of mind which turned the natives' attention toward income-earning activities. Also we must not make the mistake of supposing that these changes were taking place with great rapidity. The only rapid development was in the supply of labour for the mines. This was dictated by outside circumstances, the sudden development of a great industry. The important point is that the going out of thousands of natives for at least one period of work in the Transvaal had much less direct effect upon the Transkei's internal economy than might have been expected. For the men were able to pay their visit to the mines or to any other employment at a time in their lives when very little economically was expected from them at home. Their absence did not upset native agriculture or interfere with the economic round in any way. Its only effect was the indirect one of providing the native territory with money purchasing power. The native councils established under the Glen Grey Act were set up not merely in the districts to which the land clauses of the Act were applied, but in the whole of the Transkei. The natives in all parts obtained access to what appears to have been a very efficient service from the agricultural department. They learned the elements of dairy farming and of the use of the plough; the experience of the rinderpest taught them to appreciate European veterinary methods. But nothing is more clear than that their agriculture was not revolutionized and that their general ways of life remained remarkably similar to those of their grandfathers. The tendencies that we have described were only tendencies, and the great mass of the natives in the Transkei continued to lead their own economic lives perhaps rendered even less systematic than they had previously been by a too ready acceptance of some of the more superficial and less advantageous of western conveniences; they would sell crops after the harvest which they would have to buy back from the trader at a much increased price to feed themselves later in the year, so little did they understand the principles of commercial farming and so ready were they to fall for the temptations of ready credit. They would work their periods in the mines in order to buy more cattle and they would spend the rest of their lives in contemplation of these cattle. The tendencies were at work, but how slowly we shall realise only when we come to estimate the progress made up to the time at which our study ends.

We have assumed that the Transkei stood apart from the other native territories in South Africa in that it had been brought much more under the systematic European influence. This was the case, and the native lands in Natal and the Transvaal had scarcely begun to show the signs of advance which were at least clearly traceable in the Transkei during the nineties. In Zululand, Swaziland, and the North Transvaal even the first step, the realization that land was limited on account of surrounding white occupation, had scarcely begun to effect the native mind. For all practical purposes lands were still disposed of by the chief and taken up and dropped as the holders decided. The system remained completely primitive, and the presence of recruiters and tax collectors meant only that a certain number of young men would venture out to the mines as they had previously gone out to wars. The taxes could be met by the money that was brought back, or by disposing of some animal hides to the tax collector. In Natal this very primitive stage had passed, for the native lands had been delimited in the course of the century. There were signs that the natives were in some cases feeling over-crowded, for they overflowed on to Crown and private lands, and doubtless had a vague feeling that they were living under different conditions there, at least in respect to the paying of taxes, than they were on their own lands. Their reserved lands were a continuation of the Transkei, but mostly in more hilly country; the white government under which they found themselves was much less strong and less able to influence them than the administrators in the Cape were to influence the Transkei natives. Administration, indeed, was at the most primitive stage in which native administration can be—the recognition of loyal chiefs and the entrusting of them with the maintenance of order. White administrators were known to the natives mainly as judges and soldiers, whose power appeared in the last resort. Education by government in any of the ways practised in the Transkei, was unknown in Natal. And the native land system, the key to the whole matter, had as yet shown no sign excepting on the actual borders of cultivated European land of coming to attach importance to individual rights in lands. The Glen Grey Act would have been impossible in Natal because no approach had been made to permanent individual tenure by the natives themselves. The only evidence of a change in land practice was the inevitable one that the natives, instead of wandering to new lands on detecting some slight wearing out of the old ones, were encroaching upon the grass which lay between the cultivated spots.

### (c) *Natives Outside Reserves*

We must now deal with those natives who lived outside of the native reserves. These, in all states excepting the Orange Free State, were the conditions under which many lived, and were so varied and undefined that we can only broadly attempt to reduce the matter to a coherent description. In the first place, there were natives who lived in unoccupied Crown land. This was land which had not yet been occupied by Europeans, but which was not reserved to natives. Its quality was invariably such that at least until the advance of science it was worthless for white occupation. On the other hand, its swampy malarial nature was no disadvantage in the eyes of the natives. The chief examples of this land, were the outlying parts of the Transvaal, but similar soil was found in Natal. On land such as this natives had either lived for a considerable time or had established themselves recently on finding their reserves being overcrowded. To all intents and purposes they led an ordinary tribal life on these Crown lands, the only point of difference being that rent would be collected from them instead of taxes, and this was a meaningless distinction to most of the natives. Another difference was that white administrators were not there to guide development, but neither was this an important difference, for such administrators were found nowhere effectively except in the Transkei. The only important difference was that should the Europeans decide to clear the land, as Zululand was cleared for sugar cultivation in the early part of the twentieth century, the natives could be ordered to go elsewhere. Even this was not usually a real danger. The natives living on Crown lands tended merely to be the most backward of all natives, uninfluenced by white administrators, generally unguided by chiefs of their own, and with no security of tenure. Next we come to all of the natives living actually on lands owned or found by Europeans. These covered the greatest possible variety of modes of life. At the one extreme would be natives merely squatting without permission and in constant danger of being turned off or made to pay rent on land for which the owner at the moment would happen to have no use. These natives might be quite as backward as those squatting on unoccupied Crown lands. At the other extreme were natives with the status of bywoners, virtually partners with the farmer, and very likely with family connections in the native reserve, so that in the event of their losing their position as bywoners they would be able to return to land in the native territories. These natives would sometimes cultivate land in a better way than was done by the white farmers themselves, and would own stock which could not be distinguished from that of the owner of the farm. In between these two extremes natives lived on European farms in all sorts of informal and undefined ways, of which, however, we must attempt a classification. Some indication of the conditions has already been given in discussing the problems of European agriculture ; we must now turn our attention to the same conditions from the point of view of the native.

We must begin by repeating that many of the natives who are included in the census returns as residents on European's farms, do not live there permanently. One of the advantages enjoyed by the gold mines when they first began to recruit labour, was the practice already existing among the natives of the young males spending part of their lives in travelling, and in performing labour in return for wages in the course of their travels. So that it was common for natives to be farm labourers during part of the year on white farms, and living with their families in the reserves for the rest of the year, and perhaps after a few years, for the rest of their lives. We may take, first of all, those natives whose residence on white land was most temporary. These left their own territories to travel around the countryside at harvest and sowing time and at shearing time. In those parts of the country, such as the central districts of Cape Colony, where the resident native population was exremely small, these travelling labourers were anxiously waited for, and were certain of work and a small sum of money, or possibly a sheep in return for their services. They would then return to their own lands, and this ends their interest for us in this connection. At the other extreme, natives having practically no connections in their own land, would become farm labourers of an almost European type, staying on the same farm perhaps for several years, or perhaps for a life time, and, what is most important, having the whole of their families there. These natives, who were found on all types of farms all over South Africa, would receive a money wage of perhaps one pound per month, which would be paid to the head of the family, but which would entitle the farmer to command the services of all members of the family. Some cast-off clothing would generally be included in the natives' income, possibly in addition to the money wage, but possibly as a part substitute. The native would then have to feed himself by cultivating land wherever he was allowed to do so, and he would also, for the natives are inveterate pastoralists, possess a few head of sheep or goats, which he would be allowed to pasture. In speaking of the income of these natives it is not possible accurately to use the term " wage rates." Part of their income took the form of money ; this was essential if only to enable them to pay taxes, and to buy a few necessities which even the most primitive of peoples appear to find essential when they come into contact with Europeans. The real welfare of these people is a very elusive quality; it would almost entirely depend indeed upon the personal character of the farmer. Although the natives tend to be a roving people, it would appear that this farm labour was not mobile. The general rule was for natives, once they settled on a farm *with their families*, to stay there for many years. They had lost any original right to land of their own, and this appears to have had a very steadying influence. While a young native would travel many miles in the course

# CONTACT BETWEEN EUROPEAN & BANTU 161

of the year the married natives were afraid of becoming mere vagrants. Under the Masters' and Servants' Laws of the Roman-Dutch Code, these natives entered into, or were presumed to have entered into, contracts of service with their employers. The leaving of the employment without due notice, of which incidentally there could be no evidence beyond the native's word, entailed a breach of contract which was a crime under the Colonial Law. This further strengthened the tendency of the labourer to stay settled, and this was still further enforced by the Pass Laws, which required that every native travelling about the countryside should carry an identification pass which any policeman could call upon him to produce, and arrest him if he did not have it. In the Transvaal these passes had to be granted actually by the farmer who was the native's last employer, while in Cape Colony they had to be granted by local magistrates, who were always farmers in the neighbourhood. These laws enforced the tendency which we have mentioned of landless natives with families, to sit tight. The result was that wages and conditions could scarcely be affected by the forces of competition. The entire conditions of employment were customary. Native labour of this type was much valued by the farmers in all of those parts, which were the greater proportion of South Africa, in which native labour of a permanent type was extremely scarce.

We may next take those natives who had managed to establish some kind of customary right in the lands which they cultivated on the white farm. These are very various, ranging as they do from natives who were the equals of the white bywoners to others who were little or no better off than the farm servants whom we have just described. Generally speaking there was one difference between the best established of natives and the white bywoners; this was, that in the terms of occupation of the native, there would invariably be a clear understanding that labour service was included.

This would not apply to the white bywoner, who, in spite of uncertainties in his position, was more of a tenant cultivating land for his own benefit than the native could be. The white bywoner certainly was not expected to render labour service to a farmer; it would more probably be beneath his dignity to harvest even his own crops; he would even require a supply of native labour for himself. This difference as regards labour service had important effects upon the relative security of natives and Europeans holding land on terms, or in absence of terms, which appear on the surface to be similar. If the land became overcrowded by the growth of the white farmer's families, the white bywoner would find himself given notice to quit, and the same would happen where a progressive pastoral farmer would give new value to some of his land by fencing it, or by building a dam that would supply it with water. Indeed, anything tending to give a commercial value to land made the position of the white bywoner untenable. Such developments had different effects upon the native in the same position. In the event of the land becoming overcrowded or more closely settled, his labour would be required, if anything, more than before. An increase of arable farming as opposed to pastoral would always have this effect. On the other hand the amount of land available for the native would be less. A position of some difficulty appeared in the circumstances. On the one hand it was more than ever necessary to ensure a good labour supply; on the other hand the increasing value of arable land made it uneconomic to retain the native labour by giving him occupation of such land. The solution would depend upon a variety of circumstances. If the farm was near native reserves the farmers might rely upon getting labour when needed without having any natives permanently on their land. If the farm was far from a native's reserves the result would often be that the native would be subjected to a kind of pressure, gradually losing his rights and falling into the position of a farm labourer, this process being rendered fairly easy by the relative immobility of such natives which we have already described. The same position would ensue in the case of land being fenced or brought under irrigation. Any increase in the value of land, whether from mere overcrowding or by sub-division, or by reclamation, shifted the tendency to pay natives by means of land rights toward paying them in other ways. As regards the pastoral rights which natives invariably held along with their right to cultivate, these rights also tended to become restricted as one would expect, especially when the farmer was adopting fencing for his sheep lands. If it happened that there was still plenty of rough land on the farm, the native's flocks might just be relegated to this, but if this was not the case, the native would find that the farmer objected to his sheep and he would be obliged to get rid of them.

There is only one other mode of occupation of white farmers' land by natives that we can clearly distinguish. This was ordinary renting. It was to this that the term Kaffir farming was chiefly applied, and it was found only in those districts near to native reserves, and with land unsuitable for white cultivation. In some cases the whole of farms taken up by whites would be used for no other purpose than that of letting them out to natives in return for money rent. It really amounted to a means of dealing with land which perhaps should have been included in the native reserves and left freely at their disposal, but which, for some reason, possibly the military success of white colonists in earlier times in securing possession of it, possibly the expectation of the white farmers that they would make a good profit out of the rent paid by natives, possibly the expectation that, as agricultural methods improved, and as the land became more valuable owing to railway building, it would cease to be kept for Kaffir farming and would become real white land. This land was found especially in the Ciskei, more especially the coastal lands of the Ciskei, in which the vegetation was too rough, and the liability to cattle disease too great for these lands to be used for the cattle ranching, for which they were potentially suitable. Here much of the land was owned by absentee farmers, who drew rents which, according to many statements made by well-informed people, afforded them a much greater income than they could have obtained even by the most determined scientific culture of the soil. Rack-renting was a term frequently applied to the treatment of these natives. The term was taken to mean that the rent per acre paid by the natives was greater than any rent paid by whites on neighbouring land, either as regards annual rental or equivalent market price paid for the land. This was undoubtedly the case; the natives, largely by the ability of their young men to earn money wages in other regions, were able to pay considerable rents. The main factor in the situation appears, however, to have been the necessity of the natives to occupy this land, resulting from their ideas and their tribal customs, which prevented their making better use of the lands reserved to them in the Transkei. Their demand for the land was real in the sense that they could simply not visualize living on any other land or in any other way, and it was effective owing to their ability to get command of purchasing power in the way in which we have mentioned. This Kaffir farming was found in Natal under apparently the same conditions. In the Northern Transvaal the largest area was devoted to it, and the largest number of natives accommodated. Here the conditions were very similar excepting that in the early nineties much of these lands were bought by companies for speculative purposes. After the first flush of speculation, however, these companies were glad to obtain any income from the lands which could be got. Rent from natives who occupied the land tribally was at first the most regular of these sources of income. Later it became the policy of the best of the companies to settle white immigrants on these lands wherever possible, but the land suitable for this was very limited, and the Kaffir farming continues to this day.

In the Ciskei, more than in the Transvaal, it was frequently found that farmers would use part of their land in this way so as to draw a regular rent from the natives' families in occupation. The other parts of the farms would be used in other ways. On the same farm some of the land would be used by raw natives squatting there and paying this rent, while on other parts there would be natives who were share-farmers; on other parts again natives would be labour tenants, and on others again land would be well cultivated by means of wage labour. But the proportion of the farms devoted to each of these systems varied in relation to the nature of the soil and to its distance from native reserves. Rough soil on the borders of the reserves would have little other than Kaffir farming; useful farm land some hundreds of miles from the reserves would have little but wage labour. Actual changes in the systems were slow, and although in this, as in most other matters in South Africa, the seeds of change were found in the occurences of the nineties, actual developments were few. Although efforts were made to overcome the cattle diseases that rendered the coast lands worthless for white farming, the actual cattle plagues of the nineties were very severe; although dairy farming took on a new value through improvements in communications and efforts were made to establish co-operative creameries, only the foundations of this enterprise were laid. The main impetus to improvement came indeed from those farmers who had good land, with few native occupants, in the neighbourhood of the more doubtful land; from the farmers just inland from the coast with soil having some of the characteristics of the fertile Eastern Province. They found that they were able to respond to the changes in value in the nineties, but that their efforts were impeded by the conditions on the neighbouring land. The main effect of the semi-occupation of land by natives was to impede farming on other lands. The demand for segregation came, not from the farmers owning the semi-native lands, but from their neighbours. These more progressive farmers—more progressive by reason both of their better soil and of the absence of natives from it—found the contiguity of the other lands a distinct handicap; they needed a regular labour supply, and the more thoroughly they carried on their cultivation and the more carefully they herded their sheep, the more urgent did this supply become. But natives who could live on land so much more similar to their own, and under conditions so much closer to their tribal habits, were not available for this outside farm service. This was only one of the circumstances. Another scarcely less serious was that the presence of the outside natives interfered with the work of any native labourers who did engage themselves with the progressive farmers. Their neighbours would induce them to run away and would treat them to beer drinks so that their labour lost value. Yet another drawback was that the neighbouring natives were not always careful to distinguish between their own stock and that of the farmers, so that sheep stealing could, and did, assume dangerous proportions; finally the stock of the natives could not be prevented, excepting where the land was more carefully fenced than was generally possible at that time, from mixing with the farmer's stock and so frustrating his efforts to improve breed. As a result of these problems rising out of neighbourhood of colonists' land with semi-native land, the nineties saw the first efforts being made seriously to find a mode of segregation. The matter did not get beyond discussion excepting that the Glen Grey Act was considered at least to be an effort to prevent the problem getting worse, in that it aimed at attaching the natives to the land in their reserves in such a way that by improving cultivation they would overflow less on to the other lands. Location laws whereby farmers were to be allowed to settle a certain number of native families, and only a certain number, on any land which

# CONTACT BETWEEN EUROPEAN & BANTU 167

they owned, were also discussed, but their application was not yet enforced.

## REFERENCES

The Annual Reports of the Transvaal Chamber of Mines, which include the Reports of the Witwatersrand Native Labour Association and much correspondence between the State Secretary for Natives and the Chamber.

The Report and Evidence of the South African Native Affairs Commission of 1903 to 1905.

Report of the Transvaal Labour Commission of 1903.

The Reports of Delegates from the Transkeian Territories to Johannesburg to enquire into the conditions of labour.

Three Select Committees on the working of the Glen Grey Act are important. The dates are 1894, 1895, and 1898.

## SECTION II

## CHAPTER V

### THE INDUSTRIAL DEVELOPMENT OF THE SOUTH AFRICAN STATES FROM 1887 TO 1899

THIS is a subject which although it has caused much controversy, requires but little space in a study such as this. It is not our intention to give full details either of the diamond or of the gold mining industries. These have already been well treated by writers of much technical knowledge and considerable insight into the commercial aspect of their subject. To attempt a full description would take up the better part of this book, and, since the writer has little technical knowledge of mining it would be of little value. What has not yet been written up is the effects of these mining industries upon South Africa and this is the subject matter of this book. An enquiry into the effects of the mining industry upon the developments of manufactures in the various parts of South Africa might begin either with the Cape Colony in which elementary manufacture existed long before gold or diamonds were heard of, or with the Transvaal where, owing to its great distance from the manufacturing centres in Cape Colony and elsewhere, the impact was more immediate. We shall adopt the latter course.

In the Transvaal the existence of manufacturing industry prior to 1886 had been virtually unknown. Even household industries had not existed, for the distances between farms were so great that any kind of specialisation was impossible, and the goods which were not obtained from the traders were made by the farmers or their families. On the establishment of the Witswatersrand industry the question immediately arose as to whether all necessary supplies were to be imported through the coastal towns or whether, in the event of raw materials being found in the Transvaal, these were to be used locally, or whether again raw materials were to be imported and manufactured in the Transvaal. These matters might have been decided by price alone and very largely were ; for transport from the coast was soon seen to be very reliable. But political factors entered as well, for the Transvaal government, conscious of its insular position and also of the power which that position now gave it, showed an inclination to invest part of its revenues in industrial enterprise and to foster these enterprises by means of customs and railway protection. The difficulties in beginning any manufacturing industry were exceptional. All skilled labour coming into the district was employed at once on the mines. Raw materials were as yet scanty, and such was the concentration of effort and capital on gold prospecting that there was very little chance of supplies of other materials being proved. Coal, of course, was in a class apart ; its production was an integral part of mining enterprise, and fortunately sufficient supplies were soon found. All other raw materials lagged far behind, although belief in their existence was great. Lead had been mined by farmers for their own uses for many years. Timber was much more scarce than it ought to have been, for Boer and Bantu alike had treated it as a worthless resource, but it was available on the outskirts of the Transvaal and it was hoped that its use might be more economic than the importation either of wooden articles or uncut wood. The materials for cement making were present but not exploited, while a supply of tallow for mine candles might be induced by offering sufficient prices to the farmers. By judicious management the government, as well as private enterprise, might have caused these industries to be established. This, however, would have taken some time, and matters moved so quickly during the gold rush and the subsequent developments that the government looked about for more immediate means of widening the basis of the Transvaal's industrial life.

That this was inevitable under the circumstances is shown by the fact that whereas few or no people proposed to start the more fundamental industries, which indeed would certainly have been very difficult at that time, numbers of people proposed to the government that they should receive concessions whereby they would have the monopoly to carry on certain manufactures. A situation similar to that found in England in the sixteenth and seventeenth centuries was now found in the Transvaal. The government, as a matter of national policy, wished manufactures to be established, but the enterprisers who could do the work were in a position to demand monopolies. Add to this that the government found that by granting such monopolies it would not only involve itself in no financial risk but might actually reap immediate profit. The concessionaires required to be entrusted with the manufacture of such articles as could be made on the spot from ready available material. This generally meant imported material. Indeed in general the concessions resulted only in some assembling work being done. Concessions were granted to people who were to put jam in jars and dynamite in boxes. The system, it would appear with justice, was soon charged with corruption. The one concession which lasted throughout the nineties was that in dynamite, which caused that essential material to be very expensive to the mines, but which was necessary to a government, frequently involved in native wars and quite possibly soon to be involved in a more important one. The dynamite concession gave rise to a great amount of controversy. It was protected by a sympathetic customs policy as well as by a direct concession. At first it was claimed that certain raw materials were being produced locally; later it became known that everything was imported and little done except to add greatly to the price. Many of the mines were in sympathy with the government with regard to its general policy of attempting to foster other industries, but all of them protested loudly against the dynamite concession, with

## INDUSTRIAL DEVELOPMENT—1887 TO 1899

the result that it was withdrawn and recast and given to different people several times, but remained intact up to the outbreak of the South African War. Fortunately no effort was made to establish iron or engineering industries in this way. The customs policy of the Transvaal, although irritating in its taxation of the raw materials involved in the concessions, did not discriminate against mining machinery or house building materials. It was only in the commercial boom of 1903 that general industries began to appear. Prior to that time the only important general industry was that of building. At this stage we must attempt to analyse those features of gold mining of more immediate concern to the outside world. These were in the first place the quantity and composition of the labour supply; in the second place the amount of development in relation to the production; in the third place the contribution of the industry to taxation; in the fourth place the inflow of capital on account of the development of the gold industry.

The statistics of labour supply in the nineties are incomplete but afford us some indication of what was taking place. The numbers of white and non-white employees on the gold mines are given in the following table:*

| Year | Whites | Natives |
|---|---|---|
| 1893 | 4,046 | 29,500 |
| 1894 | 5,363 | 40,088 |
| 1895 | 6,807 | 50,648 |
| 1896 | 7,430 | 47,097 |
| 1897 | 8,060 | 50,791 |
| 1898 | 9,476 | 67,797 |

which shows to what extent the whites were outnumbered throughout the decade. The wage rates are given in the following table:*

| Year | Av. monthly wages of white employees £ s. d. | Av. monthly wages of Natives £ s. d. | |
|---|---|---|---|
| 1894 | 21 6 0 | 3 1 1 | From returns made by between 67 and 81 mines. |
| 1895 | 21 14 0 | 3 3 6 | |
| 1896 | 23 14 0 | 3 0 10 | |
| 1898 | 26 0 0 | 2 9 9 | |

*Chamber of Mines reports.

As we already know, the wages rates of the natives give no indication either of the cost of native labour to the mines, or of the native standard of life. They are given here largely as a matter of interest and partly because they did vary from time to time. After the organization of the recruiting system by the Chamber of Mines in 1897, the amalgamated mines agreed to pay the same wages to native labourers, and, in 1903, a reduction was effected. But during the nineties the figures had but little significance. Before 1897 the rates given above were adhered to only by a few mines in respect of either native or white labour. The system of payment is more significant, the white miners being paid according to contract rates in respect of the amount of work accomplished by each miner in his work place. The origin of this system was in the early mining conditions, when it was found that the best way to get work done was to entrust a given piece to a miner and to pay him a lump sum from it out of which he had to find the natives' wages. The natives, however, soon came to be managed by the mine organizations and not by the working miners. But the contract system continued and practice varied between allowing the white miner to pay the natives and the mine itself paying them. As difficulties in obtaining native labour showed themselves it became advisable for the mines themselves to pay the natives, but the contract system did not die. Even in 1914 there were several contractors who recruited labour, brought the natives to mines which contracted for them, supervised them while at work, obtained a lump sum from the mine management, and paid out the natives' wages. But the number of these contractors was few, and they had ceased to be working miners. They agreed also to pay the wage rates to natives as fixed by the Chamber of Mines. In the early days it is certain that the wages paid to natives by working men contractors were very variable; the mine management was often completely ignorant of them. The system which gradually evolved was one of paying natives according to the number of

# INDUSTRIAL DEVELOPMENT—1887 TO 1899

inches which they drilled. If they drilled less than a stipulated minimum their ticket was not marked and the day's work went for nothing. Extra pay was given for each number of inches over the minimum. The system led to endless trouble, for the contractors were able to measure the holes wrongly, and the natives only knew that for some day's work they got no pay whatsoever. Since the contracts under which they were engaged stipulated not month's work, but the number of shifts, thirty shifts being taken as normally equivalent to one month, this meant that the natives would have to stay one extra day for every card that was not marked. The complaints of natives about non-marking of cards continued right into the twentieth century and contributed to the native troubles of 1911. This piece-work system applied only to drill and hammer boys. Those engaged on shovelling and tramming were paid time rates. It was another source of difficulty that practically all natives were led by the recruiters to believe that they would be drill boys; they were told that the harder they worked the more money they would get. When they found themselves allotted to inferior work with lower and fixed pay they were dissatisfied, but of course no remedy was ever found.

The amount of development work in progress was the chief determining factor in the prosperity of the commercial community of South Africa. The coastal colonies found their imports varying in proportion to it, and to the merchants of Johannesburg it was of great though of less importance. Needless to say, it was also one of the chief and one of the most misleading factors in inducing European investors to contribute their capital. The figures relating to stamp working is given on next page along with the actual gold output.

## TRANSVAAL MINES (WITWATERSRAND)

| Year | Gold Output (000 omitted) | | No. of Stamps working through year (in single stamps) |
|---|---|---|---|
| | Amount fine (oz.) | Value (£) | |
| 1887 | 19 | 81 | 56 |
| 1888 | 171 | 729 | 525 |
| 1889 | 306 | 1,300 | 711 |
| 1890 | 408 | 1,735 | 1,805 |
| 1891 | 601 | 2,556 | 1,465 |
| 1892 | 1,011 | 4,297 | 1,907 |
| 1893 | 1,221 | 5,187 | 1,955 |
| 1894 | 1,639 | 6,963 | 2,273 |
| 1895 | 1,845 | 7,840 | 2,546 |
| 1896 | 7,851 | 7,864 | 2,949 |
| 1897 | 2,491 | 10,583 | 3,567 |
| 1898 | 3,564 | 16,044 | 5,765 |

Unfortunately no figures are available as to the numbers of employees on development and production work respectively.

The contribution of the mining industry toward the taxation of the State was another of those vexed questions which caused endless controversy at the time, but about which to this day we know very few facts. Those mining magnates who chose to indulge in controversy, could point out with perfect truth that almost the whole of the State's income arose directly or indirectly from the gold mining industry. They urged that the difference between the national income then, and before 1886, was so great, and the expenses of the government so little increased, while the cost of importing goods was so high, that the industry was clearly overtaxed, and that great reductions might be effected. There was doubtless much to be said for this point of view, but a point that was much overlooked was that the mining industry had developed so phenomenally that the State might have found itself in possession of great revenues from the application of crude and small taxes. This appears to have been the case. The most apposite remark in the controversy was that made by the *Economist*, in 1898, that the amount paid in taxation

# INDUSTRIAL DEVELOPMENT—1887 TO 1899

per ton on the Witwatersrand was only about one-third of what would have to be paid per ton raised in Rhodesia under a very modern system of development. It appears indeed that many of the mining people appreciated their good fortune and kept in the good graces of the Transvaal government. The proportion of the State revenue derived from the mining industry cannot be traced. Revenue from customs duties was not so much increased as created by the new conditions. Revenue from land taxation was also created almost out of nothing. It was the inevitable result of the sensational creation of a highly capitalized industry in a most primitive country. We may safely suppose that had a British Governor been in charge of the administration of the Transvaal, more of the revenue would have been spent in the development of roads and irrigation and agricultural research, but we cannot be sure that his expenditure would have been highly beneficial. The state of the country was so unsettled that it cannot be said even to have been experimental. Experiment came after the South African War, and even then, as we shall see, although much had been learned about the country and about the ways in which it might develop, much of the expenditure was wasted and the taxation of the mines was heavier.

The inflow of capital into the country is another question on which we have much information but little of it accurate. The capitalization of the mines and the amounts of dividend paid out together with the number of mines paying and not paying dividend, is shown in the following table :—

## GOLD AND COAL MINES*

| Year | Capitalization £ | Dividends £ | No. of Mines paying Dividends | No. not paying Dividends |
|---|---|---|---|---|
| 1893 | 40,000,000 | 1,000,000 | 54 | |
| 1896 | 55,358,000 | 1,794,000 | | |
| 1897 | 63,188,000 | 3,001,000 | 30 | 188 (N.B.—There are abour 400 companies which are not working or never have worked). |
| 1898 | (not known) | 5,089,715 | 45 | 52 (Producing but not paying dividends). 40 (Not producing). Total 92 |

Charges of over-capitalization were undoubtedly well founded, and much money was lost by the investing public of Europe, but the mining industry, as a whole, appears never to have regretted this state of affairs. It is certain that had the money not been readily forthcoming the gold resources of the Transvaal would never have been exploited to the point of establishing a gold output so high and so regular as was actually the case.

The coal mines of the Transvaal were, as we have already said, worked as an integral part of the gold mining industry. Before 1895 two mines were working in the Johannesburg and the Middelburg districts, whose total output we do not know, but which supplied the mines with all necessary fuel of a suitable quality, and owing to its proximity to the mines and to the cheapness of native labour, at what must have been a very reasonable cost. The management of the Netherlands Railway Company were accused of providing inefficient service at high rates, but this can only be taken to indicate that any work which was not in the hands of the mines themselves was sure to be the object of criticism.

It is significant that Portuguese East Africa, which

*From the files of the Economist for the years mentioned.

## INDUSTRIAL DEVELOPMENT—1887 TO 1899

now found itself in close touch with the Johannesburg market, underwent little or no industrial development. Its land was coastal and tropical, and its main hope lay in supplying the Transvaal with such commodities as sugar and tea. In spite of this, however, one might have expected that some attempt would have been made to foster manufacturing industries of some kind. This was not done. Labour was so plentiful and so well suited to industrial work that the district became the chief source of the Transvaal's labour supply, and coal could have been obtained from the Middelburg mines. But miscellaneous raw materials were absent, and capital and enterprise confined themselves, as in other parts of South Africa, to the carrying trade.

With surprisingly few qualifications the same may be said of Natal. The tropical plantation industry received a stimulus, and factories were built to work up its products. Coal was worked as well, having for its market during the nineties the Natal railway system and the bunker trade. A few manufactures appeared secondary upon the sugar industry, but these were very small, and the only remaining industry of any importance was building. Prospecting was carried on over all the inland regions and several false starts were given to a gold industry. Hopes of discovering gold were not relinquished for a long time. No assistance to local manufactures was given either by customs or by railway policy, which concentrated upon the carrying trade. The only industry of importance was coal mining, of which the output in the nineties was as follows:—

(000 omitted throughout)

| Year | Coal (tons) | Value £ | Year | Coal (tons) | Value £ |
|---|---|---|---|---|---|
| 1890 | 81 | 40 | 1895 | 160 | 80 |
| 1891 | 87 | 43 | 1896 | 216 | 108 |
| 1892 | 142 | 71 | 1897 | 243 | 121 |
| 1893 | 129 | 64 | 1898 | 387 | 175 |
| 1894 | 141 | 70 | 1899 | 328 | 139 |

The labour supply for this industry was made up as the following table shows:—

| Year | Europeans | Natives | Indians | Output in Tons |
|---|---|---|---|---|
| 1889 | * | 475 | * | 81,547 |
| 1890 | * | 475 | * | 87,774 |
| 1891 | * | 750 | * | 142,160 |
| 1892 | * | 575 | * | 128,925 |
| 1893 | * | 775 | * | 141,010 |
| 1894 | * | 850 | * | 160,115 |
| 1895 | * | 1,000 | 275 | 216,106 |
| 1896 | * | 1,050 | 475 | 243,960 |
| 1897 | 125 | 1,750 | 850 | 387,811 |
| 1898 | * | 1,200 | 750 | 328,693 |

*Under 100

It will be seen from this that the proportion of white to non-white were much as one might expect, but that even here, although the coal mines were situated within very easy reach of the native territories, and although the natives showed no special disinclination to underground work, yet the mines relied for increases in their labour supply upon immigrant Indian labour in about the same proportions as upon natives. At first the Indians refused to be indentured to the mines. They had come to Natal for plantation work, which they understood, and fought shy of any other. But as the prejudice was overcome, and as it was seen that higher wages were obtainable, the Indians took to the work.

In Cape Colony, the position of manufacturing industries was somewhat different in that it had been stimulated by the diamond discoveries in the early seventies, and that a customs policy had evolved which, though not designed to be protective of manufacture, had had that result. We have already mentioned the relations between the customs tariff and the industries. In the census of 1891 the number of factories of various kinds, with the numbers of their employees, was given as follows :—

| | No of works | No. of workers | Works with power | H.P. |
|---|---|---|---|---|
| Mines. etc. | 68 | 15,860 | 21 | 3,320 |
| All others | 2,162 | 16,875 | 316 | 3,597 |
| Total | 2,230 | 32,735 | 337 | 6,917 |

## INDUSTRIAL DEVELOPMENT—1887 TO 1899

But these are very small when compared to the diamond and agricultural industries taken together, and Rhodes incurred few protests when he made his famous reference to the "bastard industries." The treatment of these industries under the tariff in force in the nineties, continued, however, to be favourable if only incidentally so. And it is difficult to see in what ways the industries could be entirely artificial if they were enabled to grow up by means of duties collected for revenue purposes. It is true that most of the raw materials had to be imported, many of them in a semi-manufactured condition, but anyone with experience of a country like England should have known that the international exchange of raw and semi-raw materials is one of the foundations of the modern economic world. One of the reasons for the growth of these industries in Cape Colony was that quantities of raw materials already existed, though not of such regularity of quality and of supply as would have established the industries without the aids of imports. The local supplies, however, at least in favourable seasons, were low in cost. This applied to skins for leather as well as to numbers of other by-products of agriculture. These cheap supplies may be taken to have founded the industries together with the existence of the Cape half-caste or "coloured" population. These coloured people had none of the disadvantages of the tribal native as industrial workers, nor of the disadvantages of white labour, which was very scarce and expensive. They showed themselves readily capable of doing skilled and continuous work. The opening up of accessible markets in the early seventies and the late eighties completed the foundations of the Cape manufacturing industries. The need of setting up railway workshops for repairs gave another impetus to the industrial development. The possibility of fruit canning and the manufacture of preserves from the fruit was always present, and began to be realized in the later nineties. Apart from these general industries, which grew up at each of the three chief ports, the colony was as poor in industrial development as any other part of South Africa. Its coal mining was insignificant. All of its industries continued to be almost insignificant in relation to the imports of similar articles. Had this not been so the duties would not have been revenue raising and might even have been abandoned. Inside of each industry a perpetual competition went on between the local materials and the imported. The quality of local leather was very poor owing to its being gathered from great areas, being supplied by farmers who did not have large numbers of cattle of similar breed. The problems of tanning were only slowly overcome owing to the same reason. The quality of the leather tended to be of the lowest, since few cattle were killed for food purposes, and all the skins available were from animals which had lived into old age. The carriage building industry was something of an exception in that a special type of carriage had been evolved to suit South African conditions of transport. But this was an industry which was carried on all over the countryside and was not concentrated in factories. A factory production did come into existence during the nineties, but it had to use imported timber.

The Orange Free State can scarcely be dealt with in this connection. After the South African War intelligent efforts to establish household industries were talked of, but these do not concern us at present. In South Africa, as a whole, we have seen that the conditions for small scale industries existed in Cape Colony and nowhere else. The establishment of industries secondary to mining was possible in the Transvaal, but did not yet materialise. Distances, conditions of labour supply, scarcity of raw materials, difficulty in obtaining capital except for mining; all of these meant that South Africa was not an industrial country.

*A Summary of South African Development During the Nineties*

Enough may have been gathered from the foregoing

## INDUSTRIAL DEVELOPMENT—1887 TO 1899

section to see that South Africa in the nineties was too vast and complex and unexplored, and the mechanism of collecting information too defective to allow its development to be clearly summarized in any short form. We have tried, in dealing with each section, to arrange the available information into intelligible form, and to estimate the weight of various factors, so that the importance of all tendencies to development may be appreciated. At the same time our efforts will have failed if they have not left in the readers' mind a clear impression of the whole such as may be committed to paper here, in order that the reader may check his own impressions by comparing them with those of the writer. We have seen that South Africa, consisting of two British Colonies and two almost independent inland Republics, comprised a total area of 470,000 square miles. Two-thirds of this area had, in 1891, a population of less than two persons to the square mile, and the other third was more thickly populated only because it is inhabited by natives living under their own tribal organizations. Only in the immediate neighbourhood of towns did the white population exceed four persons to the square mile, and these neighbourhoods were limited to four in number in 1891 and to five in number within the next two or three years, when Johannesburg was added. The rainfall was as low as the density of the population, and scarcely any steps had yet been taken to conserve the available supply. The land itself was variable, having nowhere any extensive tracts of good soil excepting in the Karroo, where water was not available. The only hope of agriculture was to develop the good soil in those small areas scattered over the whole of South Africa where it was known to exist. The people were diverse in race, the Europeans consisting mainly of Dutch and British, who showed no tendency to fusion, the former being scattered over the countryside, and the latter living in the towns. The land had been occupied, as is the case with new land everywhere, in such a way as to make intensive farming almost impossible, but in this case the mode of occupation really seems to have fitted in with the natural conditions of the soil, which only in a few places was capable of closer settlement. But even this was known to the South African people of the nineties only in a vague way. The soil was often unexplored and untested, and although the people had a general belief, which turned out to be correct, of the very limited nature of their soil, they knew nothing accurately, and constructive experiment was consequently impossible.

Interesting developments did come about in connection with certain agricultural industries, such as fruit farming, especially in the Cape South West, ostrich farming in Oudtshoorn, sugar and tea planting in Natal, and stock improvements in the Eastern Province of Cape Colony. These developments interested commercial men in so far as they influenced oversea trade, and they also indicated to the governments various lines of activity. Yet railway lines were built which connected the new market of Johannesburg with the outside world rather than with the potential producing districts of South Africa. Branch lines would have to come later and they would almost certainly be uneconomic, at least at first. It is not certain whether the creation of the Johannesburg market stimulated or hindered South African agriculture. It was not economically connected with the main producing regions, and it did distract the farmers by offering them high pay for such unskilled and non-agricultural work as transport driving. In the Cape South West and in the Transvaal, sub-division of farms had taken place, in the former case for economic reasons, and in the latter case by sheer pressure of population unbalanced by economic opportunity. In the pastoral lands of the whole of the interior, from the south of the Karroo up to the north of the Transvaal High Veld, no sign of economic closer settlement was to be seen. The Karroo lands indeed had been allowed to deteriorate.

## INDUSTRIAL DEVELOPMENT —1887 TO 1899

The great transport system built in the early nineties consisted of three trunk lines connecting the Transvaal with five ports. Its service to the Transvaal was direct in enabling it to import the goods necessary for the development of its gold-mining industry; its service to the rest of South Africa, as we have indicated in writing of agriculture, was less direct. Import into the Transvaal tended to be made economical by the competition of the three systems, though this was modified by the fact that part of each line lay within Transvaal territory, and that the Transvaal railway administration found it in its own interest to induce the traffic by artificial means, if necessary, to travel over that line which had the greatest mileage under Transvaal control. Fortunately this line was also the shortest and connected Johannesburg with what was really its natural port, Delagoa Bay. The railway administrations of the Cape and of Natal found themselves at the mercy of the Transvaal administration, which could divert a great deal of traffic from their lines to its own by a manipulation of rates. Cape Colony pleaded for a rate agreement since it had an immense proportion of its national resources locked up in a railway system which had at first enjoyed almost a monopoly, and had fixed its rates accordingly, but which now found itself at a great geographical disadvantage with the new competitors. Natal did not join in this request since it had a geographical advantage over the Cape, and since the Transvaal administration gave it good terms on account of a considerable proportion of the line between Durban and Johannesburg lying within Transvaal territory and providing goods traffic to the Transvaal railways. A rate war followed in which the natural disadvantages of the Cape, coupled with the policy of the Transvaal administration, brought about a heavy loss in traffic and in receipts to the Cape. The immigration figures of the Cape and Natal show that fewer people entered South Africa in the nineties than the population of Johannesburg which was estimated at 30,000 in 1896 so that an actual drain of population would appear to have been felt by the rest of South Africa. This is emphasized by the fact that the population of all towns increased owing to commercial activity, so that the agricultural regions almost certainly suffered.

## REFERENCES

See references inserted on page 102, also
The Files of the *British and South African Export Gazette* are especially useful.
Census reports of the various States and Colonies in 1891 and 1892, and in the first census for the whole of South Africa, that of 1904.

## SECTION II

## CHAPTER VI

### THE RECONSTRUCTION OF SOUTH AFRICA AFTER THE ANGLO-BOER WAR

#### (a) *Introductory*

WITH the political or even the economic causes of the Boer War we cannot here concern ourselves. It is enough to say that the result of the war was to bring within the British Empire the most valuable gold-producing area in the world and some millions of square miles of land, mainly populated by Dutch people, which was of more problematical, though of considerable, potential value. The economic post-war problems may be said to have centred round making this area self-supporting, so that future peace would be ensured, and of less importance, settling it partly with a British population, so that it might in future be willing to remain an integrate part of the Empire. Dutch preference for independence was very well known, and it was felt that the permanent and peaceful membership of the two ex-republics in the British Empire could be guaranteed only by fundamentally altering the racial composition, not only of their total population, but of their agricultural population. For this reason the reconstruction of the ex-republics, which were now the two new colonies of the Transvaal and the Orange Free State, by British administration, is one of the most noticeable features in the economic history of South Africa. Both the coastal colonies, however, underwent reconstruction under the guidance of their own governments and of the high official who was commissioner for South Africa as a whole, while all four States proceeded with an attempt to reach a new stage in the development of their agricultural and mineral resources. This development, leading as it did to increased railway building and commercial intercourse between all parts of South Africa, led also to an intensified recognition of the fact that South Africa was an economic unit, and that it could only achieve permanent prosperity when the railways which had made it a unit ceased to belong to a number of rival administrations.

The reconstruction period is notable chiefly for the putting of the finances of the Transvaal upon a new footing; for the building of railway lines which did make communication between the Witwatersrand and the five ports easier than before, but which also covered many new areas, and so raised many new problems of rate fixing and the treatment of traffic; for the bringing about of a customs union which rode roughshod over the many complex problems of the various states, but which was almost universally admitted to be preferable to the paralysis of communications which must have resulted had customs problems been allowed to become as complicated as were railway problems; for the initiation in all states of land settlement schemes designed to overcome the drawbacks of the early extensive settlements so far as natural conditions permitted and scientific farming made possible; and finally for the making of an agreement with the oversea shipping companies which greatly assisted the export of South African produce. These are by no means all of the reconstructions attempted, but they are the chief ones, and they are the key to the economic development of the period.

It is desirable that we should know the post war conditions upon which this reconstruction had to follow. In the nature of things, however, only a little can be known. We know that imports flowed into the country at a great speed, attracted by high prices, to overtake arrears in building, in mining, and in other developments We know that almost the whole of the agriculture was paralysed, the inland regions having been swept by troops. Beyond this very little can be known, for populations were so transitory and exchange of goods between various parts so little recorded, that figures of internal population and trade were either not kept or must be heavily discounted.

(b) *The 1904 Census*

A census of the whole of South Africa, the first scientific census in the two inland states, was taken in 1904. The desire for a means of comparing the four States and of guiding the new administration is quite understandable, but the impatience shown in taking the census before the post-war settlement of the people was completed is a matter for permanent regret. While the census was being taken the agricultural areas were still in process of repopulation. During the war many inhabitants of the interior had travelled to the coastal towns for safety. A general aggregation of people in the towns apart from these refugees was inevitable after the war, when demobilization was taking place and bonuses were being spent. The Dutch women and children had been gathered into concentration camps while the men were on military service. Their lands had been so devastated that they had not by any means been able to take up their old holdings within a couple of years and, indeed, a drought had slowed down matters still further. The blocking of railway lines during the import boom had contributed to making re-settlement a slow process, and the total loss of bullocks and other stock had not only rendered the farming population unable, owing to lack of transport, to reach their old homes, but had convinced them that it was not worth while trying to return until they received compensation to enable them to re-stock their farms. To take a census under these conditions was very difficult, especially in the inland colonies, where machinery had to be created for the first time, and was certain to make the results of very little value. The best we can do is to give the census figures for what they are worth. As giving a total for South Africa they may have some value, though even this is doubtful. As providing comparisons between town and country they must be almost worthless, and as indicating the proportions of white to non-white they must be equally so. Even immigration and emigration figures were not kept during the war. We have already pointed out some of the dangers to be avoided in using even those earlier censuses, such as those of Cape Colony, which had some experience behind them. It will be seen at once that comparisons between the 1891 and the 1904 census figures, which have so often been made, must be almost worthless, and we shall not make them here excepting as regards totals.

The following tables gives the chief results of the 1904 census:—

### NATAL CENSUS

| | |
|---|---|
| European | 97,109 |
| Indian and Asiatic | 100,918 |
| Mixed and other | 6,686 |
| Bantu | 904,041 |
| Total other than White | 1,011,645 |
| Total | 1,108,754 |

### CAPE COLONY CENSUS

| | |
|---|---|
| European | 568,000 |
| Bantu | 1,158,000 |
| Mixed | 394,000 |
| Total other than Whites | 1,552,000 |
| Total | 2,122,000 |

### TRANSVAAL

| | |
|---|---:|
| European | 289,000 |
| Bantu | 1,021,000 |
| Asiatics | 12,000 |
| Mixed | 23,000 |
| Total non White | 1,056,000 |
| Total | 1,346,627 |

### ORANGE RIVER COLONY

| | |
|---|---:|
| European | 142,670 |
| Bantu | 229,000 |
| Mixed | 15,000 |
| Total non White | 244,000 |
| Total | 387,000 |

The proportion of male to female had increased considerably, but whether this can be taken as a result of genuine immigration is very doubtful. The numbered natives also increased in about the same proportion as the European totals. Comparison in any case would only be possible in Cape Colony and Natal, and even here of very doubtful value, since the native peoples were almost as scattered as the whites in the upheavals caused by the war. The Transvaal native population was, of course, included in a census for the first time.

The oversea trade returns, though of course more accurately kept, show only that the country was re-stocking itself with all kinds of goods. Imports through the various ports into the Transvaal are given in the following table, showing 1898 as the last normal year, and showing the great decline after 1905, and also showing the imports through the various ports.

## TONNAGE OF PRINCIPAL CLASSES OF TRAFFIC FROM THE COAST PORT TO THE TRANSVAAL

(000 omitted in tonnage figures)

| Year | Cape Town | | Port Elizabeth | | East London | | Total Cape Ports | |
|---|---|---|---|---|---|---|---|---|
| | tons | per cent. | tons | per cent. | tons | per cent. | tons | per cent. |
| 1898* | — | — | — | — | — | — | — | — |
| 1903 | 14 | 1.3 | 63 | 10.1 | 81 | 13.2 | 157 | 25.6 |
| 1904 | 8 | 1.7 | 35 | 7.3 | 45 | 8.9 | 88 | 17.9 |
| 1905 | 8 | 1.4 | 37 | 8.1 | 33 | 5.5 | 70 | 13.0 |
| 1906 | 7 | 1.5 | 30 | 6.5 | 30 | 6.6 | 66 | 14.6 |

| Year | Durban | | Delagoa Bay | | Total tons | All Ports per cent. |
|---|---|---|---|---|---|---|
| | tons | per cent. | tons | per cent. | | |
| 1898* | — | — | — | — | 421 | 100.0 |
| 1903 | 271 | 44.1 | 186 | 30.3 | 616 | 100.0 |
| 1904 | 196 | 89.9 | 208 | 42.2 | 493 | 100.0 |
| 1905 | 219 | 36.1 | 309 | 50.9 | 608 | 100.0 |
| 1906 | 152 | 52.7 | 244 | 52.7 | 464 | 100.0 |

*This figure is for the whole of the Transvaal through traffic.

Figures of internal trade, so far as they are available, are given in the table on p. 191, which serves to show that a great proportion of the total imports taken into the Transvaal were from abroad, and which gives some illustrations of the exchange of goods other than goods from oversea between the various states.

Returns of industrial development in the census may be taken as being more accurate than those of population. Remembering, of course, that manufacturing industry was greatly expanded during the post-war activity, and that it did retain this expansion, the following table may give some indication of the number of factories, the number of work-people employed, and the details of horse power used in the factories found in the four States.

| | No. of Institutions | No. of Institutions where Engines are used | H.P. used | No. of persons employed |
|---|---|---|---|---|
| Cape | 2,617 | 615 | 31,587 | 52,730 |
| Natal | 794 | 415 | 16,943 | 29,111 |
| Transvaal | | | | |
| Mines, etc. | 273 | 198 | 179,627 | 108,220 |
| Others | 1,357 | 316 | 1,627 | 19,818 |
| O. F. S. | 164 | 76 | 4,240 | 7,117 |

## TRADE WITHIN THE CUSTOMS UNION, 1906-9
(000 omitted throughout)

### GOODS NOT THE PRODUCE OF SOUTH AFRICA

| | To Transvaal. | | | | From Transvaal. | | | |
|---|---|---|---|---|---|---|---|---|
| | 1906 | 1907 | 1908 | 1909 | 1906 | 1907 | 1908 | 1909 |
| From C. Colony | 2,535 | 2,790 | 2,947 | 3,501 | To C. Colony 137 | 143 | 105 | 88 |
| ,, O. R. C. | 74 | 63 | 66 | 35 | ,, O. R. C. 203 | 203 | 183 | 169 |
| ,, Natal | 3,003 | 3,702 | 3,079 | 3,380 | ,, Natal 83 | 107 | 98 | 75 |
| ,, Swaziland | — | — | * | — | ,, Swaziland — | 22 | 17 | 23 |
| ,, S. Rhodesia | 1 | 1 | 1 | 1 | ,, S. Rhodesia 11 | 19 | 30 | 27 |
| ,, N.W. Rhodesia | — | * | * | * | ,, N.W. Rhodesia — | 1 | 1 | 1 |
| ,, Basutoland | * | * | * | * | ,, Basutoland 4 | 8 | 4 | 5 |
| ,, Bechuanaland | * | 1 | * | * | ,, Bechuanaland 2 | 1 | 3 | 3 |
| Totals | 5,614 | 6,560 | 6,094 | 6,919 | 443 | 507 | 444 | 391 |

### GOODS THE PRODUCE OF SOUTH AFRICA

| | 1906 | 1907 | 1908 | 1909 | | 1906 | 1907 | 1908 | 1909 |
|---|---|---|---|---|---|---|---|---|---|
| From C. Colony | 1,635 | 1,835 | 1,812 | 2,665 | To C. Colony | 442 | 398 | 336 | 355 |
| ,, O. R. C. | 686 | 809 | 1,058 | 1,135 | ,, O. R. C. | 134 | 133 | 119 | 170 |
| ,, Natal | 855 | 900 | 1,033 | 1,220 | ,, Natal | 201 | 279 | 306 | 414 |
| ,, Swaziland | — | — | * | * | ,, Swaziland | — | 12 | 14 | 14 |
| ,, S. Rhodesia | 1 | 3 | * 3 | 5 | ,, S. Rhodesia | 12 | 20 | 26 | 29 |
| ,, N.W. Rhodesia | — | 1 | * | 1 | ,, N.W. Rhodesia | * | * | * | 1 |
| ,, Basutoland | 9 | 18 | 4 | 5 | ,, Basutoland | * | * | * | 1 |
| ,, Bechuanaland | 4 | 5 | 8 | 5 | ,, Bechuanaland | 1 | 1 | 2 | 1 |
| Totals | 3,191 | 3,573 | 3,922 | 5,039 | | 792 | 847 | 806 | 988 |
| Grand Totals | 8,806 | 10,134 | 10,017 | 11,958 | | 1,235 | 1,354 | 1,250 | 1,382 |

* Below £500.

## REFERENCES

Files of *Economist* and the *Statist*.
Report of the Census of 1904.
Minutes of the Bloemfontein Conference, 1903.
Reports of the Proceedings of the Inter-Colonial Council of the Transvaal and the Orange River Colony.
Reports of the South African Customs Statistics Bureau.
*The Reconstruction of the New Colonies under Lord Milner*, by Worsfold.

# SECTION II

## CHAPTER VII

### THE RAILWAYS AND FINANCES OF THE FOUR COLONIES

EACH of the four States had a programme of railway building drawn up in readiness for the coming of peace In the case of the Cape Colony and Natal these programmes consisted almost entirely in the strengthening of the trunk line systems with a view to increasing their competitive power. The programmes went slightly further, however, in that they visualised the connecting up of the main lines with each other in such ways that fresh agricultural lands would be served and the various parts of the colonies brought into more direct contact with each other. The two new colonies, which were immediately brought under a single railway administration, included in their programme the building of lines of two quite distinct natures both for the cheapening of imports brought to Johannesburg and for the development of areas which previously had been unserved. The dual nature of railway building was much more pronounced in the interior than in the coastal colonies The coastal colonies, and more especially the Cape, already had points of economic activity hundreds of miles apart, such as Cape Town and Port Elizabeth, which, although the route between them lay through much good agricultural land had not been directly connected by rail. In the Transvaal, on the other hand, development was still centred at one point, and the building of railways into other parts was still a case of building lines to nowhere, and the economic advisability of this was still disputable.

Reconstruction in each of the States depended upon their borrowing power and their revenue resources. In the last resort this depended upon their railway earnings and customs receipts. Had the railways been in private hands, or had the governments abstained from using them as instruments of taxation, it is certain that the reconstruction would have been much more slow than it was. Railways and customs together accounted for some two-fifths of the income of the Cape government, some three-fifths of the income of the Natal government, and a similar proportion in respect of the Transvaal. The Transvaal administration was able to institute a tax upon mining profits and to persuade the Chamber of Mines, in order to avoid further taxes, to underwrite a loan. All of the States raised money in England. But the coastal colonies had no mining tax which they could impose and no equivalent of the mining industry to strengthen their borrowing position. Nor had they the secure railway resources of the Transvaal; they were competitors for a trade controlled at the source by the Transvaal. When the post-war boom ended in 1905, even the Transvaal, fearing a reduction of her revenue from railways, was obliged to curtail her reconstruction programme. The Cape and Natal, however, when faced with this slump were almost faced with bankruptcy, for in addition to the ordinary reduction of revenue they were both losing traffic to Delagoa Bay. This is illustrated in the following table, where it will be seen that the amount of revenue paid over by railways to the State fell in the coastal, while actually maintaining an increase on the others.

| Year | Transvaal and Free State £ | Cape Colony £ | Natal £ |
|---|---|---|---|
| 1903 | 1,839 | 807 | 2,561 |
| 1904 | 1,702 | 428 | 1,933 |
| 1905 | 2,546 | 973 | 2,052 |
| 1906 | 2,584 | 796 | 1,836 |

(ooo omitted throughout).

The Cape figures are based on a rough calculation.

The Transvaal had sacrificed customs revenue entirely by joining the customs union. But this loss was more than balanced by the strong position of the Transvaal in respect of her railways. The full strength of this position was illustrated in two ways, first of all by the fact that the Transvaal, in order to obtain a labour supply for the mines from Portuguese East Africa, was able to enter into an agreement with that state whereby it was to receive the work of carrying at least 55 per cent. of the total imports into the Transvaal. In the second place it is seen in the fact that the coastal colonies were glad to be allocated the remainder of the traffic in definite proportions. It had by now been fully realised that free competition between the railway systems would mean a war of rates which none of them could face; by manipulating the rates on the lines under their control, the Transvaal administration could ruin not only the vulnerable Cape railways but even the Portuguese line. Under an agreement of 1904 the Cape railways were guaranteed 20 per cent. of the total imports into the Transvaal; this, however, was a minimum which would only just enable the lines to pay and would practically render them valueless as a source of revenue. In 1905 and 1906 it was seen that as a revenue-earning instrument the Cape railway system was in danger of being played out. Her only hope was to concentrate the Transvaal traffic in such a way that it might be more economically distributed between the three Cape lines. Mail and passenger traffic was of course guaranteed by the necessity for speed to the main Cape Town—Johannesburg line. It was in goods traffic of all descriptions that competition was being felt, and it was an unfortunate fact from the point of view of the Cape government that two Cape lines were competing against each other. These were the lines from East London and Port Elizabeth. The only remedy was to discover which of these was the more economically situated as regards the Transvaal traffic, and by means of rate manipulation to cause the traffic to be concentrated on to that line. The two systems had held their own very evenly in the past. Even the existing depression was felt equally by both. If the government had been autocratic it might simply have decided that any one of them was to be used in the future as the "fighting" line. Since local interests had to be considered, and since it was in any case advisable to analyse costs as far as possible, a number of tests were carried out to determine which of the lines could carry at the cheapest rate. The Cape government was able to claim that it was receiving less traffic than it was in the interest of the Johannesburg merchants that it should receive. This is highly probable, for the Transvaal administration was bound to make its own railways pay as well as possible, and this could only be done by concentrating traffic upon that line, the greatest proportion of which lay within its own territory, and by charging possibly uneconomically high rates upon those lines connecting the termini of the Cape, and in a less degree of Natal with Johannesburg. The railway users in Johannesburg were quite aware of this, but the government could not escape from the necessity of earning the greatest possible revenue.

## *Finances*

For the purposes of our study we may begin by giving tables of the budgetary position of each colony during this period. The following table gives the income and expenditure of the four colonies in each of the five years under review :

| Year | CAPE COLONY | | ORANGE FREE STATE | | NATAL | | TRANSVAAL | |
|---|---|---|---|---|---|---|---|---|
| | Revenue | Expen. | Rev. | Expen. | Rev. | Expen. | Rev. | Expen. |
| | £ | £ | £ | £ | £ | £ | £ | £ |
| 1902–3 | 11,701 | 11,197 | 956 | 839 | 3,439 | 5,039 | 5,427 | 4,608 |
| 1903–4 | 9,913 | 10,862 | 875 | 807 | 4,334 | 4,071 | 5,813 | 4,538 |
| 1904–5 | 8,472 | 9,149 | 786 | 780 | 4,160 | 3,829 | 4,404 | 4,261 |
| 1905–6 | 8,236 | 8,231 | 768 | 769 | 3,384 | — | 4,670 | 4,829 |
| 1906–7 | 7,701 | 10,158 | 787 | 774 | 3,665 | — | — | — |

(000 omitted throughout)

It will be seen that after the close of the war each state

had substantial surplus which, however, even in the Transvaal, was much reduced by 1905. The significance of this reduction can be seen more fully in the following table, which states in the case of each colony what proportion of its total income was derived from railways, from customs, from direct taxation and from all other sources taken together:

|  | Railways | Customs | Direct Taxation | Other Sources | Totals |
|---|---|---|---|---|---|
| CAPE COLONY | £ | £ | £ | £ | £ |
| 1902-3 | 5,617 | 3,503 | 32 | 2,659 | 11,701 |
| 1903-4 | 5,120 | 2,396 | 28 | 2,369 | 9,913 |
| 1904-5 | 4,033 | 1,925 | 27 | 2,487 | 8,472 |
| 1905-6 | 3,940 | 1,870 | 45 | 2,381 | 8,236 |
| 1906-7 | — | — | — | — | — |
| TRANSVAAL |  |  |  |  |  |
| 1902 | 2,176 | — | 508 | 3,743 | 5,427 |
| 1903 | 1,759 | — | 720 | 2,854 | 5,333 |
| 1904 | 1,590 | — | 791 | 2,030 | 4,411 |
| 1905 | 1,699 | — | 983 | 1,988 | 4,670 |
| 1906 | 1,638 | — | 1,156 | 1,877 | 4,651 |
| NATAL |  |  |  |  |  |
| 1902 | 1,726 | 889 | — | 818 | 3,439 |
| 1903 | 2,286 | 1,068 | — | 974 | 4,334 |
| 1904 | 2,499 | 800 | — | 855 | 4,160 |
| 1905 | 1,884 | 605 | 6 | 885 | 3,384 |
| 1906 | 2,085 | 569 | 8 | 1,004 | 3,665 |

(000 omitted throughout)

It will be seen from this that at the beginning of the period none of the states had any considerable income from direct taxation, but that before 1905 the Transvaal had begun to draw a considerable income from this while the Cape drew a small income. Even the Transvaal income, however, showed signs of falling off in 1905 and this is explained by the fact that it consisted entirely of a tax on mining profits and that a depression in gold mining had set in in 1903 and was very deep by 1905. The collapse of revenue from railways is seen to be acute in Cape Colony, and felt considerably even in the Transvaal.

The first considerable factor in determining the financial position of the four colonies had been the customs union, which was concluded almost immediately after the close of the war. This, as we have seen, involved some sacrifice of revenue in the case of the inland colonies. Prior to the war the Orange Free State had received considerable sums annually from the Cape government while the Transvaal had had its own customs duties. The coastal colonies had passed all the goods destined for the interior free of duty, excepting for a slight transit charge. After the customs union these same goods obtained access to the Transvaal on payment of the same transit duty but free across the Transvaal border. The Cape and Natal were able to continue their customs policy as before. No duties were seriously altered and no increases occurred. In the customs bargaining the inland colonies had made the bigger sacrifices and the coastal colonies had in consequence to agree to impose no extra charges.

An enquiry was held into the finances of the Transvaal as a result of which it was decided either to impose a tax on gold profits sufficient to finance a reconstruction scheme or to obtain the support of the Chamber of Mines in the raising of a loan sufficient to finance the reconstruction of the whole of the Transvaal. As will be remembered from the table given above, the actual sum received as a result of the gold tax was very small compared to the profits from the railways. The intention at first, however, had been different; the mines had been claiming a cheaper railway service and this it was thought would weaken the railways as an instrument of taxation. Like many schemes of post-war reconstruction this one reckoned without the slump which was bound to follow the over-active years 1902 and 1903. The slump in this case not only came in all its natural intensity but was augmented by an inability of the Transvaal mines to obtain sufficient labour to carry out the development work for which they had imported machinery. This failure altered the whole complexion of Transvaal finance. The gold profits tax yielded less than had been expected and the railways remained the main source of revenue. The railway building was curtailed, only about two-fifths of the lines which had been approved by the Inter-Colonial Council being actually started before 1905.

In Cape Colony the fate of the proposed lines was even worse. Apart from two lines to shorten the distance between the two goods-traffic ports and the Transvaal, and a few very minor constructions, no building was undertaken. A great programme was almost entirely dropped excepting for renovations. In Natal a very similar state of affairs existed. Lines had been proposed in all directions, from Durban north-east into the sugar rands, from Petermaritzburg outwards into potential agricultural lands on one side and to native lands on the other. Actually the House of Assembly nearly passed a ludicrous scheme of doubling the trunk line to Johannesburg. The pressure of traffic immediately after the war was very great and might have involved Natal in a huge futile expenditure, but the development lines were less urgent and were allowed to wait.

The important features in railway development at this time in South Africa appear to have been in the first place that all the administrations considered the advisability of using the profits of the trunk lines not only as contributions to general revenue, but more precisely to make them contribute to the general development of the country by supporting a number of non-paying branch lines. It was only this turning of their attention to the agricultural regions, which could not themselves support lines, that enabled people in all the South African states to begin to talk of not using the railways for taxation. When this was mentioned it meant very different things to different people. To the Transvaal mineowner it meant the railways being run only to cover cost and so his having the advantage of a cheaper service; to the farmer it meant a supply of branch lines of the value of which he was well aware. The South African lines were almost unique among state owned lines in their payability. Profits, which if they had been made by private companies would have aroused no problems, became bones of contention when they were at the disposal of the states. It was a true sign of development that it could be suggested, as it was at this time, that no profits should be made on the railway systems as a whole, but that they should be reinvested in the lines either for reduction in cost of service or for development of new traffic by lower rates. In the second place the post-war period was significant on account of changes and experiments in systems of management. In the inland colonies it is important to realise that the whole of the railway system, including that in the Orange Free State, was nationalized. The Transvaal lines were bought from the Dutch company and were now run by the administration after being amalgamated into one system with those of the Orange Free State. This necessitated the taking over and absorbing of the Free State administration and the creation of a new Transvaal administration. This was done without the usual disadvantage of Parliamentary control, by an autocratic administration. At the same time it was known that this regime would probably last only a few years so that it would be necessary to create a machine which could be taken over by a democratic government. The Cape and Natal had the advantage of watching this experiment as closely as they wished. In the third place all relationships between the lines of the different administrations underwent a development. Under a railway convention of 1904 the Transvaal had agreed so to regulate rates as to maintain fixed proportions between the Cape and Natal and Delagoa Bay. But while this had been fairly easy so long as only the three main lines entered the Transvaal it became extremely difficult when several more lines crossed the border and was further complicated by the efforts of the two coastal colonies to change their routes so as to take advantage of these lines. A short cut in Cape Colony might necessitate a change of rates inside the Transvaal in order to preserve the balance according to the agreement; the Cape would have the advantage of carrying its given share at a lower cost. These changes

## RAILWAYS AND FINANCES

involved endless discussion between the administrations as to the rate fixing rights of their members. It was these discussions in the main which showed the impossibility of South Africa being served with reasonable efficiency by three or four different systems. The managers of all the systems met and discussed not only the contentious matters such as rate fixing but also technical matters such as line gauges and waggon weights on which it was essential for all to agree. This led to the South African railways being worked technically as a whole though administratively in conflicting groups.

There can be no doubt that the whole of the post-war reconstruction centred upon railway building. It will readily be appreciated that efforts, for example, to promote agricultural experiment would be impossible without in the first place the experts of the departments being able to keep in easy touch with the farmers spread over great areas, and in the second place without these farmers being induced by finding themselves able to sell goods in new markets to adopt the experts' suggestions. This importance of communication enters into absolutely every branch of administration in which reconstruction was attempted, and was in most cases not merely one of the factors but the determining factor. Navigable rivers did not exist; areas were swept by drought; mechanical communications were the only means of opening up a sub-continent which in spite of certain sensational developments was still largely desert, or unbroken scrub land, and, where occupied by whites, almost entirely the roughest type of pasture land. A land settlement had to be initiated in the inland colonies and this was impossible without railway communications which would make settlement by cultivating farmers a feasible proposition where it never had been before. Native administration had to be put on a new basis and this obviously meant that communications would have to be built. Even in matters such as education, communications were the key. In most of these matters all efforts at reconstruction would be rendered futile if not preceded by railway building. It was absurd to think of agricultural improvement without this prior condition. Enormous sums of money might be unproductively spent and the best administrative efforts discouraged. On the other hand, with mechanical transport provided, many developments would ensue without any other special administrative effort. Good agricultural lands connected with markets would quite automatically attract new settlers and improve their agriculture. Railway building was not only a preliminary essential to administrative efforts but would in many cases save these efforts altogether.

## REFERENCES

Minutes of the Bloemfontein Railway Conference, 1903.
The Cape Government Report on Trial Trains, 1906, between Port Elizabeth, East London, and an inland centre.
Report by Mr. Conacher on the Distribution of Rail Traffic in South Africa, 1906.
Text of the Selborne Memorandum.
Text of the Modus Vivendi with Portugal.
Minutes of the Inter Colonial Conference, 1906.
Correspondence published by the Cape Government concerning Railway Rates between Durban and Cape Ports and inland centres.
Report of the Cape Commission on Railway Management and the Construction of New Railways, 1907.
Newspaper Files, especially those of the *Cape Times*, are valuable.

## SECTION II

## CHAPTER VIII

### LAND SETTLEMENT AND AGRICULTURE IN THE RECONSTRUCTION

It is common to treat land settlement as a subject in itself, which, of course, it is administratively. To the administrator the settlement of people for the first time either on unoccupied land or on land which has been obtained for settlement purposes from other settlers, is a piece of work in itself. For a study such as this, however, even settlement of new land cannot be separated from general agricultural development, entailing as it does closer settlement on almost all types of land, the bringing into the market for private buying by new settlers of land which previously had been locked up owing to its occupation by unprogressive pastoral farmers, and also the state-aided settlement of immigrants on all types of land. To examine the land settlement policy of the Transvaal administration may lead to understanding an important part, but only a part, of the transition in land values that was going on at the time. The Cape Colony and Natal evolved no real land settlement policy until about the time when they joined the Union of South Africa, yet commercial land settlement was proceeded with, both as regards the reclaiming of land, which previously had been regarded as unsuitable for whites, and as regards the closer settlement of all lands with reasonable soil which were influenced by railway building. Land settlement was regarded as a matter of great importance in all parts of South Africa as a step from the extensive farming dictated by the very large holdings of the pioneer farmers. It was thought that the time had now come to change the delimitation of the land and the type of agriculture resulting from it, which had been inherited from early pioneering times. The fact that State policy in land settlement had literally not existed previously was fully realized; the question was whether the new values created by railway building and by customs union would automatically make a wholesale re-settlement possible. The next question was whether this re-settlement would take place automatically by new farmers with capital being attracted, or whether government assistance would be needed to encourage a new type of farmer. The main conclusion reached at the time was that state assistance would be needed to develop the more difficult land. Regions such as the Cape Eastern Province and Oudtshoorn would require no assistance, for these were already being bought by farmers who knew the full value of the land. But in other parts, and especially in the Transvaal where uneconomic pastoral farming had been succeeded by uneconomic sub-division, it was felt that agriculture would have to be begun almost afresh by means, first of all of the government buying the land, then of experimental farms being established to discover its real possibilities and the means of realizing them, and finally by introducing settlers new to the country who could be relied upon to make use of the experimental farms, and to be uninfluenced by local tradition.

Any land settlement policy had to face the fact that all good land and most bad land in every part of South Africa had been already occupied by the early settlers and used by them for some generations. In the Cape the only land available for new settlers was in the Namaqualand Desert, and in the Transvaal the only available land was in the bush veld to the north. The buying of land by the State was an essential preliminary to land settlement, and this was so difficult on account of the fact that in general the old settlers were so attached

## LAND SETTLEMENT AND AGRICULTURE 205

to their holdings that they could be induced to sell only by quite uneconomic prices being offered. If the government in any colony were to go about the country buying land, as was said, "with a big drum," they would be offered a great amount of the most useless parts of the present farms. It was this difficulty more than anything else which led the Cape and Natal to promote closer settlement by general agricultural assistance only, and prevented their developing an actual land settlement policy. The Transvaal administration was more happily situated, as many of the settlers there, especially in the Transvaal, but to a lesser degree in the Free State, had already sold to companies. Much of this company land could be bought at comparatively reasonable rates. A large sum of money was set apart for this purpose, and considerable areas made available for government settlers. The government was able to obtain full value from these lands by seeing to it that railways were built to serve them. This at once raised their value. Great care was taken in choosing the settlers who were to receive state support and in seeing that they were agriculturists of experience in ways of culture, which would enable them to benefit by the government experimental farms and not to fall back upon the old Transvaal methods. The areas given out to these farmers were only between 300 and 500 acres each, and the settlers were required to pay for them in the course of a definite number of years. The first of these provisions, making the farms only the size of English farms, insured that the farmers would not degenerate into mere sheep farmers, while the second provision meant that they would have to produce marketable crops. These settlers were distributed about the Transvaal and the Orange Free State in small groups, but all within easy reach of railways. At the same time that they were being settled, Boer farmers were being returned with the assistance of State compensation to their previous holdings. This re-settlement or repatriation of the Boers was done without any conditions being imposed ; it was a political necessity. But it was something of a surrender, since the returned farmers were able by means of compensation money, and by establishing their claims to lands which they had previously held, to take up their former vast holdings and so to become re-instated not only in their lands, but also in their methods. The government settlers and experimental farms were merely spots of progress from which it was hoped that good agriculture would spread.

One measure was proposed in order to improve the agriculture of the returned Dutch population. This was a land bank. The proposal was not adopted until 1908, but it aroused much interest in the reconstruction period, and serves to illustrate some of the conditions which prevailed. The Dutch farmers, it was pointed out, owned land which represented the whole of their capital. They had no surplus capital with which to undertake developments. They could not be induced to sell, since sentimental reasons were present. Yet they might improve their agriculture, and more especially their stock farming if they could fence their lands and carry out irrigation schemes. The new government settlers were leaving untouched the wider problem of improving sheep farming on those big farms, which, at any rate, at the present, seemed destined to remain some three thousand to five thousand acres. Railway development could not be sufficiently wide-spread to make mixed farming payable on all these lands, but they were now brought into contact with markets, at least for their wool, such as they had not known previously. The first essential was fencing, which would enable the farmers to paddock the land and so exterminate vermin and graze the sheep scientifically. This would indeed be a revolution in pastoral farming. Trekking would be abandoned ; the grasses would receive periodical rests, the sheep would be left peacefully in the paddocks day and night instead of being herded in kraals each evening. Whether much of this

## LAND SETTLEMENT AND AGRICULTURE 207

improvement could not have been carried without State assistance we must remain in doubt. It would appear to be certain that most farmers, at least after good seasons, and after being able to dispose of what wool they had at better prices than ever before, should have been able themselves to finance the development. The first three years after the war, however, were years of drought, and it was claimed for the farmers that the whole of their resources had been absorbed in the mere re-stocking of their lands and in the building of farm houses demolished during the war. The drought years left them without resources, and very possibly in debt to the storekeepers. The re-stocking after the war had been a great opportunity to introduce improved breeds, and this had been encouraged by the government importing stud animals. It would appear that the effect of these stud animals had been very slight, excepting on the farms of the new settlers, where scientific breeding was appreciated and the result of the experiment made on the government farms made use of. But it was feared that Boer farming might, without some direct assistance, degenerate into what it had been before the war. Had this happened, the gap between the farms of the new settlers and the surrounding lands would have been so great that commercial farming might never have spread outwards. Whatever the rights of the case it was felt that the introduction of a land bank would bring a new feature into Dutch farming. It was fully realized that no parallel could be drawn between this farming and the farming in Europe, which had so benefited from land banks. It was never proposed that a co-operative system might be introduced. But it was held, and possibly rightly, that to place any new source of capital within reach of the farmers, coupled with ample safe-guards that they should make full use of it, would be beneficial.

The Transvaal experimental farms were established on the best American model, and each farm was accompanied with an agricultural college, where new settlers were persuaded whenever possible to study for at least two years before taking up their farms. The first settlers after the war lacked this advantage, and consequently some of them found the difficulties too great. It cannot be repeated too often that the qualities of the soil were almost quite unknown. One of the chief disadvantages in the situation was that newcomers to the country were unable to get experience of agriculture, partly by reason of the fact that scientific farms did not exist, but partly also because it was impossible for newcomers to the country to get practical experience without actually buying land of their own. Commercial tenancy was unknown under the old Boer system since the farmers had considered it quite good enough to allow their friends and relations merely to occupy unwanted pieces of land without giving them any definite title. The newcomers, on the other hand, would in any case have been unable to take up title in the absence of any markets for their produce. It was also impossible for newcomers to begin as agricultural labourers and then to proceed to take up land of their own, for agricultural labour was relegated by strong social custom to the native and no white man could undertake it. On the lands owned by companies it would appear that some kind of tenancy had been tried. But this always seems to have been short term with no guarantee of compensation for improvements. There were honourable exceptions to this, for some companies set aside good pieces of land, but these would appear to have accommodated very few people since they were generally far from railways, and the companies were generally able to draw good incomes from their lands merely by letting them out without any permanency of title to the many landless whites, who were only too glad to occupy them on any terms. Agricultural colleges were, therefore, of the greatest importance.

It is common to talk of the colonization of the Transvaal after the South African War. But the

# LAND SETTLEMENT AND AGRICULTURE

settlement of some 500 families in an area of some thousands of square miles can scarcely be termed colonization. What happened was that a much-talked-of land settlement policy had very few results actually in settling the land, but, as part of an agricultural policy, had considerable results in enabling the Transvaal, which for generations had been wild pastoral land, and then had been paralysed by the very sudden introduction of a highly capitalized industry into its midst, to settle down and to begin to benefit from the markets created by this industry. The development would have come about in any case. Nothing can be more certain than that agriculturalists would gradually have explored the possibilities of good land within the reach of the Johannesburg market, and that then they would have made use of the excellent railway services between that market and the coast, to develop an export trade. The export trade came later. The government efforts worked in with natural tendencies and quickened these tendencies.

While the agriculture of the coastal colonies had much in common with that of the interior, the same methods of development were, generally speaking, not applicable. The preliminary phase of extensive settlement was very similar but the general quality of the land was much less problematical. The settlers in Cape Colony had never been so completely out of touch with markets as had those of the Transvaal. Although all the land had not been scientifically explored almost all parts of it had been kept in touch with by at least one of the main ports, and the farmers had all been accustomed to some degree of commerciality in their day-to-day business. The land of the Karroo was further different to that of the high veld in that it was uniform land, of which the properties were well known. It was land with only drought-resisting grasses, and it was nowhere stimulated into showing the signs of fertility which had been seen in the watered parts of the Transvaal. The Eastern end was known to have a better rainfall than the rest of the Karroo, but even this was not experimental land. The only experiments which could be proceeded with would be in the direction of fencing land so as to improve its natural vegetation and consequently its powers of natural water conservation. None of it had been brought into the market by the action of land companies. It was generally tightly held by the farmers, who looked to the future of their families by providing that they should continue to farm in the same way, if possible. Experimental stations and land settlement experiments would have been wasteful under any such conditions. In those parts of Cape Colony which were in more immediate contact with the ports commercial influence had been at work for generations, in some cases for centuries, and no sudden improvements, no revolution in method, could be looked for. Even if the farmers there were not succeeding in finding the very best crops to grow, or the very best means of growing them, yet they were making a success of their work and they would not have been likely to sell their best land; nor would it have been advisable to buy this from them. They had gradually learned to adjust themselves to a very complex set of conditions; they had no great stretches of uniform land; they had learned simply to direct water, wherever it was available, on to small fields. In no part of Cape Colony could land settlement be the integral part of agricultural re-organization that it had been in the Transvaal. Nor could agricultural re-organization begin with a blank page as it had in the new colonies. The two systematic efforts made in the nineties to survey the agricultural possibilities of Cape Colony had served only to emphasize its great diversity. The south-west districts had nothing in common with Oudtshoorn nor had these with the Eastern Province, while the Ciskei again was a case in itself, and the one or two fertile regions found in the Karroo required treatment and experience all their own. The government might assist for example dairy farming, but it would

## LAND SETTLEMENT AND AGRICULTURE

find methods congenial to Swellendam quite out of place near Port Elizabeth. And similar differences existed in the case of almost every possible crop. The Transvaal was able to act differently; it was able to look for tobacco land or fruit land and to supply the farmers there with the appropriate seeds, but this was impossible in the Cape. It is sometimes supposed that reconstruction in agriculture was much more thorough-going in the Transvaal because the administration there was autocratic, while in Cape Colony a Parliament had to be satisfied. But we have indicated differences far more fundamental than this.

Natal was in a condition very similar to Cape Colony. She had, however, one great group of agricultural industries, which required no government assistance of any of the types discussed here. The tea and sugar production was quite able to look after itself, and although the government did encourage new settlers to take up sugar lands, this was really a commercial process of which all the terms were fixed by the development already in existence. In the rest of Natal, throughout its mid-lands and up-lands, the land was occupied on the same primitive extensive terms as in most other parts of South Africa. The farms were large and reformers were keen on an immigration policy which would cause them to be sub-divided so as to make cultivation possible. It was said, and doubtless with truth, that most of the large farms were used partly for harbouring natives and rack-renting them, while the remainder were as uncultivated as the farms of the Transvaal. It was only the high cost of buying land and the impossibility of the Natal government buying back a considerable proportion of its own territory that prevented a systematic land-settlement policy being adopted. But this difficulty was insurmountable, and it is probably fortunate that it was so. For the mere sub-dividing of the land would have done little to develop it. The cost of clearing and of beginning new operations would have been even greater than the cost of buying the land, and would doubtless either have bankrupted the government or broken the settlers. Though fertile, the land was difficult and needed clearing. When in 1906 an outlet was found for maize, great areas of land were at once brought under cultivation.

Each of the coastal colonies improved its agricultural department but could do very little more. Even in respect of irrigation, although much interest was taken in it, very little progress was made with government assistance. One experiment deserves attention, namely agricultural co-operation. This was felt in all four colonies to be one of the few ways in which the government could really assist agricultural development. An Act was passed whereby any group of farmers might form themselves into a co-operative society, and would then be entitled to receive both advice and financial assistance from the State. It was a natural re-action against the store-keeper system, which was quite unable to market anything other than staple commodities, such as wool and grain. Many farmers were able to dispose, in small quantities, of dairy produce and tobacco and wine. To make this possible central depots were necessary at which the products could be accumulated and prepared for market. These facilities were not forthcoming from private enterprise excepting in the immediate neighbourhood of towns. Yet they were of considerable importance to the farmer as giving him an increased source of income, and were of no less importance to the State in promising to turn the attention of farmers to the improvement of their stock, especially of their cattle, and to encourage them to fence land and to grow winter fodder. Dairy farming in its various branches was the one direction which any large agricultural development might take place in the Colonies. Co-operation appeared to be the key to this development. It was necessary for the government to supply the capital, but given that, success seemed quite possible. Numbers of societies were formed, but in a few years nearly all of them were in difficulties. They found

# LAND SETTLEMENT AND AGRICULTURE

themselves unable to pay interest upon the capital invested. The chief reason was that the farmers were too far apart to make common management a success. Most of the companies were liquidated and co-operation continued only on the smallest scale, the desired development taking place wherever communications made ordinary marketing possible.

The post-war reconstruction in agriculture in each of the colonies had the important effect of making South Africa known as a country in which farmers with capital could often get a good start. Together with railway development it changed the South African imports of foodstuffs into a slight export of certain products. It improved government departments dealing with agriculture so that any progressive farmer was now able to get good advice as to crops and methods. It made the use of dipping almost universal and so made stock farming on the coastal lands much more economic than ever before. But it did not discover any vast possibilities of South Africa becoming a contributor to the world's food supply. Maize was a later development. Wool could be improved. The turning of South Africa into a self-sufficing country with a prosperous agriculture was the end aimed at and largely achieved

## REFERENCES

The Annual Reports of the Transvaal, Cape, and Natal Departments of Agriculture. Those of the Transvaal Department are especially valuable.

The Report of the Transvaal Indigency Commission and also the Report of the South African Drought Investigation Commission of 1923 and Irrigation Finance Commission of 1925, are all very good on this period.

The Report and Evidence of the South African Irrigation Congress, 1906.

Report and Evidence of the Select Committee of the Union House of Assembly on the Irrigation Act of 1911.

Report and Evidence of Senate Select Committee on Closer Land Settlement, 1912.

Reports of the Union of South Africa Department of Lands.

Report of the Transvaal Land Bank Commission, 1908.

# SECTION II

## CHAPTER IX

### MINING AND LABOUR QUESTIONS IN THE POST WAR PERIOD

GOLD production during the South African War had come to a complete standstill. A few mines had commenced production in 1902 after the occupation of Johannesburg by British troops, but full production practically had to be begun afresh after the end of the war. Two distinct policies had been opened to the gold companies, one to develop gradually as labour became available, and the other to make an effort to attract as much capital as possible during the post-war boom, and to develop the mines at once so as to justify this raising of capital. The latter policy, dictated by a natural desire to take the tide at the flood, was adopted. Each company began development on every one of its mines. The result was that a great demand for labour was at once created. This demand for labour and the efforts made to satisfy it formed the centre of a prolonged controversy and virtually set the rate at which the whole of the Transvaal reconstruction programme could proceed. As we have seen, the original programme was based upon a calculation as to what sums the mines could afford to pay in taxation and as to what profits would result from the operation of the railways, which depended upon the mines. In 1903 it became evident that the mines were finding it difficult to carry out their programmes. Native labour was not forthcoming. The war had broken all the valuable connections established by recruiters, and had broken the habit which the natives were forming of coming out to work. More, it had enabled the natives to earn considerable sums of money by rendering services to the troops. The natives were now very unwilling to start to come out again, and the result was a labour shortage of very serious dimensions. This had been intensified by an agreement between the mines taken in 1903 to reduce native wages to a lower level than before the war. It had been thought that now that the mines were organized, and since it had been learned from experience that lower wages might improve the total labour supply, and it was thought that this was the appropriate time to make the change. Whether or not this change intensified the difficulties which were soon found to exist, we cannot be sure; it is quite possible that the natives had become accustomed to handling larger sums of money than ever before, and that the new wages did not attract them. However this may be, the shortage was such that the whole of the Transvaal and consequently of South Africa, was plunged into a depression which was only partly attributable to a reaction from the post-war boom. All parts of Africa were scoured for labour, and suggestions brought forward for importing unskilled white labour from Europe and coolie labour from the East. The dislike of the mining companies for white unskilled labour was very pronounced. White men were essential for the skilled and supervisory work, but they were much less valuable per pound spent in unskilled work, while the formation of a new political party, based upon the votes of a large number of white labourers, was yet another danger to be avoided. The amount of native labour available in Africa within reach of the mines, was reckoned to fall considerably short of the requirements of the mines alone, while thousands of natives were needed also for the farms and the railways. Recruiting was restarted in the Transkei and started in Natal. The supply from Portuguese East Africa was assured by the Modus Vivendi Treaty of 1901, and while it was an

P

excellent supply, it was known that it could not be increased. It remained to obtain labour from the East, and enquiries were made in China, where it was ascertained that a sufficient number of Chinese might be persuaded to indenture themselves for periods of labour in the Transvaal. An intense agitation was carried on to secure the consent of the general public to this importation. All concerned were convinced beyond a shadow of doubt that the chief need of the moment was to recover from the depression, of which the results were being felt by everyone, and public opinion was soon won over. The measure was agreed to in spite of determined opposition both from the Dutch population, who did not wish to have yet another racial element introduced into that country, and from the white artisans, who feared that the Chinese would not merely prevent the introduction of more white labour into the country, but might encroach upon the scope of employment of those already there. Up to that time there had been very little competition between coloured and white labour on the mines, but Chinese labour might be much more skilled than that of the natives and the employers might be tempted to displace the whites. The Chinese were imported only on the understanding that they were definitely to be sent back again at the end of their indenture periods. Much of the controversy centred round the question whether or not the Chinese would displace white labour; but a more immediate question was whether they would enable the mining industry to return to its former output. As regards the former question, it would appear that the opponents of Chinese labour were substantially correct in their claim that it would limit the field for the employment of Europeans  But the importation of some kind of labour was clearly necessary, given the development policy to which the mines had committed themselves. And revival did come—the railway building programme which had been suspended when depression first set in, was now resumed and other reconstruction proceeded with.

Upon the mines the Chinese labour was a complete success. Once it was recruited in China, which was very far away, there was no difficulty about supply, and the total cost was very low. With the community at large the Chinese were less popular, for the mines did not succeed in enclosing them all in compounds, and a wave of crime terrorized the Witwatersrand. The mines were made to promise that as soon as possible they would rely upon African labour, and they did proceed to devote a good deal of attention to re-establishing recruiting in prepartaion for the time when the Chinese would go. Controversy with white labour became embittered as it was seen that the relationships between Chinese and whites had in it a clear element of the competitive. An important element in the situation was that the natives on the mines were becoming more acclimatized and more skilful. Their death rate, though still high, was being reduced, and it was noticeable that those who returned to the mines after their first period were not only immune from most diseases, but were skilful workmen from the first. Recruiting was now being put upon a level far above that of its early days. Private recruiters were much reduced in numbers. The whole of the recruiters in Cape Colony were members of a limited company, the Native Recruiting Corporation, which paid them by salary and commission, thus abolishing the capitation fees which in early times had induced recruiters to bring natives to the mines by false representations as to the wages they would receive. Natives were now required to sign a uniform contract which was attested before the magistrate in each district. Supply was rendered more plentiful by droughts, which were occurring in the native regions, which the natives, now that they had experience of the mines, were fighting against by going out to work so as to be able to buy food for their families. The number of natives at work steadily rose, and in 1907 the import of Chinese ceased, and by 1909 the last Chinese had left the country.

On the gold mines the accident and sick list rates among workmen of all races were still very high. Both white and coloured were subject to miners pthisis, a form of consumption caused by dampness and exposure to dust and fumes. A commission had sat, and many enquiries had been made as to the means of reducing this disease, but little progress had been made. It was now that workmen's compensation was introduced for the white employees. No such measure was suggested for the natives, mainly, it would seem, because the cost of insurance would have been prohibitive. The many problems arising out of the employment of natives had by no means been solved. Periodic discontent expressed maladjustments, which continued for a considerable time, and are by no means non-existent to-day.

## REFERENCES

Most of the more important documents have already been referred to and the reader will require no introduction to them. In addition we have :—

The Report and Evidence of the Natal Native Affairs Commission, 1906.

The Report of the Cape Colony Native Affairs Commission, 1910.

Report of Cape Colony Departmental Commission on Native Land Occupation, 1906.

The Native Administration Reports issued by Cape Colony, Transvaal, and Natal, before Union are very valuable.

The Select Committee (Union of South Africa) on the Native Labour Regulation Bill, 1911, gives much extremely useful information.

The Select Committee of 1913 which considered the Deferred Pay System and the Period of Contract is also useful.

Two volumes, entitled *The Natives of South Africa*, issued respectively in 1901, and 1909, by a London Committee, contain the best investigation made up to that time.

The Report of the Transvaal Mining Commission, 1908.

Report of the Mining Regulations Commission, 1908.

## SECTION II

## CHAPTER X

CUSTOMS PROBLEMS WITHIN THE CUSTOMS UNION

THE final stage in customs union was carried through almost without discussion immediately after the South African War. This done, the matter was out of politics at least for a time. The agreement was that the Union might be denounced by any one party at one year's notice. It had cut a great many knots, for by 1903 the Transvaal had shown every sign of becoming a complex state with mineowners, merchants, manufacturers, and farmers, each expressing his views of customs questions. It was the Transvaal that in 1907 denounced the Customs Union. As we have seen, the colony had made sacrifices in accepting the Union. Her power as the important centre of South Africa had become thoroughly established in the few years after the war, and while the mineowners and the merchants approved of the customs union, the farmers and manufacturers who were beginning to become influential expressed strong disapproval. This denouncing of the Union led to a conference to be held in 1908 for which all parties began to prepare. The situation was one of some complexity, since in each of the colonies a manufacturing interest had succeeded in establishing itself during the post-war activities. Thus in each of the four colonies the Union was strongly objected to by one or more parties, while it was actually supported by very few interests except the merchants. The basis of the customs union had been the adoption of the Cape seven per cent. tariff in operation before the South African War. This had applied only to imported goods, and one of the main results of the tariff was to enable South African goods of all descriptions to t rave freely from one part of South Africa to another. The benefits of this to trade in general were undoubted, but everywhere local interests which had in the past been sheltered from the competition of other producers perhaps two or three miles away by a tariff wall in between, began to complain that they were exposed to new competition. The existence of tariff boundaries had undoubtedly brought about a distribution of manufacturers and a system of relations between farmers and markets which could not survive the abolition of the tariffs. The building trade in the Transvaal had in the last century imported all its raw timber, and had manufactured it on the spot ; but now it had to be realized that raw timber was an article very bulky in relation to the finished product to be extracted from it, and, now that the consideration was no longer counteracted by a duty on the finished products, these were imported. The furniture makers of Johannesburg complained loudly, and so did the printers, and the shoemakers, and the tailors, and many other manufacturers or semi-manufacturers. These complaints were joined by those of the farmers who were able to say that they were being undersold in the Johannesburg market by grain and potatoes " dumped " by the Cape Colony producers. It appears to have been the case that vegetable farming in the neighbourhood of Johannesburg had reached a stage at which it was able to supply all of that town's needs. The farmers in the outlying districts still, however, sent in potatoes and other produce which they grew in a small way. All the usual arguments against dumping were brought up against allowing potatoes from Cape Colony to compete in the same market with those of the Transvaal. A railway journey of nearly 1,000 miles was not thought sufficient protection. The same objections were raised in respect of Cape wheat. The Transvaal farmers indeed, or some few of them, had learned at some time to expect that the Johannesburg market would be reserved for them alone and for their friends of the Free State, and any disturbance of this state of affairs

## CUSTOMS UNION PROBLEMS

was resented. Curiously enough the mercantile opinion of the Transvaal was not unanimous in favour of Customs Union. As a result of the barriers of the past, Johannesburg had become a distributing centre for goods, which it was now more economical to store at and distribute from the coast. It is probable that only a slight readjustment was needed, but the disturbance was there, and disagreement among the merchants added to the general discontent. The Transvaal did not severely feel the loss of revenue from the customs collections. While the coastal colonies still had their customs ideas dictated very largely by considerations of revenue the Transvaal was very independent in this matter. The final denunciation of the union came indeed almost entirely as a result of the agitations of the farmers, supported by the manufacturers, on account of their desire to be cut off once more from the coastal colonies. The Transvaal producers felt that they had everything to gain by being self contained; they could develop their own agriculture and manufacture their own goods, thus maintaining a white population. But if goods were to be allowed to come in freely both from oversea and from the coastal colonies, then Transvaal agriculture would be undersold and Transvaal manufacture would be done in Cape Colony or even in Europe. It was a fact indeed that Cape Colony and Natal were better prepared at the time to benefit from Customs Union than were the interior colonies. Production in Cape Town of such articles as furniture, boots and shoes, had reached quite an economic level. The interchangeability of white and coloured labour had made costs relatively low, while in the Transvaal the reservation of skilled work for the whites had maintained the cost of production at a high level. Cape Colony agriculture was also able to respond to the opening up of a new market, and the distress of the Transvaal commerce which we have already described was doubtless real. The Transvaal attitude to Natal was practically the same as to Cape Colony. The same descriptions of the dumping of Natal goods were indulged in as were applied to Cape goods. In the coastal colonies the attitude was one of satisfaction with the union, but was accompanied by the demands of the producers for a higher tariff. The denunciation of the Union gave the opportunity to all parties concerned for more bargaining, and while statesmen were determined that the complications ensuing upon the abolition of the customs union could never be defaced, the manufacturing and farming interests were at least prepared to bargain to the limit of destroying the Union in order to enjoy a more favourable tariff in any future tariff that might be drawn up. The governments of the coastal colonies were in a situation different equally from that of the various merchants and manufacturers and from that of the administrations of the interior colonies. They depended upon the customs tariff for a large part of their revenues. The reduction of railway profits was throwing the weight more and more upon the customs. Their interest lay in maintaining the customs union as it was, but if possible with higher duties of the revenue-raising type. Actually the four colonies never bargained about the customs union at all. Before the conference was called the railway conference met in 1908, and complete unification was agreed upon. It is true that in the discussion of railway unification, customs were always kept in mind; how important they were we can never know, but open bargaining was avoided and the next customs tariff to be drawn up was one for the Union of South Africa.

## REFERENCES

In addition to the references already given on Customs matters, each of the four States held an enquiry by means of Commission between 1906 and 1908. Thus we have
Reports and Evidence of the
    Cape Colony Customs Tariff Commission, 1908.
    Transvaal Customs and Industries Commission, 1908.
    Natal Customs and Industries Commission, 1906.
    Orange River Colony Customs Commission, 1906.
The files of the *South African Manufacturer' Record* are of value.

## SECTION III

## CHAPTER I

### NATIVE LAND AND RECRUITMENT

*Recent Developments*

EVER since the report of the commission of 1905, the need had been growing for a clearing up of the conditions under which natives occupied land. As we saw earlier in this book, land was occupied by natives in almost every possible mode, ranging from complete private ownership (chiefly in the Cape Colony) down to the most unregulated squatting and the most insecure tenancy-at-will in all parts of the Union. The impossibility of allowing matters to remain in this confusion has already been indicated, and rapidly became intensified with the passing of time. The purchase of land by natives was proceeding on a small scale in several parts of the Union, and was creating dissatisfaction among white farmers, who, with some exceptions, strongly objected to being neighbours of native landowners, even though the cultural difference between the native and the white might be very small. In other cases the settlement of whites on the land, either by government or by private enterprise, was proceeding fairly rapidly, assisted by water boring and anti-malarial measures, and frequently involved the taking over of land which was supporting natives. In other cases again, dairy farming was promising to take on a new value, and the keeping of herds of cattle was now possible, since the eradication of East Coast fever, on much coastal land on which natives were living under various forms of tenancy. In almost all parts of the Union the value of land was rising, and in consequence farmers were adopting more advanced methods of cultivation, and of sheep management. As this advance went on, the farmers objected more strenuously to the nebulous ways in which the natives were scattered on and around their farms. They objected to natives squatting on unoccupied land near their farms, for this meant stock-stealing and very possibly a shortage of labour; they objected to the natives living on their farms as tenants-at-will, for although they wanted the labour, they were beginning to wish to pay for it in other forms than by granting use of land to the natives.

For the sake of clearness we may say that the problem was made up of the following points:—In the first place, it was necessary to regulate the actual purchase of land by natives; in the second place it was necessary to regulate the purchase of land by Europeans in areas which were essentially native, and which, if lost to the native, would drive him to press more upon white farmers' land; in the third place the question of Crown land had to be investigated, so that the natives living on it would be recognized tenants of the Crown, and not mere drifting aggregations causing uneasiness to neighbouring farmers; next, native tendency on the basis of a monetary rent had to be regulated so as to diminish the dangers of natives being rack-rented by absentee white landowners, and then turned loose without other provision being made for them when the owner wished to put the land to other uses; lastly, the natives living on farms actually worked by whites had to be clearly defined either as labourers, or as labour-tenants, or as squatters, so that each farmer would be allowed a fair share of labour, but the more backward farmers would not be allowed to fill their farms with superfluous natives.

The problem was extremely complex, and even to-day, twenty years after Union, only the first steps have been taken toward defining it clearly in practice. It will be seen then, that the historian cannot analyse it completely, he can only indicate the material factors.

At the time of union each of the four colonies had its own native land legislation and its own administrative principles. These continued in force after union, and the conditions were not materially simplified until the Land Act of 1913 attempted to regulate native purchase throughout the whole country. Even then the attempt was not successful, except in providing a basis for discussion and administrative action. These are proceeding to this day. The main provisions of the Act were simple; they were that outside certain defined native areas, no native might purchase land, and inside these areas no white might purchase land. So far the Act aimed merely at maintaining the existing state of affairs. It would prevent native buyers spreading into land which was eligible for white settlement; it would also prevent white buyers from buying land which was really needed by the black population. The Act as thus worded would merely prevent the buying of land by natives outside of their statutory reserves, such as the Transkei in Cape Colony. It would do nothing to prevent the buying of Crown land by whites, even though that land should be absolutely necessary to maintain native populations. The next step of the Act, therefore, was to provide that a commission that should be set up for the purpose of deciding what land, in addition to the reserves, should be set aside definitely for native occupation It was recognised that the reserves which had been set apart for natives by treaties during the nineteenth century were definitely insufficient. There was much unoccupied Crown land generally inaccessible and unwanted by whites which was occupied by natives, and would have to be set aside definitely for their benefit. There was other land which was partly occupied by whites but in which white settlement would have to be stopped. A schedule to the Act defined the land which was definitely native; outside of this no landed property might change hands except by expressed permission of the Governor-General until the commission had reported.

The Act applied directly only to actual purchase. It also had the effect, in the Orange Free State at least, of making illegal the share-farming, or farming "on halves," which was prevalent there. In the Cape Colony its effects were quickly rendered nugatory by the fact that the Act of Union had provided that the natives there should enjoy certain privileges, and it was held by the High Court that the Land Act could not deprive them of the right to purchase any land whatever. Despite this, however, for reasons which we shall see later, the commission which was set up enquired into Cape Colony conditions as well as into those of the other Provinces.

It was not only in Cape Colony that constitutional difficulties were met with. In Natal the natives, with considerable justice, regarded the Act as an infringement of the proclamation annexing the country to Great Britain. This proclamation had enabled the natives to purchase land freely through the medium of the paramount chief, that is to say, the Governor General of Natal. This amounted not to a restriction, but to a safeguard, in that the Governor General could refuse to sanction transfers on terms which, to him, seemed unfair to the native purchaser. Land had been bought in almost all parts of Natal excepting the coast land. By the time the Act was passed, no fewer than 359,000 acres were privately owned and supported 37,000 inhabitants. Much of this land was in the inaccessible thorn country, but much of it intermingled with European land. The position in Natal appeared to be that white farmers, upon obtaining tital to land which they did not wish themselves to cultivate, had been in the practice not of settling natives indiscriminately, but of selling the land to them. The natives had in this way regained possession of land which doubtless should never have been alienated from them. The result was satisfactory to the white farmers, and at least enabled the natives to occupy land on secure terms. Both white and native in Natal declared their opposition to the Act

# NATIVE LAND AND RECRUITMENT

The various commissions and committees which have sat for the purpose of defining native areas have been able to draw certain arbitrary lines, but these have had little effect beyond displeasing both sections of the population. Wherever a piece of country has been set aside as a native area, the neighbouring white farmers have objected that it is fairly valuable land, and might at least in the future be used for cattle grazing. The natives, on the other hand, have protested that it is "baboon" country, and that if they are to be confined to it, all opportunities of progress will be denied them. Areas have been scheduled, but most of the doubtful land has been left open. Purchase by natives is still permitted by special permission of the Governor General of the Union, and in nearly all cases applications made by natives to purchase land there are acceded to.

In the Transvaal a different state of affairs was found. Very little land had been bought by natives. The little that had been bought had generally been transferred not to individual natives but to Europeans in trust for groups of natives, portions of tribes, who had gathered together enough mnoey to buy land on which they could live tribally. This tribal purchase means, in some cases, that the natives succeeded in enjoying extra reserves ; in other cases it meant only that mission stations were established on which numbers of native families were allowed to live under the surveyance of the missionaries. The Act of 1913 had, however, a real function in the Transvaal, in that great areas in the low veld were in a doubtful condition as to their future development. On the one hand, white settlers were gradually carrying agriculture into these areas ; on the other hand, natives who had accumulated some savings on the Witwatersrand were showing signs of wishing to invest these savings in land on the borders of the low country. It was here that delimitation might be very useful. The Crown lands all carried considerable numbers of natives. They were short of water in many parts ; in many parts they were malarial ; but the boundary between cultivable and useless land was constantly receding as water boring was carried on, and as progress was made against malaria. Nor was there any fixed boundary between Crown and private land. Surveying was unknown, and farmers and companies had taken effective possession of much ground, with or without the full knowledge of government. The land to which private claim was admitted, in most cases, remained white land, and then came under the Squatters' Law, which entitled the government to order the owner to keep only as many natives on land as he needed actually for labour purposes. This meant that the white owners lost the old value which the land had had to them in enabling them to collect rent from great numbers of natives. Considerable areas were set aside in which white people could buy no land. These areas may be taken to represent the minimum necessary for the native tribes in the North Transvaal. The natives already there continued to occupy the lands in tribal fashion ; land purchase by natives is made virtually impossible. Service has undoubtedly been done in guaranteeing reserved land for the native. Opportunities for progress by investing savings in land have almost undoubtedly been closed down. In the Transvaal, a certain number of applications to purchase land have been made by natives and, as in Natal, these have been generally acceded to. But they have been relatively insignificant. Private purchase by natives has never played the same part in the Transvaal as it has done in Natal. Cape Colony had been well provided with native reserves from early in the nineteenth century, and her natives had always enjoyed the fullest right to purchase land outside these reserves. This right had been embodied in the Act of Union in 1910, and so could not be taken away by means of ordinary legislation. A supreme court case upheld the right so that legally one half of the law, namely, that forbidding the natives to buy land outside of certain scheduled native areas, was declared unconstitutional. The other half still held good ; it was to the effect that no white man might buy land inside a native area. It was, therefore, possible to proceed with the marking out of areas for each race. The native areas would be definitely reserved, and native purchase outside of these areas could be discouraged by administrative action. In Cape Colony there had been a small but steady purchase of land by natives. It had been an outlet for the most prosperous of the native family. There was a prospect that as the Cape natives came to earn more money on the mines, and as they felt increasing difficulty in investing their savings within the limited boundaries of the reserve, they would proceed to buy up land in the neighbouring district of the Ciskei. How far this process would have gone, we do not know. The overcrowding of the reserves by an increasing population, and the over-stocking of them by the cattle, which are still the chief investment of the native, seem to indicate that had outside purchase been left quite free, numbers of natives would have had both the desire and the means to take advantage of it. There is, however, one important factor which must be kept in mind ; that is, that the natives at least in these areas were in the habit of leasing rather than of buying the land. Leasing was a much more easy process than buying. The native himself probably did not realise the essential difference between the two. He wanted the use of the land, and it was not easy for him to take the further step of desiring to make it his property. And the purchase of land was hedged round by many practical difficulties. There were the expenses of survey. The transfer documents had to be signed. A lump sum of money had to be found such as surpassed the comprehension of most natives. And even if all these steps were taken, the native was still not the absolute owner of the land. He found he had taken it by means of what was known as a mortgage. He had to keep on paying sums of money every six months, and if he failed to pay on any occasion, he might lose the land. The native, indeed, was a natural victim of the land shark. It was entirely in the natives' interest that the old Transvaal government had made it illegal for natives to take transfer excepting through the Native Affairs Department, or some other trustee. The right to purchase was in itself a doubtful advantage.

In the eastern portions of the Cape Colony, the portions with which the Native Land Act was chiefly concerned, leasing was much more common than selling to natives. As we have seen earlier in this book, the land between the Great Fish and the Kei Rivers was of doubtful value to white cultivators, but much sought after by natives. All of it, however, was owned by whites, and none of it was inaccessible. The fact of its being eagerly desired by the comparatively advanced Transkei natives, gave it a definite monetary value. Unlike the land of the Northern Transvaal, it was not given over merely to numbers of native squatters. It was mostly leased to natives for definite money payment. The native population in the district had increased greatly between 1904 and 1911, and continued to increase, while the white population remained almost stationary. This extra native population was accommodated as lessees. But they were liable to eviction on only sufficient notice to enable them to gather the crops in the ground. This complete insecurity made the system extremely unsatisfactory. It was obviously unsatisfactory to the native, in that he could be made to pay rent up to the value of all that he realized from his holding. For the family could actually live very largely on money brought from the Rand by the young men. It is possible that the natives were often obliged to draw upon this money also to pay the rent. And there were two factors at work to increase the difficulties in the natives' position. In the first place, the increase in the native population meant that the rents would be steadily raised and kept near the level at which the most prosperous natives could afford to pay, and in order to pay the rent, the natives would either lease smaller pieces of land, or would attempt to keep numbers of

## NATIVE LAND AND RECRUITMENT

their friends and relatives on their holdings. In the second place, east coast fever had been overcome by means of the dipping tank, and the land could in consequence be used for cattle grazing by the European owners.

Numbers of natives had succeeded in buying land outside of this area given over to leasing. But they were a very select few. There is no evidence that they were more backward as cultivators than their white neighbours, and no bad feeling appears to have been present. The real land problem did not concern these, or even those who might be expected to join them. It concerned the insecure tenants of the Ciskei farms, whose transition from the status of rent-paying lessees to that of superfluous farm hands was only a question of time. Fortunately, the development of cattle grazing was not phenomenally fast. At the moment of writing, in 1930, no decisive legislative steps had been taken, but the Hertzog Bills are under discussion, which will limit the number of natives on each farm to those actually required for service.

The Native Land Act meant different things to all the different parts of the Union. In Cape Colony it had meant mainly that attention had been drawn toward the Ciskei problem; in the Orange Free State it meant that attention was drawn toward yet another mode of settling natives on the land. In this state, only a very little land had been set aside as native reserves. This was largely due, as we have already seen, to the convenient proximity of Basutoland. Outside of these reserves it had always been illegal for any native to acquire property in land. Yet the Free State had a considerable population of natives over its whole area, and it had proceeded to settle these in a way of its own. Crude squatting, as practised in the Northern Transvaal, was out of the question in this district of uniformly good grazing land. Likewise, the leasing of the Ciskei was out of place and completely unknown. Every farmer had land which he knew to be good; but his farm was usually too large for him to make full use of the land himself. The practice had therefore grown up of accommodating natives on what was known as the share-system. We have already described this system, and now we need deal only with its developments at the time when the Native Land Act was passed, and with the effects of this Act upon it. The Act included a provision to make the system illegal. It had long been agitated against by the more progressive farmers, and had practically been driven underground by sheer weight of opinion. The natives accommodated under it were all owners of stock, and as farmers improved their grazing land, the presence of native stock, whether on their own or their neighbours' farms, was increasingly a cause of loss. The native stock, apart from running loose and trampling and grazing the land, mixed with the herds of the white farmers and made selective breeding impossible. Ever since the country had recovered from the Anglo-Boer War, there had been a distinct tendency to improve the grazing. This had been due partly to improved marketing opportunities, but largely to the increasing white population which caused the farms to be sub-divided into areas more economic for pastoral farming. This had not led to any kind of real poor white problem, since the land was too valuable to be cut up into uneconomic patches as it had been in the old Transvaal. But it had meant that white bywoners were displacing the native sharefarmers. Labour was still required, and natives without stock were welcomed. But the native sheep owner was doomed. "To put it quite bluntly," as was said at the time, " the natives have become too rich." With the practice made illegal in 1913, natives had either to dispose of their stock or to trek in search of other land. The former course meant great loss ; the latter was almost impossible. It was held that most of the natives being Basutos would be able to accommodate their stock by handing it over to their relatives in Basutoland. This, however, was possible to only a slight extent, for Basutoland, in common with most native areas, was showing clear signs of congestion by 1913.

Many of the natives, however, were not Basutos, but Baralongs, having no tribal land. Some extra provision was made in the form of land near the reserves, which was scheduled as open for native purchase. But here, as in other parts of South Africa, the right to purchase land solves no problems. A few purchases took place, but the net result of the Act was a further congesting of Basutoland, a loss to the natives through depreciation in the value of their stock, and the remaining of the bulk of the native population on the Free State farms with the status of farm labourers.

The native land question in South Africa may be said to consist of the necessity of accommodating a constant or increasing number of natives upon the land in some ways suitable to their present stage of culture, and in making provisions for their proceeding to a more advanced stage. It is generally admitted, by all except the frontier farmers, that the actual reserves made for native habitation are too small by almost any standard. The only possible doubt regarding this is one arising from the fact that native methods of agriculture are still nearly everywhere extremely primitive. It is possible that by intensive education, the natives would be able to increase considerably the yield per acre of most of their reserves, and if this were done without the native developing pari-passu a desire for the standard of life of the European peasantry, the situation might be eased. This may very possibly be done, and, coupled with the introduction of individual tenure, might practically solve the native question so far as the reserves are concerned. The real problem, however, lies outside of the reserves. About three-sevenths of the total native population are on white land. A growing proportion of these, numbering perhaps half a million (mostly adult males), are outside of our present calculations in that they have come to depend directly and permanently on the industries of the towns. A considerable proportion again are provided for as permanent farm labourers living a life different only in details from that of the English farm labourer. The remainder constitute the main problem. They vary in numbers from time to time, and in characteristics from place to place. They include the natives squatting on Crown and company land in the Transvaal, and those living precariously as tenants-cum-labourers—in the Ciskei. Their position becomes insecure in proportion to the advance of white settlement in the Northern Transvaal, and the progress of cattle farming in the Ciskei. As individual tenure becomes more prevalent inside the reserves, these cease to offer scope for the refugee population. The very existence of these natives retreating into the reserves forces the natives already there to adopt individual tenure. The tendency of legislation to-day (1930), in agreement with economic tendencies as they are seen in European farming, is to make the position of these natives ever less secure ; to require that they shall be classed as full-time labourers, and to make the definition of a " full-time labourer " ever more exacting. The stage has not yet been reached at which the reserves can prevent the influx of further natives. Individual tenure is the only real means of doing this, and it can be adopted only by relatively advanced natives such as are to be found in parts of the Transkei. A beginning has been made to apply it in Natal, but only a beginning. It could of course be forced by administrative measures, entirely from above, without waiting for the development of the natives, but this would require an expenditure both of money and of administrative effort such as is regarded as out of the question.

It should be noted that the problem in general derives much of its acuteness from the very fact that the natives are increasing in wealth and in standard of life. Much of the over-crowding in the reserves is not of people, but of cattle. The reserve natives making money as wage earners in industries return to their reserves, and, since all other avenues are closed, invest their savings in cattle. This in itself indicates that they have not yet learnt to allow their incomes to be absorbed in improving their standard of life. The natives outside the reserves on the other hand cannot accumulate cattle, but they are under the necessity of providing themselves with some kind of European clothing and often of buying European food. This fact, in addition to the fact that they have to pay rent in cash, brings them up against the difficulty of approaching a European standard of life without acquiring the Europeans' resources. Those who are farm labourers are in the same position to a certain extent; their main income is from payment in kind in the form of a little land to cultivate, or some grain, and an occasional sheep. But their taxes, and generally their clothes, have to be paid in cash, and, generally speaking, the cash payment is a fixed sum of from twenty to forty shillings a month, which has scarcely altered since the late nineteenth century, while the cost of commodities has of course increased greatly.

At this stage we may pass on to the development of the non-agricultural resources of the natives since the time of union. The connecting link between the natives' original home and the mines on which he first learned the meaning of wage labour is recruiting. Nothing indicates so clearly the deep social differences between the native and even the most primitive European workmen, as the fact that until very recently a supply of native labour could be obtained only by means of a specially designed recruiting organization. Comparable in kind, it is true, to such bodies as the Industrial Transference Board in Great Britain, but in scope, and in the nature of the transference made, not in any way similar. The development of this organization, concerned as it was with the kraal life of the native at one end, and with his wage-earning industrial life at the other, reflects clearly the whole mechanism by which native kraal life became connected with European industry.

We have attempted earlier in this book to outline

the forces at work changing the economic basis of native life. We saw how the native land system was changing, and native customs with it, so as to leave the people more dependent upon supplies of wealth from outside. We saw also how European traders in the territories hastened the process. We have now to see how these processes have shaped themselves in more recent years.

Once Cape Colony and the Transvaal were united under one government, no time was lost in setting up administrative machinery to facilitate a more intensive recruitment of labour for the mines. The same machinery was applied to Natal, though somewhat less intensively. These steps were taken under the Native Labour Regulation Act of 1911, which provided for the control of recruiting, for the provision of uniform contracts so that the natives would not be misled when indenturing themselves, for the setting up of recruiting stations under salaried government officials whose work it was to see that the natives understood the contracts, and that they were safely despatched to the Rand. The Act, indeed, attempted to regulate what had previously been a most unregulated business. The old recruiting method had consisted, in districts like the Transkei, in getting the native into debt and then in obliging him to go to work to pay off the debt. Recruiting had come to depend upon this; so much so that practical people seem to have believed that in no other way could the native be brought out to work. Whether or not these people were right we shall attempt to see later on. In lands which were less developed than those of the Transkei, such as those of Natal and Portuguese East Africa, the trader and his debts played a much smaller part, and recruiting was done on what was really a voluntary system; the natives learned to value the money which they could get for working on the mines, and presented themselves to the recruiters in ample numbers. This was especially the case in Portuguese territory. Recruiting was quite different

## NATIVE LAND AND RECRUITMENT 237

in these latter areas to what it was in the Transkei. In the Transkei, the recruiter was in every case a trader; in the other territory, he was a forwarding agent. It seems to be quite clear that if the extremely backward natives of Portuguese East Africa felt the need of money sufficiently to offer themselves to recruiters, then those of the Transkei, with their really developed needs, would certainly have come out to work without the use of the debt mechanism. It appears, indeed, that the Transkei traders had been thrust by the chances of economic development into a position in which they exercised considerable power without performing any necessary service. It was only in the Transkei and in those parts of Natal where white traders had established themselves, that the " advance " system had grown up. Under this system, sums of money or quantities of goods were given to the natives, nominally in order to enable them to buy the necessary clothing, and to lay in stocks of food for their families to enable themselves to go away to work. The debt was secured against the natives' future earning power. These advances were in addition to any other debt which the traders might choose to allow the natives to contract. In 1911 these advances were limited to two pounds each, but the law allowed them on occasion* to go up to five pounds. They had become customary, so that scarcely any native would go to the mines without having first got his advance. The effect of this was, that only those employers who could afford to put up the advance money could hope to obtain labour. This money was provided by the employer, not by the trader. An employer wishing to engage a thousand natives, must have a capital, if the five pound advance was the general practice, of five thousand pounds. Thus scarcely any except the wealthier mining companies could afford to recruit. Farmers found it quite impossible, and small industries were at a great disadvantage.

The expenses of recruiting forced the gold-mining

* As in seasons of drought.

companies to adopt some organization which would prevent their raising the costs by competing against each other. The Native Recruiting Corporation had been formed to operate mainly in Cape Colony. This was a limited company whose capital was subscribed by nearly all gold-mining companies. It made no profit, rendering the service at cost. It distributed the natives after they were recruited among the mines according to an agreed quota. By this means, the recruiters in Cape Colony, were to a large extent prevented from competing against each other by such illegitimate means as misrepresenting contract terms or making illegally high advances. The Native Recruiting Corporation worked within the terms of the Native Labour Regulation Act. All its recruiters were registered under this Act. They were all traders and they all received salaries and commissions from the recruiting corporation. So that the Act confirmed, whereas it might have been more advantageous had it weakened, the connection between trading and recruiting.

The expenses of recruiting in the Transkei were, in 1910, not accurately known, but were probably about one-third of the amount paid in wages. In Portuguese territory, the cost seems to have been considerably less. These costs remain practically unaltered to the present day. The disadvantages of the recruiting system, no matter how well it may be administered, are very serious. Even in Portuguese territory, where, as we have seen, it is reduced to a minimum, and is practically a forwarding agency, it is still open to abuse, in that undue pressure may be brought to bear upon chiefs, and misrepresentations may be made by underlings such as touts and runners. In the Transkei, where the system is applied to relatively civilized natives, its abuses are more in number and more acutely felt. In the first place, the recruited native is indentured for a considerable period under conditions which necessarily deprive him of much freedom. He cannot choose which mine he shall go to, nor the type of work which he shall perform. The expense of recruiting makes the time indenture necessary; for once the mine has spent money in recruiting a native, it wishes to tie him for as long as possible in order to recover that money, and to defer the time when it will be necessary to spend a similar sum on recruiting another native. A twelve months' contract would very nearly halve the costs of recruiting on a six months' contract. This contract means that the native is unable to consult his own desires and needs in the matter of working on the mines. The voluntary native can return home when he feels that he needs a change of condition, or when his family need him. He would probably work just as long, year in year out, as the recruited native. His needs would compel him to do this. But he would do it with a sense of freedom. In the second place, recruiting absorbs money which, or so the natives feel, might be added to their wages. Whether this is so or not, the expense is certainly a burden which limits the sphere of activity of all but the richest mines. In the third place, the recruiting system, where it is bound up with trading, encourages the tendency of natives to run into debt and consequently is a cause of unrest.

A further disadvantage of recruiting by traders, is that the traders are impelled to grant the maximum credit to the natives merely in order to ensure that the earnings are spent with them in the territories, rather than with the storekeepers at the labour centres. It has always been a mystery as to how much of their money the natives spent while at work, and how much they brought back home. Many estimates have been made and round sums put forward as to the probable amount brought home by each native. It seems to the present writer, that these estimates lack all significance in view of the immense variations between individual natives, between natives of different tribes, and between natives from widely different territories. Generally speaking, the proportion of the total wage brought home seems to depend upon two factors: first, the stage of civilization which the native family has reached; second, the extent to which the trader has seen to it that the money must be brought home to pay debts. As regards the first factor, the more advanced towards civilization the family is, the more will the native tend to spend his money on his own needs. Really primitive natives will take home almost every penny of what they earn, and will spend it on their family's needs or will invest it in cattle. Storekeepers on the Rand have been known to plead or insist that the mine should employ less Pondos, and more advanced natives, because the Pondos, being the rawest of all Transkei natives, had not learnt to spend a penny with the storekeeper. But even these broadest of rules break down in important instances. The Portuguese natives have the most backward home life of any natives on the Rand; yet they appear to be the freest spenders. It would appear that their tribal life is much nearer to what is known as the hunting stage, whereas the Pondos have become settled pastoralists. The Portuguese native therefore, may still regard himself as going out for his youthful adventures, and thus spend his money freely. But even he does not spend it all. He sends considerable sums home by means of remittance agencies and deferred pay. The Portuguese authorities have calculated that their natives must bring £800,000 per annum back into the territory. Traders have always squabbled as to their share of the natives' earnings. An agitation to limit the number of Portuguese natives, has been carried on for many years. This agitation has been the work mainly of the Transkei traders, who hoped that if the numbers of Portuguese natives were limited by law, more Cape natives would have to be recruited, and so more money would come into the Cape native territories. The agitation has been opposed by the Witwatersrand storekeepers, who knew the Portuguese boys to be their more profitable customers.

The Transkei traders have always been able to urge that the real interest of the native lay in his spending his money at home, and that consequently they did him a real service in granting him credits which at least insured that he would have no money to spend anywhere else. This contention does not meet the point that debt among natives is a serious evil. It was realized by about 1912 that some other way of inducing the native to spend his money at home would have to be found, and ways and means were sought of assisting him to take his money home. The Native Recruiting Corporation established a remittance agency which enabled natives to send part of their wages home when paid at the end of the month. Deferred pay was also tried and with very considerable success. Advances were limited by law to the sum actually necessary to provide the native with his travelling equipment. In these ways some of the worst features of the recruiting system were overcome, and it was enabled to approach its ideal of a means of assisting voluntary natives to proceed to work.

## REFERENCES

The Reports and Evidence of the Native Land Commission, 1916, and the Subsequent Land Committees in the various Provinces.

Report of the Native Grievances Commission, 1914. The Evidence is unfortunately unpublished but was put at my disposal by the Native Affairs Department of the Union.

The Report of the Low Grade Mines Commission, 1919.

The following also are available:

Census Report (1924) on Non-European Races.

Report on Native Location Surveys, 1923.

Report and Evidence of Select Committee on Native Bills, 1928.

# SECTION III

## CHAPTER II

### LAND SETTLEMENT, AGRICULTURE AND IRRIGATION

THE period since Union has seen many experiments and much development in land settlement, irrigation and agriculture. The Land Act of 1913 has been responsible for buying up some thousands of morgen of land, and for placing thereon settlers of all types. The Milner Land Settlement schemes had had very small results. At the time of union there were only about 1,000 settlers working under them, about half each in the Free State and the Transvaal. No pronounced success had attended their efforts. Those in the Free State had settled down to become prosperous farmers, but it is not certain that their methods were very different to those of the surrounding old-fashioned population. They seemed to have become rather an addition to that population than a stimulating new element. They had been fortunate in being settled on good land, but this fact, although it made for their prosperity, meant that the scheme had but little significance as an experimental step intended to lead to the formulation of a new policy. In the Transvaal things had been very different. Some of the government's land had failed to attract a single settler; other schemes had attracted settlers who had in time given up an unequal struggle against drought. All of the schemes had been on a much smaller scale than in the Free State, the areas of the farms averaging only 500 acres. The Transvaal schemes had undoubtedly been experimental. They had put settlers upon dry land

## LAND SETTLEMENT AND IRRIGATION

with only 500 acres apiece, while the surrounding farmers had been able to make a living only from 5,000 acre farms. They had put other settlers upon practically uninhabited land, in the hope that they would succeed by boring for water; the settlers had, in nearly all cases, spent the whole of their small capitals in the attempt, and then had to surrender their farms. The fact that there was a plentiful demand for land was clearly illustrated by the fact that when these farms were surrendered, there were other settlers ready and willing to risk everything in taking them over. The Transvaal settlement cannot be said to have been successful in putting people on the land, but it did lay the foundation for up-to-date enquiry as to the properties of the soil, and the best means of putting new settlers upon it.

It was shown that for land settlement to progress new means of cultivation had to be taught, and practical means of improving the water supply had to be found. They had also shown that there was a good supply of potential farmers present in the Union. Most of these were living on their father's farms as bywoners. A few were living as tenants on company land. Many of them had already become something approaching "poor whites," and most of them had no idea of farming except the Boer conception, which required vast farms which, simply because of their great size, could be trusted to yield a bare living year in, year out. But many of them were young and educable; the mere fact of their applying for small farms was hopeful. It was with these, rather than with immigrants, that South African land settlement policy came to be concerned. Immigration was, unfortunately, mixed up with politics. The Milner schemes had quite openly aimed at settling Englishmen in the new colonies, in order to increase the English vote. The results were held to justify the prejudice against introducing farmers from abroad. Immigrants with capital would be able to look after themselves, but it would be worse than useless to encourage small working farmers to come into the Union when the supply among the resident agricultural population was already more than could be coped with. Consequently land settlement was proceeded with, but it differed from that in almost all other new countries. in that it was not connected with immigration schemes. Large-scale immigration, such as Canada had known, was never thought of.

The Milner experiments had shown that future policy must keep several points in view. In the first place, land settlement on unoccupied land was very nearly out of the question. For this to be successful great amounts of money would have to be spent in finding water, and in supporting the settlers, possibly for years, until they reaped paying crops. In the second place, settlement of existing farm land was only slightly easier. This involved what was known as closer settlement, and this could not be successful without either finding new water, or developing new methods of cultivation, such as dry-farming, and supervising the settlers to see that they adopted these methods. In the third place, the problem of irrigation was seen to be involved. And fourthly, the all important question of costs, both the initial cost of the land and the further cost of supplying water, farming implements, and the right kinds of stock and seen on favourable terms to the settlers, dominated the whole.

In 1913 a comprehensive Land Act was passed, designed to apply to the whole Union. It aimed at assisting carefully selected applicants from the rural districts to obtain freehold tenure of areas of land of not more than about 500 morgen. It provided for advances to be made to them in respect of the purchase price of the land, and of practically all other expenses to be incurred during several years, while the settlers were finding their feet. The land was to be selected by the Lands Department from among farms which were advertised in the ordinary way. The department was to make its enquiries secretly, so as not to give the

## LAND SETTLEMENT AND IRRIGATION

impression of " going round the country buying land with a big drum." But this was the only step taken to prevent an undue rise in the price of land. It is significant that despite warm advocacy rom certain quarters, no provision for a land tax was included, and no provision for compulsory expropriation. These were resisted hotly by the whole of the land owning interest, as they always had been, doubtless partly by fear of immigration as a result of a too effective land policy, but partly also, no doubt, because of the extremely deep roots which the existing mode of occupation had taken. It cannot be over-emphasized that as regards its land, and the landed population, South Africa is, in many respects, an old rather than a new country. Comparatively new settlers can be forced to dispose of their land by compulsory sale or by taxes on unimproved values. But an old population cannot be so easily dealt with. The history of South Africa in this respect is in decided contrast to the history say of New Zealand, and this fact undoubtedly supplies the greater part of the explanation.

The new policy of land settlement happened to be launched to the accompaniment of new ideas in irrigation. Up to that time irrigation schemes had been carried on in the two colonies in which they were suitable, Cape Colony and the Transvaal, but they had been more closely linked with ordinary agriculture than with land settlement. In the Cape Colony schemes had been carried out with government assistance, on which settlers had been placed ; this had been an incidental result, but the experience gained had led many people to believe that irrigation and land settlement would be closely linked together in the future. There is evidence now that this belief had been established on insufficient information, and indeed the results of the Cape irrigation schemes were none too promising. They had shown that cultivators with irrigation may require many years in which to establish themselves, and some of the schemes were already threatening to become permanent government concerns. But irrigation had a great popular appeal; the land was crying out for water. This developed into a powerful political appeal, of the same nature as agricultural railway lines, and local Members of Parliament speeded on irrigation by claiming it for their own districts. This was assisted by the Cape Department of Irrigation, which, with the technical experts' keenness on projects apart from their financial results, led the belief that a new era of water conservation was about to come. Irrigation up to then had consisted mainly in flood schemes. In the rainy season, the water collecting in the river beds was held up by the construction of simple dams, and was then led out in furrows over the fields. Conservation on a large scale had been attempted only in two or three schemes, for which the government was entirely responsible. These are the schemes to which we have already referred, and although they had not been financially successful, they were held to have proved the possibilities of large scale conservation all over South Africa.

The irrigation department was ready at the date of Union to promote conservation works in many other places. The flood schemes, as we have already seen, were connected almost entirely with lucerne growing in the southern parts of Cape Colony. Later, similar flood schemes were resorted to in the Midlands to grow lucerne for sheep. But this irrigation could be extended to few other crops. The rivers were in flood at the right time of the year for lucerne, but not for many other crops. Wheat and other cereals required water when it was not available from the rivers. So that the irrigation department hoped that by means of conservation, completely new strides in farming could be made. The attention of the country was also drawn to this possibility by the somewhat sudden collapse of the ostrich feather market in 1913. Other types of agriculture would have to be developed. This made a good opportunity for the irrigation department.

## LAND SETTLEMENT AND IRRIGATION 247

From that date great conservation works were proceeded with. The work was held up by the European war, but by 1923 considerable areas had been brought under irrigation. It then began to become clear that irrigation in itself was not enough. In the first place it could be made to apply to only a very small proportion of the total area of South Africa. This was made clear by the Drought Investigation Commission of 1923, which for the first time made a complete survey of climatic conditions in the Union in relation to soil fertility. The result of this investigation was to show that large parts of the potentially good land could not be materially affected by irrigation. While those areas that might have responded to irrigation schemes were not within suitable catchment areas. The Karroo lands did not have the water supply for irrigation schemes to deal with. The coast lands, excepting on one or two rivers, could not benefit from permanent conservation schemes. Natal could scarcely be affected by irrigation, since it already had good summer rains on the coast, and rains on the upland, under the Drakensburgs, which made wheat growing quite possible. The Orange Free State had its pastoral economy which depended upon the even fall of rain over the whole of its area. The Transvaal had areas which could be affected by irrigation, but there was much evidence to the effect that the land in these areas could be made to conserve the water, without expensive schemes, by means of careful cultivation on dry-farming lines. Irrigation could not convert the whole of the Union into a fertile garden. It could be of use only in a few selected places, and even there the cost of the works might not be commensurate with the produce yielded.

In the second place, the actual wastage of water in the Union was found to be surprisingly small. Irrigation depends not upon rainfall but upon run off. It is only the water which runs off the land that can be caught and conserved, and it was found that the total run off or wastage was only some $4\frac{1}{2}$ per cent of the total rainfall.

R

Irrigation schemes of great cost had been devised to deal with this comparatively small run off. In the meantime the 95½ per cent. of the rainfall was receiving very little attention. This, the commission determined, was the real problem. This water was falling over a great area and was being allowed in many cases to evaporate or to sink to sub-soil, or to escape as flood water without having been economically used. The change in the vegetal covering of many parts of the Union, which we have described earlier in this book, was proceeding apace. Over-stocking was depriving the land of its natural covering; veld burning by farmers, who thought only of breaking in new parts of their land, was having the further effect, especially when the land was on hillsides, of still further weakening the natural conserving powers of the country. The real problem consisted in making better natural use of the rainfall. This was to be done by State action in preventing the denudation of catchment areas and by the use of paddocking and scientific grazing by sheep farmers. Irrigation would still have its part to play, but mainly in the form of simple flood works on each farm which would allow that farm to grow winter fodder for the sheep. This growing of winter fodder was indeed one of the really important points in the agricultural development of South Africa. It was the real test as to whether farming was departing from pioneer methods. It was the basis of the mixed farming which was the only possible line of progress in nearly all parts of the Union. To attempt pure arable farming on comparatively small areas, say from 300 to 500 morgen, was extremely precarious in that two or three successive years of drought would exhaust the water resources as well as the cash resources of the best irrigation scheme, and of the most scientific dry farming cultivation. But the production of winter fodder, especially lucerne, oats, and potatoes, as part of the activities of a pastoral farm would have the all-important effect of strengthening that farm against drought.

# LAND SETTLEMENT AND IRRIGATION

In the third place the enthusiasm of experts and public alike had caused the cost of conservation schemes to be underrated. The first cost for land, it is true, was low. But the works themselves in nearly all cases were extremely expensive. The time necessary to break in the land after the completion of the reservoir, during which the irrigator would not reap a single paying crop, was much under-rated. Above all, great difficulty was encountered in finding capable irrigators. The people with experience only of South African farms knew nothing of the economical use of water and were as likely to ruin the land by over-flooding as to produce crops. The few immigrants who came to the country with capital and scientific knowledge went to private schemes. The difficulty of finding good irrigators was much intensified by the fact that most of the schemes were carried out on ordinary farms by associations of owners, all of the farmers whose lands would come under a single scheme forming themselves into a Land-Board which was responsible for its management. The water was then taken to the farms. But the farms remained the full property of the irrigators. The result was that each irrigator found himself still in possession of his farm of pioneer size, but now under the necessity of cultivating in an entirely new way and of paying water rates which could only be paid if this cultivation was successful. In most cases it was not. The farmers had no superfluous capital with which to provide themselves with the many adjuncts of scientific farming; the State found it necessary to become more and more liberal in advancing money for fencing, for seed, for agricultural implements, and also to postpone again and again the payment of the water-rate. The only successful schemes were those in which cultivators had farms of a hundred morgen or less. But few of the farmers under the schemes had farms of less than 500 morgen.

The development which ensued was one of very considerable interest. Closer settlement had long been the aim of progressive agriculturalists. This had not been approached by means either of State expropriation or tax on unimproved land values. It had been impossible to reduce the size of the farms. Now, however, water rates may take the place of these expedients. There are two alternatives in the future of the irrigation schemes; one is that they should remain for all practicable purposes government concerns. This was the fate of several of the early schemes. The government remained the chief proprietor of the capital which was locked up in them, and recovered only what it could in the form of irrigation rates. The other alternative is that the farmers who are unable to meet the rates should be obliged to dispose of part of their farms. A permanent commission has been appointed to deal with cases on their merits. It remains to be seen which direction affairs will take.

The agricultural development of South Africa, from the date of Union up to the present day, may be summed up by saying that efforts are still being made to introduce mixed farming to supersede the large-area pastoral farming which is the legacy of the past. The mixed farming must vary according to the type of soil. In the most favourable regions in the Transvaal it tends to take the form of a farm of about 500 morgen, of which the greater proportion is given up to arable farming, while a little live stock is scientifically grazed on the remainder. In the Cape North West, to take the opposite extreme, the most that can be hoped for is that enough bore-holes will be sunk to enable sheep to be carefully paddocked so that the vegetation may periodically be rested. On all types of farms between these two extremes, progress may be measured by the extent to which farms are being divided up, by the extent to which fodder crops are grown, and by the amount of fencing which is done. As will be gathered from the preceding section, the sub-division of farms has not made great progress. If it takes place only slowly under irrigation schemes, it takes place even

## LAND SETTLEMENT AND IRRIGATION

more slowly elsewhere. There is clear evidence that the growing of fodder is increasing. At the date of Union, it was known only in the most progressive parts. Now, however, there are few farms without the protection against drought which the growing of winter feed affords. Fencing, encouraged by government, has made the most definite strides of all. Recent droughts, though they have been severe, have been better resisted than ever before, while the improved quality of the wool market indicates not only the better feeding of the sheep, but the keeping of them clean by leaving them in paddocks instead of kraaling them every night, as was the early practice. It is significant, however, that this improvement in pastoral practice has not yet led to the successful establishment of dairy farming or the protection of beef and mutton for export. The pig is still almost negligible. The greater part of all maize grown is exported. The hopes that South Africa would develop as the Argentine had done and export its maize in the form of beef and mutton, has not been realized. This cannot be entirely accounted for by the railway policy of giving specially cheap rates, which amount to a bonus on the export of maize. It is certain that this policy increases the value on the farm of maize, and in consequence makes it less likely that efforts will be made to feed it to the animals. But this is far from being the only factor in the situation. One great underlying factor is that South African herds are generally small and must be until some radical improvement in grazing has been brought about; great stretches of rich natural pasture do not exist. Apart from this, a ranching industry in South Africa has the same difficulties to contend with that manufacturing industries have. Centres of consumption are small, with the exception of some five large towns, and are great distances from most of the farms. The grazing industry, in consequence, cannot find a market for its by-products. Despite great efforts to establish co-operative creameries, butter has never been produced in a sufficiently concentrated manner to enable it to be graded and sold to regular markets so as to support its production by the bulk of the farmers. In the case of milk, the problem is even more acute; only a few of the most enterprising farmers, with the assistance of railway lines practically touching their land, have succeeded in establishing a milk trade. The home demands for meat and dairy produce have been successfully met, with seasonal exceptions, for some time past. But this only shows that the home market is not large enough in itself to support scientific grazing and cattle farming. And in the foreign market the South African producer is helpless against the more fortunate farmers in other countries. Maize is the most easily grown grain in South Africa, and it is the only large agricultural export. As we have seen, this export cannot be blamed for preventing the development of mixed farming in South Africa, but we may say that when the export begins to fall, without a corresponding diminution in the production, it will in all probability be a sign of progress. One of the problems of exports in South Africa is to know just when it will be advisable to withdraw the bonus on maize export. If it were withdrawn now, it would in all probability discourage the production of maize without causing a corresponding increase in the production of animal food-stuffs. Other agricultural products in South Africa have made considerable progress since Union, yet still reflect the fundamental disadvantage of the country, namely, that its good land is in small patches. The quantities exported, of such articles as fruit and wine, have not increased so greatly that they can be said to be exported on a larger scale. The policy of the fruit exporters is still only to catch the cream of the European markets by sending the best of fruit at exactly the right season. Whether large sales could be found for inferior fruit, which at present is sold extremely cheaply inside the Union, without spoiling the market for the established brands, is still a moot point. The view of practical

## LAND SETTLEMENT AND IRRIGATION 253

exporters is that the existing markets should not be risked.

### REFERENCES

The most important sources have already been mentioned, the two chief being the Drought Investigation Commission Report, 1923, and the Reports of the Irrigation Finance Commission, 1925.

# SECTION III

## CHAPTER III

### CONCLUSION

THE customs policy which at the time of Union was still a revenue raising consideration, became by 1925 a definite policy of protection of manufacturing industries. The main consideration is whether the primary industries should or should not be taxed in order to promote a group of secondary industries. The protectionist policy is based definitely on the belief that general manufactures are necessary for the well being of the State, and that it is economically advisable to tax the other industries in order to promote them. The policy is simplified by the fact that the primary industries, agriculture and mining, are in a very taxable position. Agriculture depends so largely on the home market that an increase in its cost of production does not cause it to lose foreign markets, excepting in the case of wool, maize, and those other products which, as we have seen, are exported on a small scale. And the farmers who depend upon these exports can be recompensed for the higher costs of production resulting from protection by means of measures, such as low export rates, which amount to bonuses on export. The farmers producing only for the home market also receive similar compensation for the taxation which the protectionist policy imposes upon them  They have low rates for the railway transport of their produce to the inland consuming centres, and also assistance by means of land banks and other similar devices  The industry which is really taxed is mining, gold and diamond. The whole policy is, as it has been for forty years, to regard the mining industry as a temporary industry, which will yield very high profits for a number of years and will then disappear. When the mines give out the country will then have to depend upon its other primary industry, agriculture, and whatever secondary industries have been established and promoted to a paying basis. In consequence the State takes a very large proportion of the wealth produced by the mines and devotes it to the scientific development of agriculture, and to the promotion of a set of manufacturing industries which may hope to be at least self supporting by the time the mines give out. This taxation of the mines is conducted largely through the protective duties, which raise commodity prices and in consequence the cost of labour.

Agriculture, it is felt, no matter how prosperous it may become, should not be relied on in the future to support the whole population. In the meantime this outlook is intensified by the fact that the progress of agriculture itself takes the form of a " rationalization," which diminishes the need for population on the land. The fencing of farms entails the displacement of white bywoners as well as black share-farmers. The re-settlement of these white bywoners on the land is an expensive process and an uncertain one. In addition, the normal increase of population in the farming districts, unless it is to cause a quite uneconomic cutting up of farms, such as the old Transvaal experienced, must be provided for by town industries to which the youths can be apprenticed. The children of the white artisans in the existing industries must also be provided for. Up to the present time the tendency has been for these to drift into blind alley occupations. Consequently the protectionist policy has been accompanied by legislative measures to encourage the apprenticeship of white children. The colour bar will, it is assumed, be maintained as it is on the mines, and extended to the manufacturing industries.

This taxation of the mining industry is admittedly done largely by rule of thumb. It is done, not only through protection given to other industries, but also through railway policy. The Act of Union attempted to prevent this by stipulating that the railways should be run only at cost and should make no profit. This succeeded in wiping out the large surplus which the railways had hitherto given, in every State, to the general revenue. But it has not succeeded in very high profits being made on mining traffic and being used to subsidise traffic for the benefit of agriculture and some manufacturing industries. The Act indeed attempted to some extent to forestall this by providing that no railway lines might be built unless a Railway Commission sanctioned them. If any lines were built without this sanction, the deficit on them must be met out of general revenue. This provision has not succeeded in preventing a considerable mileage of non-paying agricultural line from being built. The losses on these lines are met out of the profits on the mining traffic. The advisability or otherwise of this cannot easily be determined. It is easy to prove that certain of the lines serving the gold mines must be paying so highly that the administration taking the profits can be accused of levying taxation upon the users. It is held that this policy is a direct contravention of another provision in the Act of Union to the effect that the lines must be conducted on business principles. On the other hand the term "business principles" is held to be an indefinite one. It may be said to be contradicted by the Act of Union itself when it provides that no profits are to be made. Also it is not fundamentally against business principles to build lines "to nowhere." These branch lines will in time develop their areas and will increase the payability of the whole system by bringing extra traffic to the main lines. In South Africa especially, with its great distances and with the very high cost of building roads, mere main lines alone would do extremely little to develop agriculture. The branch lines have been built as cheaply

# CONCLUSION

as possible, at a cost considerably below the average for South Africa. It is true that, as in the case of irrigation, mere political considerations may have been the cause of some of the lines being built. It is undoubtedly unfortunate that no kind of local financial responsibility can be placed upon the actual users. If that were possible the necessity for finding money would compel the development of the land; as it is the value of the land is undoubtedly raised, and this, while giving an unearned increment to the farmers who are fortunately situated, also acts in such a way as to induce the least progressive of the farmers to realize the increment by selling. This must draw energetic and commercially-minded farmers into the area.

The dangers of taxing one primary industry for the benefit of the other primary industry, and of the secondary industries, cannot be overlooked. The Witwatersrand mines are mostly of low grade, periodically at least near to the border of payability. This is constantly impressed upon those responsible for the protectionist policy. It is largely due to historical causes that it falls upon somewhat deaf ears. The gold mines are known to have been guilty in the past, if not to be guilty to-day, of inefficient organization and of gross over-capitilization. It is held that to give the mines an easy time by lowering their costs as much as possible, would be merely to enable them to continue their internal inefficiency to the immediate loss of the country and to the ultimate benefit of no one. By raising their costs in one way, they may be forced to lower them in other ways, and it is probable that this has actually happened. To induce lowering of some costs by raising others is certainly a dubious process from the point of view of the industry itself; but since the higher costs are reaped by the treasury, the object aimed at is achieved. The secondary industries are to-day being quite consciously developed by the State in this way, on the principle that " no bird ever flew on one wing." State activity, in the directions which we have indicated, has in recent years involved an extra expenditure which has almost certainly exceeded the increase in the national income. The ratio between imports and exports has, however, been well maintained. Budget surpluses have been the rule. A beginning has been made to revise the tariff so as to tax only those articles which are being produced in South Africa, so that the customs tariff may be said to be moving clear away from pure revenue considerations toward actual development of industry. The high government expenditure must be very largely regarded as productive, especially if a long view is taken, for it must be kept in mind that South Africa is one of the most difficult pieces of land which white people have ever attempted to settle, and it is not surprising that the chance discovery of precious metals should be seized upon in order to assist in the general development.

## REFERENCES

Report on Trade and Industry of South Africa, 1912.
Reports of the Board of Trade and Industries.
Report of the Economic and Wages Commission, 1925.
Annual Reports of His Majesty's Trade Commissioners.
Professor Lehfelt's Estimates of the National Wealth of South Africa.

# INDEX

Absentee farmers, 164
Advance system, 144-45, 237
Advances, limited by law, 241
Agricultural co-operation, 119, 212-13
Agricultural credit, 118
Agricultural department, fruit farming experiments of, 112
Agricultural education, importance of, 243-44
Agricultural marketing, 117-19
Agricultural transport, impediments to, 98
Agriculture, before 1892, 40-51; effect of diffusion of population on, 40-1; effect of nature of water supply on, 41-5; ostrich farming, 48; suitability of Karroo for, 45; methods in Western Province, 45-6; wine industry, 46-7; on the Eastern Coast, 49; in the Eastern Province, 50; and tariffs, 96; effect of systems of transport on development of, 97; in mining development period, 103-37; and lack of survey of lands, 103; land syndicates, 104; in the Karroo, 106; effect of railways on in Eastern Province, 108; State encouragement of, 135; development of in nineties, 182; paralysed by war, 187; government assistance to, 206-8; results of post-war reconstruction in, 213; developments in since Union, 250-53; not wished to be sole support of population, 255; in Cape Colony, protection of in 'eighties, 27-8; fenced land in 1891 and 1904, 107; types of land and methods, 103-14; in Transvaal, 132-36; in Natal, 50-1, 124-27; in Orange Free State, 127-30; economy of large farms in, 130; in Native Areas, 119-24; share-farming, 50; effects of Kaffir farming on methods, 76-8; native methods, 121-22; effect on S. African development, 136-37
Apprenticeship, of white children, 255
Arable cultivation, distribution of, 4; in the Karroo, 4; in Basutoland, Free State, Natal, Transvaal, 5
Australia, imports from, 101; committee of farmers sent to, 135

Basutoland, arable cultivation in, 5; admission to customs union of objected to by farmers, 96; as source of Free State's labour supply, 129
Beaumont Commission, 1916, 225-26
Bechuanaland, annexation of, 8; economic importance of, 10; census in, 16
Bedford, 109
Boer War, results of, 185
Botha, General, 104
Boundaries, state, in early period, 7
British Empire, imports from, 101
Building, Industry in the Transvaal, 171

## INDEX

Bywoners, non-appearance of in Free State, 129; in Transvaal, 131

Cape Colony, agriculture of, in South-West, 109-12; re-construction conditions compared with Transvaal, 209-11; customs duties of, in 'eighties, 25-6; benefits of customs union to, 221; exports of, 1850-90, 21-2; imports of, 1850-90, 21-2; Land Act rendered inapplicable in, 226; manufacturing industries, 1891 178-80, 1904 192; population, 14, 16, 17, 188; occupations of 1891, 17-18; emigration of to Transvaal, 18; railways of, 11, 29-30, 82, 86, 195-96; railways and revenue on, 84-7, 91-2; railway agreement of, with Free State, 83, with Transvaal, 194; revenue of from sale of crown lands, 134-35; tariff revision of after customs union with Free State, 30-1; transport in before 1892, 33-40
Cape coloured labour, 179
Capitalization of gold mines, 175-76
Carriage building, 180
Cattle, change of function of, 122; as native form of currency, 150
Cattle dipping, in the Ciskei, 120
Census, 1904, 187-92; Cape Colony, 14; in Orange Free State before 1892, 15; in Transvaal before 1892, 15
Ceylon, importation of coffee seed from, 125
Chamber of mines, and native labour, 140; loan to Transvaal administration by, 193
Chinese labour, 216-17
Ciskei, agriculture in, 119-20; Kaffir-farming in, 163-67
Clanwilliam, 109

Coal mines, in the Transvaal, 176; in Natal, 177; output, 1890-94, 177; labour supply of, and output, 1889-98, 178
Coffee, experimental industry in Natal, 125
Colour bar, 255
Commerce in the interior (early period), 6
Concessions in Transvaal industries, 170
Contract system, 172-73
Craddock, 109
Credit, of farmers with storekeepers, 7; in recruiting, 239-40
Crown lands, occupation by natives of, 158
Customs, Cape negotiations with Free State, 1855, 24; effect of building of railways on, 24; reduction of by Natal in railway bargaining, 86; in the gold discovery period 94-102
Customs department, of South African Republic before 1892, 24
Customs duties, in Cape Colony before diamond discoveries, 25; in Cape Colony in the 'eighties, 26; in the Transvaal, 175; in Cape Colony, 179
Customs policies, of Transvaal and Free State in early period, 13; before 1892, 24-33
Customs policy, revision of Cape tariff after union with Free State, 30-1; of Natal in competition with Delagoa Bay, 31; of Transvaal, 31-2; concurrent with railway policy, 94-5; since the union, 255-58
Customs protection, of Cape industries in the 'eighties, 26-7; of agriculture in the 'eighties, 27-8
Customs revenue, in Cape, Transvaal and Natal, 1902-07, 197

# INDEX

Customs Statistical Bureau, established for union 1905, 20
Customs unification, 20
Customs union, 197-98, 219-22, between O.F.S. and Cape simultaneous with Railway Union, 83; loss of revenue by Transvaal in joining, 195

Dairy farming, 251-52
Deferred pay, as means of counteracting native debts, 241
Delagoa Bay, as port for Transvaal, 9; as railway competitor of Cape and Natal, 194
Development work, determines amount of imports and capital invested in mines, 173
Diamonds, boundary dispute on discovery of, 7; effect of discovery of on balance of occupations, 18
Drakensberg, effect of on Free State rainfall, 127
Dynamite concession, 170-71

Economist, on mining taxation, 174-75
Expenditure, of the four States, 1902-07, 196
Experimental farms, in Transvaal, 207-8
Exports, classification of, 20-1; of the Cape Colony, 1850-90, 21-2; of Natal, 1850-90, 22; general character of before 1892, 23; per head of population, 101; organized, of fruit, 111-12

Family, as unit of cultivation among natives, 121
Fingos, as traders, 122; difficulty of recruiting among, 142-43
Fire-arms, used in recruiting for diamond mines, 139
Foreign trade, 96-102
Fruit, export of, 252-3
Fruit farming, 111-12
Fruit industry, 179

Glen-Grey, and the Glen-Grey Act, 152
Glen-Grey Act, 123, 145-6, 148-57; as an attempt to make natives contribute to food supply, 136-7; comparison of working of, in Glen-Grey and Fingo district, 153-4; and existing tendencies in native land tenure, 154
Gold, discovered in Transvaal, 10; effect of discovery of on balance of occupations, 18
Gold mines conditions of labour supply, 140-1; taxed to support secondary industries, 257-8
Gold mining industry, related to agriculture, 137
Gold output, 1887-98, 174
Griqualand West, population table, 16

Harvest, effect on native census results, 15
Hertzog, Bills, 231

Imports, effects of existing communications on, 96-7; effect of gold and diamond discoveries on, 96-7; of mining machinery, 98-9; from non-British countries, 1890-98, 99-101; from the British Empire, 101; railway plans for cheapening of, 193: in Cape Colony, table of, 1850-90, 21-2; in Natal, 1850-90, 22
Indentures, 239
India, importation of tea and sugar plants from, 125
Indian labour, 124; in Natal, 126; regulated immigration of, 135
Individual land tenure, and the Glen-Grey Act, 151-2; before the Glen-Grey Act, 152-3; economic changes caused by, 154-6
Industry, protection of in Cape Colony in the 'eighties, 26-7

# INDEX

Inheritance, of land among natives, 121
Inoculation, of cattle in native territories, 123
Irrigation, 114-19, 245-50; experiments in a result of ostrich-farming, 114; and Roman-Dutch law, 116-17; encouraged by Cape Government, 135; department of, 246; by flood methods, 246; by conservation, 246-9; cost of, 249; state assistance, for, 249; as a cause of closer settlement, 249-50
Irrigation Act, in Cape 1876, 115
Irrigation associations, 116
Irrigation loans, 115

Johannesburg, as a market for Cape fruit, 111

Kaffir-farming, 158-63; effect of on labour supply to farms, 162-7; proportion of land devoted to affected by agricultural conditions, 165-6; and the Glen-Grey Act, 166; and location laws, 166-7; in Natal, 127; in Northern Transvaal, 134; in Orange Free State, 129-30
Karroo, arable cultivation in, 4; type of land in, 105; irrigation in, 115
Kimberley, as a market for wine, 110
Kroonstadt, agricultural development of by railways, 128

Labour conditions, on gold mines, 218
Labour supply, of white and non-white employees on gold mines, 1893-98, 171; to manufacturing industries in four States, 1904, 192; shortage of augments post-war slump in mines, 198; in Natal, 126; on coal-mines, 1889-98, 178
Labour tax, 152; effects of, outside Transkei, 157

Land, occupation of by natives, 223-4; purchasable by natives defined, 225; purchase of by natives in Transvaal, 228; difficulties of purchase, of by natives, 229-30; purchase of by natives outside native areas, 231; occupation of by natives on undefined terms, 233-5
Land Act, 1913, 225; 244-5
Land Banks, 119
Land settlement, before 1892, 51-62; subdivision of farms in the Transvaal and Cape Colony, 56-8; summary of early policy in South Africa, 61-2; development of a State policy, 203-6; promoted by general agricultural assistance only, 205; after war important as part of an agricultural policy, 208-9; only possible by closer settlement, 244
  in Cape Colony, 58-61; loan tenure in, 52; individual tenure, 52-3; policy in the Nineties, 134-5
  in Natal, 61; 125
  in Transvaal, 53-6, 131; re-distribution of, made possible by land companies, 134; achieved by government purchase and selection of settlers, 205; reinstatement of Boers on large farms, 205-6
  in Orange Free State, before 1892, 53
Land survey, in the 'nineties, 135; and Glen-Grey Act, 153-4
Location Acts, 78, 137
Lucerne, a by-product of ostrich farming, 112-14

Maize, grown in uplands of Natal, 127; development of export of, 251-2
Malmesbury, 110
Manufacturing industries, 1904 census, 192
Marketing of produce, in the 'nineties, 136

# INDEX 263

Masters' and servants' laws, 161
Middleburg, overcrowding of land at, 132
Milner land settlement schemes, results of, 242-3
Milner, Lord, and development of Transvaal agriculture, 133
Mines, effect on imports of, 98-9
Modus Vivendi Treaty, 215
Molteno, 109
Money, in agricultural dealings, 117-18

Natal, agriculture in 5, 124-7; boundaries of, 8; population of, 1891, 19; 1904, 188; occupations of white and Asiatic population in 1891, 19; imports of, 1850-90, 22; exports of, 1850-90, 22; tariffs of in 1891, 30; tariff competition with Delagoa Bay of, 31; first railway to Transvaal from, 85; railway agreement with Transvaal of, 86; public debt and railway debt, 1881-96, 88; native land tenure in, 124; large scale farming in, 125; Kaffir-farming in, 164; industries of and Transvaal mines, 177; difficulties of re-settlement of land in, 211-12; benefits of customs union to, 221-2; Land Act in, 226-7
Native administration, in Natal, 157
Native Affairs Commission, 1903, 137
Native agriculture, 49, 149-50; government assistance to, 156
Native areas, defined by Land Act, 225; allocation of in Cape Colony, 228-31
Native chiefs, influence of on labour supply, 144; and the land system, 148-9
Native councils, influence on agriculture of, 155-6
Native family, and labour supply, 145-6; and the land system, 149-50
Native inheritance laws, 150-1

Native labour, and political boundaries, 8; failure of in Natal plantations, 126; good supply of in Free State, 129; supply of in Transvaal in the 'nineties, 134; employment before 1890, 138; length of contract on the mines, 146-7; and the Glen-Grey Act, 148; from European farms on gold mines, 159-60; on farms, 160; shortage of on mines after war, 214-5
Native labour conditions, on the mines, 172-3
Native labour costs, in relation to native wages on the gold mines, 147-8
Native labour supply, 141; shortage of owing to agricultural prosperity, 141; to mines from Cape Colony, 1896-1905, 142; replaces Chinese, 217
Native Labour Regulation Act, 236
Native land, effect of nature of demand for on rents, 164
Native land occupation, outside reserves, 73-8, 158-67
Native land settlement, 62-5
Native land system and the Glen-Grey Act, 148-50
Native land tenure, in the Transkei, 120-1; growth of individual tenure, 123; in Natal, 124, 157; effect of system on recruiting, 143; effect on, of limitation of land, 151; in reserves outside the Transkei, 156-7; by leasing, in Eastern Province, 230-1
Native marriage system, and land sytsem, 150
Native policy, before 1892, 62-78; efforts to control labour supply, 68-9; comparison of that of the Cape and Natal, 70; in the Transvaal, 71-2; objects of the policy in South Africa as a whole,

S

72-3; summary of situation before opening up of gold mines, 78
Native population, unreliability of the census on, 65; effect of increase of on fixity of land tenure, 123
Native Recruiting Corporation, 238
Native tenants, compared with bywoners, 161-2
Native territories, population of, 16; economic system of (Transkei), 65-70
Natives, difficulty of taking census of, 15; agriculture of in reserves, 119-24; collection of rent from by Transvaal companies, 134; development of contact of with Europeans, 1890-99, 138-67; non-agriculture resources of, 235-41
Native wage rates, on gold mine 147-8
Natives' wages, attitude of natives towards, 147-8; on farms, 160
Netherlands Railway Company, and transport of coal, 176
New Zealand, comparison of South African land problems with, 245
Northern Transvaal, Kaffir-farming in, 164-5

Occupations, of white population in Cape Colony, 1891, 17-18; of white and Asiatic populations in Natal, 1891, 19
Orange Free State, arable cultivation in, 5; boundaries of, 8; early customs policy of, 13; censuses in before 1892, 15; stimulus to agriculture of from Johannesburg market, 20; Customs' agreement of with Cape Colony, 1855, 24; position of in railway agreements, 83; agriculture in, 1887-99, 127-30
Orange River Colony, population of, 1904, 189; manufacturing industries of, 1904, 192

Ostrich farming, 112-14,
Oudtshoorn, tobacco farming at, 112; ostrich farming at, 112-14; farmers introduce irrigation at, 114-17
Overstocking, 248

Pass laws, 161
Pass system, and attempts to estimate labour supply, 142
Pastoral industry, distribution and conditions of, 2
Phylloxera, 110
Ploughs, introduction of among natives, 122
Polygamy, and native land system, 150
Pondoland, annexation of, 8; census in, 16
Pondos, agricultural methods of, 123
Population, distribution of, 7; up to census of 1891, 14-20; relative increases and decreases of native and white, 19; effect of diffusion of on agriculture, 40-1; of Indians in Natal, 1876-1900, 126; density of, 181; of Natal, 1904, 188; of Cape Colony, 188; of Transvaal, 188; of Orange River Colony, 189
Portuguese East Africa, recruiting agreements with, 140; not developed industrially through Transvaal mines, 176-7; as source of labour, 177; railway agreement of Transvaal with, 195
Portuguese natives, attitude to money of, 240
Prospectors, traders facilitate work of, 6
Public Debt, of Cape Colony, proportion of, invested in railways, 87; of Natal, compared with railway debt, 88

Queenstown, 109

Rack Renting, of natives, 164
Railway Administration, in 1876, 37

# INDEX

Railway agreements, first made, 82-3 ; between O.F.S. and Cape Colony, 83
Railway competition, position of Cape Colony in, 90 ; position of South African Republic in, 91
Railway Conference, 1908, 222
Railway Convention, 1904, 200-201
Railway rates, preference on agricultural produce, 39 ; differentiated policies of the three systems, 39
Railway workshops in Cape Colony, 179
Railway revenue, in four States, 1903-06, 194 ; in Cape, Transvaal and Natal, 1902-1907, 197
Railways, built on discovery of gold, create new economic unit, 11 ; not built to serve agriculture, 23 ; development after diamond discoveries, 36 ; difficulties of State management, rate policy, 37-8 ; outside Cape Colony before 1892, 40 ; early agreements, 81-93 ; as instrument of taxation, 85 ; political control of policy of, 86-7 ; position before South African War, 91-2 ; value and tonnage carried by competing administrations, 1897-1906, 91 ; effect of position of on South Africa's food supplies, 97 ; effect of building of branch lines on agriculture, 97-8 ; demanded by Free State wheat area, 128 ; inducements offered to native labour by, 139 ; summary of development in nineties, 183 ; post - war reconstruction plans, 193 ; and post-war slump, 198-9 ; as means of taxation, protested against, 199-201 ; as basis for post-war reconstruction, 201-2 ; policies since union, 256-7 ; of Cape Colony, 86 ; before 1887, 11 ; competition with Natal, 29-30 ; commencement of South Western system, 33-4 ; of Eastern Province system, 34-6 ; of Port Elizabeth system, 36 ; three systems run financially as one, 85 ; amount invested in, 1874-94, 87 ; railway revenue and total revenue, 1874-94, 87 ; tonnage carried on three systems, 1874-94, 88 ; effect of rate war, 91
in Transvaal, 9, 81-2, 83-4 ; negotiations with Delagoa Bay, 85-6 ; re-organization, 200 ; tonnage of traffic from coast, 191 ; possibility of development lines compared with Cape Colony, 193
in Orange Free State, re-organization of, 200
Raw Materials, in Cape Colony, 179 ; competition of imported and local, 180
Reconstruction, 185-6
Recruiting, methods of, 138-41 ; effect of on native life, 138-48 ; for mines, prohibited in Natal, 141-2 ; in Transkei, 142 ; in Pondoland, 142 ; among the Fingos, 142-3 ; by advances system, 144-5 ; in Portuguese territory and Transkei compared, 236-7 ; abuses of, 238-41 ; effect of development of civilized needs on, 240
Remittance agency, as means of counteracting native debt, 241
Revenue, dependent on railway and customs, 193 ; sources of in Cape Colony, Transvaal, and Natal, 1902-07, 197 ; of the four States, 1902-09, 196
Rhodes, C. J., and annexation of Pondoland, 8 ; his experiments in fruit farming, 111-12 ; and the Glen-Grey Act, 152 ; and manufacturing industries, 179

Roman-Dutch law, and irrigation, 116-17; and native labour, 161
Rotation of crops, in native agriculture, 150
Rustenburg, overcrowding of land at, 132

St. Lucia Bay, as port for Transvaal, 9
Sexual division of labour, 149
Share-farming, made illegal in Free State, 226; effect of native land act on, 231-3
Sheep farming, conditions of before 1892, 42-4; effect on the soil of methods used, 44; in the Karroo, 106; in the Eastern Province, 107; improved methods of, 107-8, 248, 251; in the Orange Free State, 127-8; in the Transvaal, 132; improvement of in the Free State, 136; improvement of breed prevented by Kaffir farming, 166
Sheep stealing, a result of Kaffir-farming, 166
Soil erosion, 106-7, 248
Somerset East, 109
South Africa, development before 1886, 1; area of, 7; development up to 1892, 13; position of before outbreak of war, 92-3; economic importance of native territories to before 1899, 123; summary of agricultural development of in 'nineties, 134-7; industrial development of, 1887-99, 168-84; summary of general development during 'nineties, 180-4
South African produce, used by mines, 99
South African Republic, Customs department of, 24; position in relation to railways, 81-2
Southey, Mr., attacks on soil erosion of, 108

Stamps, working on gold mines, 1887-98, 174
Statistics, defects of up to time of union, 13
Stock diseases, 138
Store-keepers, dealings of farmers with, 7; as commercial agents, 117; in O.F.S. 128; local monopoly of, 136
Sub-division of farms, 250-1; in Cape Colony, 56-8, 104; non-appearance of in Free State, 129; in the Transvaal, 56-8, 131-2
Sugar, Natal industry, 124
Swaziland, as corridor for Transvaal, 10

Tanning industry, 180
Tariff boundaries, difficulties in the result of the removal of, 220-1
Tariffs, select committee on, 1883, 28; select committee on in 1891, 29; inter-colonial relations, 94-6; and South African produce, 95-6; of South Africa compared with other colonies, 101-2; in the 'nineties a revenue concern, 102; Natal duty on sugar, 124; in Transvaal, 171; becoming developmental rather than revenue raising, 258
Taxation, through railway revenue, 85; of mines, 174-5, 194, 198, 255; of land, 175, direct, in Transvaal and Cape, 197
Tea, Natal industry, 124-5
Tobacco farming, 112
Trade, in the interior at early periods, 6; inter-colonial, 98; foreign, 96-102; development of among natives, 122-3, with natives, effect of on recruiting, 143; within the Customs Union, 1906-09, 190; before 1892, 20.
Trade statistics, before 1892, 20-3

# INDEX

Transkei, census in, 16; agriculture in, 120-3, and the Glen-Grey Act, 152; effect of recruitment on internal economy of, 155-6

Transkeian Native Councils, 123

Transport, in the pre-railway period, 2; before 1892, in Cape Colony, 33-40: effect on imports of existing forms of, 96-7; from O.F.S. to Cape ports, 128

Transport riding, by natives, 122; in Transvaal, 132

Transvaal, arable cultivation in, 5; boundaries of, 9; access to the sea of, 9; early customs policy of, 13; census before 1892 of, 15; food supply of in 1892, 23; advantage to of railway competition between Cape and Natal, 32-3; customs policy of, 31-2; finances of railway system of, 89; land companies in, 104; agriculture of, 1887-99, 130-4; decay of agriculture of in 'nineties, 131; manufacturing industries in, before 1886, 168-9; raw materials available for manufacture in, 1886, 169; revenue of, 175; increase of population of, at expense of other States, 183-4; population of 1904, 188; manufacturing industries of, 1904, 192; strong position of in railway bargaining, 195; position of after customs union, 221; and Land Act, 227-8

Wage rates, of white and non-white employees, 1894-98, 171-2

Wallace, Professor, report of on Cape Colony agriculture, 135

Wheat, production of in Free State, 128

Wine farming, in Western Cape, 110-11

Winter fodder, importance of production of, 248

Witwatersrand, wealth of Transvaal farmers due to development of, 132

Witwatersrand Native Labour Association, 140

Wool, early conditions of trade in, 3; exports of from Cape Colony, 4; classification, of, 118; sales at Bloemfontein of, 128; sales of in Transvaal and Free State, 136

Wool trade, 118-9

Zululand, added to Natal, 8

For Product Safety Concerns and Information please contact our EU representative GPSR@taylorandfrancis.com
Taylor & Francis Verlag GmbH, Kaufingerstraße 24, 80331 München, Germany

www.ingramcontent.com/pod-product-compliance
Lightning Source LLC
Chambersburg PA
CBHW052219300426
44115CB00011B/1755